ROUTLEDGE LIBRARY EDITIONS:
ACCOUNTING

Volume 44

MANAGEMENT ACCOUNTING RESEARCH

MANAGEMENT ACCOUNTING RESEARCH

A Review and Annotated Bibliography

CHARLES F. KLEMSTINE
& MICHAEL W. MAHER

Routledge
Taylor & Francis Group
LONDON AND NEW YORK

First published in 1984

This edition first published in 2014
by Routledge
4 Park Square, Milton Park, Abingdon, Oxon OX14 4RN
605 Third Avenue, New York, NY 10017

Routledge is an imprint of the Taylor & Francis Group, an informa business

British Library Cataloguing in Publication Data
A catalogue record for this book is available from the British Library

ISBN 13: 978-0-415-53081-1 (Set)
ISBN 13: 978-1-315-88628-2 (ebk) (Set)
ISBN 13: 978-0-415-71554-6 (hbk) (Volume 44)
ISBN 13: 978-1-315-88162-1 (ebk) (Volume 44)

Publisher's Note
The publisher has gone to great lengths to ensure the quality of this book but points out that some imperfections in the original copies may be apparent.

Disclaimer
The publisher has made every effort to trace copyright holders and would welcome correspondence from those they have been unable to trace.

Management Accounting Research

A Review and Annotated Bibliography

Charles F. Klemstine &
Michael W. Maher

GARLAND PUBLISHING, INC.
NEW YORK & LONDON 1984

For a complete list of the titles in this series
see the final pages of this volume.

Library of Congress Cataloging in Publication Data

Klemstine, Charles F.
Management accounting research.

(Accounting history and the development of a profession)
1. Managerial accounting—Bibliography.
2. Accounting literature. I. Maher, Michael, 1946–
II. Title. III. Series.
Z7164.C81K72 1984 [HF5635] 016.6581'511 83-49434
ISBN 0-8240-6300-7 (alk. paper)

The volumes in this series are printed on
acid-free, 250-year-life paper.

Printed in the United States of America

We hope this document is helpful in reducing barriers to entry to the managerial accounting literature. Numerous colleagues commented on earlier drafts of this review and to them we are grateful. We are particularly grateful to Richard Brief for his input and for introducing us to Garland Publishing.

C. F. Klemstine
M. W. Maher

TABLE OF CONTENTS

Page

INTRODUCTION. 1

TRENDS IN MANAGEMENT ACCOUNTING RESEARCH. 11

1. GENERAL LITERATURE. 27

1.1 Fundamental Concepts 28

1.2 Information Economics/Value of Information 44

1.3 Descriptions of Firm/Industry Practices. 52

1.4 Human Resource Accounting. 58

1.5 International Comparisons. 61

1.6 Systems. 63

1.7 Economics of Internal Organization 68

1.8 General-Miscellaneous. 72

2. PRODUCT COSTING 79

2.1 Direct/Absorption Costing. 80

2.2 Distribution Costs 89

2.3 Product Costing-General. 93

3. COST ALLOCATION 100

4. COST ESTIMATION 113

5. DECISION MAKING 118

5.1 Cost-Volume-Profit Analysis. 119

5.2 Capital Budgeting. 128

5.3 Decision Making-Behavioral 137

5.4 Decision Making-General. 145

6. PLANNING AND CONTROL. 156

6.1 Budgeting. 157

6.2 Variance Analysis and Investigation. 171

6.3 Transfer Pricing 184

6.4 Principal-Agent. 190

6.5 Planning and Control-General 193

7. REVIEW PAPERS 213

ALPHABETICAL BIBLIOGRAPHY 218

INTRODUCTION

INTRODUCTION

Objective

This bibliography presents a review of trends in management accounting research and a classified annotated listing of over 600 works in the area. It was written as an aid to the accounting researcher or student who wishes to review the development of the literature in management accounting over many years.

Set of Management Accounting Literature

The subject area of management accounting is somewhat difficult to bound, but we used the traditional areas of information for planning and control, product costing, and information for decision making. Using this definition, we traced the development over time, 1926 to 1982, of management accounting research through the primary scholarly academic journals. The search was generally limited to academic journals because of the research orientation of the book. While many articles in practitioner journals contributed greatly to these areas their primary orientation was not toward research expansion of management accounting. Developments of research areas that did appear in these publications would be included in other articles in academic journals. Additionally, only main articles from these journals were reviewed and annotated; teaching notes and comments and replies relating to main articles reviewed generally were not included to keep the number of articles to a manageable level.

Scholarly journals in other disciplines were not generally included. Many ideas and theories of management accounting have been imported into the accounting literature from other disciplines, most notably economics, operations research, behavioral sciences, and decision theory. Nevertheless, to search all such areas would have been an overwhelming task. This review has focused on the accounting literature and includes only those works from outside the accounting literature that were seminal in defining and introducing a research area, and were frequently referenced in the accounting literature.

The journals surveyed were The Accounting Review, The Journal of Accounting Research, The Journal of Accounting and Economics, Accounting Research [1948-1958], Abacus, and Accounting, Organizations and Society. The search was limited to these because they are/were generally regarded as the major academic journals. Also included in the review are AAA Studies in Accounting Research which pertain to management accounting, significant books in the area, and a few articles from Management Accounting and nonaccounting literature. We have excluded unpublished work, except for a few review papers.

Caveats

By limiting the review to the three areas listed above we have excluded articles that may have fit another individual's broader definition of management accounting. Nevertheless, we have included more than 600 works spanning the years 1926 to 1982 in reviewing the area. We believe this represents a great portion of the research literature in management accounting.

Organization

This book is organized as follows. First, a review of some trends apparent in management accounting research is presented. This provides an overview of the literature covered in the bibliography and some insight into why the literature developed as it did. The annotated bibliography follows this review. The bibliography has been divided into six main topical categories representing the main areas listed above and within some of the broader categories they are further divided into subcategories. For example under category 5, Decision Making, there are four subcategories: 5.1, CVP Analysis; 5.2, Capital Budgeting; 5.3, Behavioral Studies; 5.4, Other Articles

Within each topical category or subcategory the articles are arranged in chronological order to enable the reader to see the development of an area over time. For example, CVP Analysis begins with an article in 1943--L. Brush, "Graphic Analysis of Expense," The Accounting Review (October 1943))--and continues chronologically with 31 articles to the last piece listed in 1979--W. Shih, "A General Decision Model for Cost-Volume-Profit Analysis Under Uncertainty," The Accounting Review (October 1979).

While the chronological listing is useful to show how the literature on a topic has developed over time, we also found it useful to have an alphabetical list at the end of the paper which shows the reference and where it can be found in the annotated bibliography. Therefore, there are two primary ways this document can be used: (1) by going through a category or subcategory of interest and (2) by using the alphebetical index to locate particular articles or books.

The following categories and subcategories are used:

1. GENERAL LITERATURE: This category includes works dealing with many general topics and those not easily classified by topic. The following eight subcategories make up the General Literature category:

1.1 Fundamental Concepts - Included in this section are those works discussing certain fundamental concepts in management accounting (e.g., AAA reports). The articles span the years 1926 to 1981 and are primarily an a priori search for cost and managerial accounting principles.

1.2 Information Economics/Value of Information - The articles in this section deal explicitly with the value of information. They span the years 1968 to 1981. Other articles related to this topic are included in subcategory 6.4, Principal-Agent.

1.3 Descriptions of Firm/Industry Practices - These articles address practices in organizations and industries and are primarily descriptive. They span the years from 1930 to 1968.

1.4 Human Resource Accounting - This section contains articles in HRA. They begin in 1968 and continue until 1980.

1.5 International Comparisons - These articles describe management accounting practice in foreign countries.

1.6 Systems - The works in this section take a systems perspective of management accounting. They cover the period 1946-1982.

1.7 Economics of Internal Organization - The works in this section address the economic theory of organizations and span the years 1937 to 1982. All but three are from outside the accounting literature.

1.8 General-Miscellaneous - This section contains those articles not otherwise categorized. Included are works on the role of accountants in organizations and the impact of regulation on management accounting.

2. PRODUCT COSTING: Included in this category are those works dealing with product costing. The following three subcategories make up the Product Costing category:

2.1 Direct/Absorption Costing - The articles in this section trace the direct/absorption controversy from 1945 to 1973. This topic dominated the managerial accounting literature in the 1950's and early 1960's.

2.2 Distribution Costs - This section contains a set of articles on the control of these costs and whether or not they should be inventoried. This is a fairly large set of articles on a shortlived topic (all but one were published before 1935).

2.3 Product Costing-General - This section contains those works on product costing not included in the two categories above, including works on standard costs, spoilage, and process costing.

3. COST ALLOCATION: This category contains all the works pertaining to the allocation of costs, both overhead allocation and joint product cost allocation. The articles span the years from 1945 to 1982 and include a priori and conceptual pieces and applications of modeling to cost allocation problems. Certain articles on the allocation of fixed and variable costs are included in subcategory 2.1, Direct/Absorption Costing.

4. COST ESTIMATION: The works in this category all pertain to the estimation of costs. The articles run from 1945 to 1974 and include considerable imports of methodology from economics, statistics, and mathematics. The CVP Section, subcategory 5.1, also has some papers related to cost estimation.

5. DECISION MAKING: This category contains those works in the area of decision making. The following four subcategories make up the Decision Making category.

5.1 Cost-Volume-Profit Analysis - The articles in this section address CVP analysis. They span the years 1943 to 1979 and include several modeling papers incorporating uncertainty and resource constraints. Some papers in the Cost Estimation category use CVP examples.

5.2 Capital Budgeting - The articles in this section deal with capital budgeting and run from 1947 to 1981. Most of the work is a priori conceptual and modeling.

5.3 Decision Making-Behavioral - This section contains the articles addressing the behavioral aspects of decision making. Nearly all use laboratory experiments. These articles cover the period 1964 through 1982. Recent articles deal mostly with human information processing.

5.4 Decision Making-General - The decision making articles in this section are those not included in one of the above categories. Included are articles on opportunity and differential costing, inventory models, pricing, and product mix decisions.

6. PLANNING AND CONTROL: This category contains articles dealing with the various aspects of planning and control. The following five subcategories make up the Planning and Control category. Some of the works in Information Economics--subcategory 1.2--are also related to Planning and Control.

6.1 Budgeting - All the articles dealing with the various aspects of budgeting are included in this section. The articles span the years from 1929 to 1982 and include discussion pieces, field studies, and laboratory experiments.

6.2 Variance Analysis and Investigation - This section contains articles relating to the analysis of variances and to investigation decisions. The articles in this area begin in 1937 and continue to the present. Some articles on standard costs and performance evaluation related to this topic are included in subcategory 6.5, Planning and Control-General.

6.3 Transfer Pricing - The articles in this section address the various aspects of transfer pricing. They are primarily a priori discussions, but some modeling papers and one survey paper are also included. Articles on decentralization and performance evaluation in general, without specific reference to transfer pricing, are included in subcategory 6.5, Planning and Control-General.

6.4 Principal-Agent - This section contains those works explicitly using the principal-agent model. Some of these papers could be classified as information economics or in other planning and control topics (e.g., budgeting). As this is a new, rapidly growing literature, we decided to give it a separate subcategory.

6.5 Planning and Control-General - This section contains those articles in the areas of planning and control not included in one of the above subcategories. The articles cover such topics as standard costs, cost control, and performance evaluation.

Annotation

Each reference has a brief description of the research. Also, each reference has the following categories:

A -- Source discipline, to describe the researcher's source of ideas, if they are based on a discipline besides accounting, and methods. Example source disciplines are economics, psychology, and statistics. "Unspecified" indicates there was no dominant outside source discipline.

B -- Method of analysis, to indicate the method used by the researchers. Examples include modeling, laboratory experiment, and field study. "A priori" means the paper is based mostly on conceptual reasoning without an explicit model manipulation, experiment, or emprical analysis. We differentiate a field study from a survey. For our purposes, a field study incorporates an active manipulation of data to find hypothesized relationships, whereas a survey collects data, only.

C -- Topic refers to the topic addressed by the researcher (these topics are listed above).

Iere is an example:

Jaedicke, R. K., and A. A. Robichek, "Cost-Volume-Profit Analysis Under Conditions of Uncertainty," The Accounting Review (October 1964), pp. 917-926.

(1) Discusses the use of cost-volume-profit analysis when the volume of product is unknown and a probability distribution for the volume is used. The technique is illustrated using both an actual distribution and a general distribution (normal). Introduces uncertainty to C-V-P analysis (a landmark piece).

(2) Categories: A. Mathematics/Statistics B. Modeling C. CVP

A. Mathematics/Statistics	B. Modeling	C. CVP
↑	↑	↑
Source disciplines	Method of Analysis	Topic

TRENDS IN MANAGEMENT ACCOUNTING RESEARCH

TRENDS IN MANAGEMENT ACCOUNTING RESEARCH

A major finding of our review of the literature presented in this bibliography is that there was a significant change in the character and quantity of the literature in the 1960s. Table 1 presents an overview using 1960 as a

TABLE 1

Comparison of Management Accounting Literature
Before and After 1960

	Before 1960	After 1960
Average number of management accounting academic articles per year[a]..............	4.9	18.3
Percentage of articles relying primarily on *a priori* and descriptive research methods[b]................................	90%	44%
Percent of articles relying primarily on modeling, experimental and empirical methods.................................	10%	56%
Percent of articles relying on an outside source discipline for key concepts (e.g., economics, psychology)..................	20%	55%

somewhat arbitrary cutoff point. Not only was there a marked increase in the quantity of management accounting articles, but also the nature of the literature changed. The two major changes were a change in research methods from

---

[a]Academic articles include managerial accounting articles published in *The Accounting Review*; *Journal of Accounting Research*: *Journal of Accounting and Economics*; *Abacus*; *Accounting, Organizations and Society*; and *Accounting Research*.

[b]"*A priori*" means the article was based on conceptual reasoning without an explicit model manipulation, experiment or empirical analysis. "Descriptive" includes both case studies and questionnaire surveys that collected data but did not manipulate data to test hypothesized relations.

mostly a priori and descriptive to modeling, experimentation, and field studies, and an increase in the reliance on outside disciplines for theory and methods.

Table 2 gives more details about the development of the literature by topic. (Figure 1 presents the same data for a subset of the topics.) The large number of articles on product costing published between 1950 and 1965 dealt mostly with the direct versus absorption costing controversy. Since the mid-1960s, the research has focused more on planning and control and decision making topics, and less on product costing.

The change from a priori and descriptive work to modeling, experimental and empirical research methods is shown in Table 3 and Figure 2. The proportion of research relying on outside disciplines like statistics, economics and psychology, for theories is shown in Table 4 and Figure 3. (We refer to this as "importing" research ideas.)

In short, the nature of management accounting research changed dramatically in the 1960s. Prior to 1960, the literature was dominated by a search for fundamental concepts and truths. Horngren [1975] and others have referred to the pre-1960 period as one in which accountants searched for True Costs (i.e., the one true religion), while in later periods we looked at accounting in terms of user decision models (i.e., pick the religion that works) and the economics of information. Of course, the preoccupation with finding True Costs paralleled the search for True Income in the financial accounting literature.

The pre-1960 literature also contained many definitional pieces, observations about practices, and other works that have become an established part of textbook folklore. Much of the material in current cost accounting textbooks was originally developed in the literature. For example, a 1928 article on differential costs that could be the basis for any "modern" cost or managerial

TABLE 2

Management Accounting Articles by Topic[a]

Year	Product Costing	Decision Making	Planning and Control (Inc. Agency Theory)	Cost Allocation	Cost Estimation	Information Economics	Description of Firm & Industry Practices	All Others	Total
1926-30	5	3	3				1	4	16
1931-35	11		6				3	2	22
1936-40	3		5				1	2	11
1941-45	1	3		1	1		1	12	19
1946-50	5	3	3		2		6	4	23
1951-55	10	9	7	3			4	8	41
1956-60	10	5	8				1	16	40
1961-65	17	26	19	4	3			16	85
1966-70	4	25	46	6	4	6	2	10	103
1971-75		25	33	7	2	7		15	89
1976-80	1	24	45	10		6		16	102
1981-82		5	15	7	—	2	—	8	37
Total	67	128	190	38	12	21	19	113	588

[a]Includes only articles published in The Accounting Review, The Journal of Accounting Research, The Journal of Accounting and Economics, Abacus, Accounting, Organizations, and Society, and Accounting Research. Research monographs and articles in nonaccounting journals are excluded here but included in the bibliography.

Figure 1
Management Accounting Literature by Topic

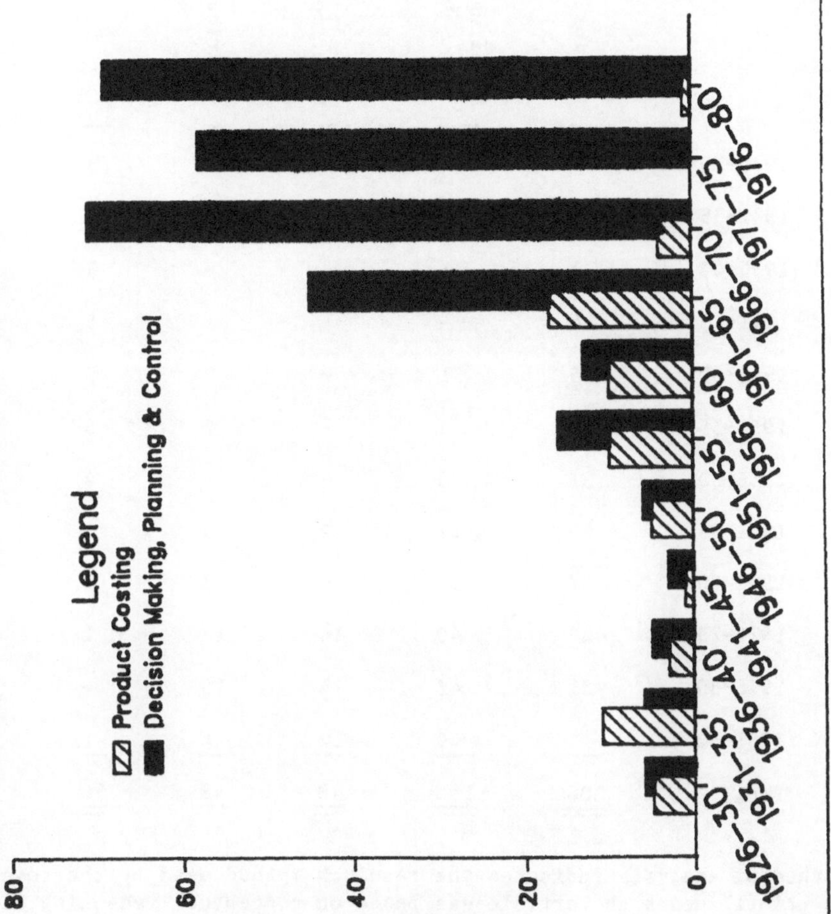

TABLE 3

Management Accounting Articles
by Method of Analysis[a]

	A Priori	Modeling (Inc. Simulation)	Experimental	Empirical	Descriptive	Total
1926-30	13	-	-	-	3	16
1931-35	13	1	-	2	6	22
1936-40	7	1	-	-	3	11
1941-45	14	-	-	-	5	19
1946-50	15	1	-	2	5	23
1951-55	32	4	-	2	3	41
1956-60	31	5	-	-	4	40
1961-65	60	17	2	3	3	85
1966-70	57	35	6	3	2	103
1971-75	22	40	14	12	1	89
1976-80	31	42	14	15	-	102
1981-82	11	9	12	4	1	37
Total	306	155	48	43	36	588

[a]Method of analysis indicates the research method used by the researcher. "A priori" means the article was based on conceptual reasoning without an explicit model manipulation, experiment or empirical analysis. "Descriptive" includes both surveys that only collected data and case studies. Questionnaire based research that involved data manipulation as part of the study to test hypothesized relations are included in the "empirical" category.

Figure 2
Management Accounting Literature by Research Method

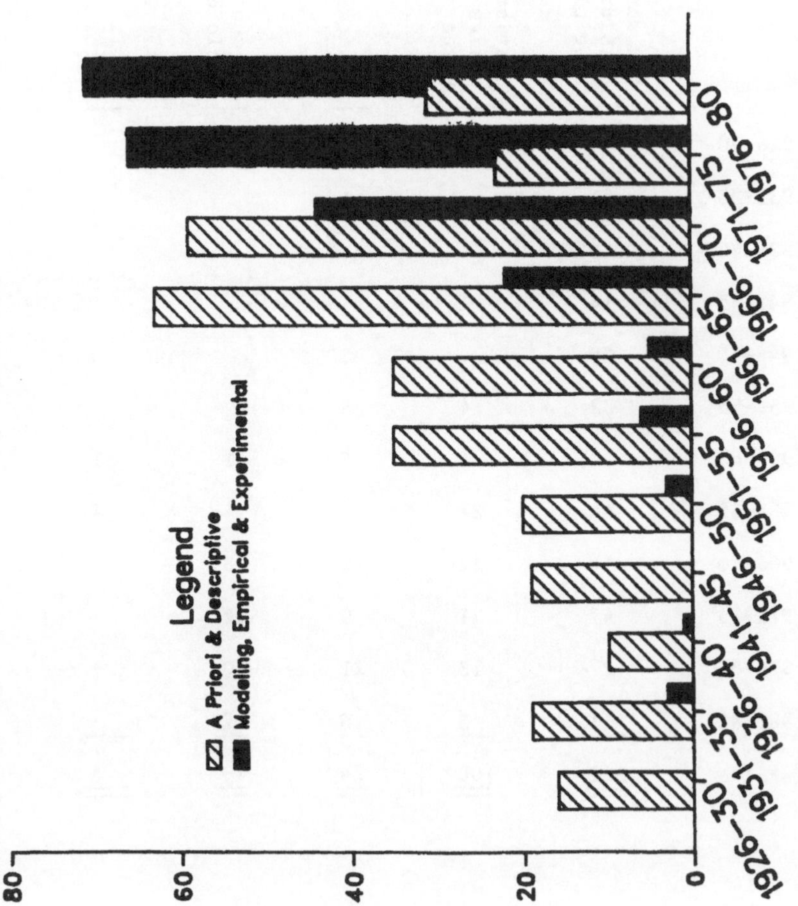

TABLE 4

Management Accounting Articles
by Source Discipline

	Did not rely on outside source discipline	Statistics, mathematics and operations research	Economics	Psychology and Sociology	Other	Total
1926-30	13		3			16
1931-35	21		1			22
1936-40	10	1				11
1941-45	14	1	4			19
1946-50	20		3			23
1951-55	32	4	5			41
1956-60	27	6	5	1	1	40
1961-65	46	27	5	4	3	85
1966-70	54	32	12	5		103
1971-75	47	21	9	12		89
1976-80	27	13	21	40	1	102
1981-82	11	3	6	17	—	37
Total	322	108	74	79	5	588

Figure 3
Management Accounting Literature by Source Discipline

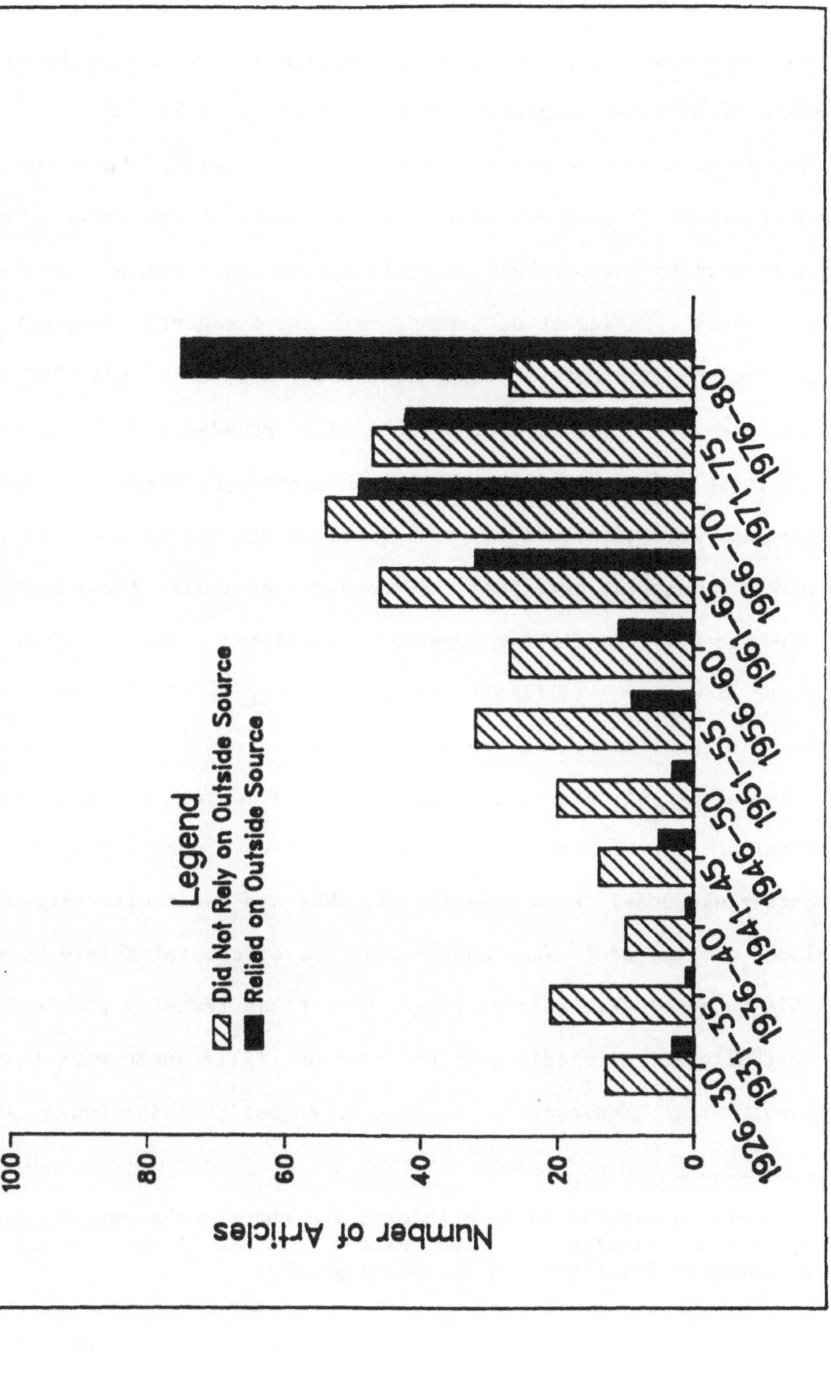

accounting textbook's chapter(s) on relevant or differential, average, and "sunk" costs, and had a clear user orientation: "Accounting is useful to business mainly to the extent that it provides data which can be used in the formation of business judgments" (Rorem [1928], p. 335).

The point can be summarized by stating that nearly all of the topics and issues discussed in cost and managerial textbooks of the 1960s vintage had been discussed in the pre-1960 academic literature. Perhaps this point was not previously apparent to us because cost and managerial accounting textbooks are not replete with references, particularly not to the pre-1960 literature.

The pre-1960 literature also included an abundance of "case studies" which describe cost and managerial practices in particular firms or industries.[1] These papers were descriptive -- they made no attempt to theorize about <u>why</u> particular accounting practices developed in particular firms or industries.

The pre-1960 descriptive papers, if published today, would be criticized for their lack of generalizablility. They were, in effect, case studies characterized by considerable depth compared to current surveys and field studies. While the number of observations was small, we learned a lot about each observation. However, very little systematic work on the "why" of managerial accounting was done. Such questions as, Why are particular accounting methods developed as they are? What characteristics of companies lead to the use of flexible budgets? Variable costing? Cost-based transfer picking? Why and how are cost allocations used? were not systematically dealt with then, nor have they been since. The answers to these questions -- which could lead to a

---

[1]For readers interested in more information about these papers, they are listed chronologically under the heading "GENERAL LITERATURE-Descriptions of Firm/ Industry Practices" in the bibliography.

"positive" theory of management accounting -- might be found in a more sophisticated application of the research methods in the early descriptive literature.

While importing ideas from other disciplines has been a major feature of our literature from the beginning, there is an important difference in what was imported before and after 1960. The former was limited to general concepts. Examples include Rorem's [1928] import of differential cost notions from economics and Matz's [1946] report on the development of the computer at the University of Pennsylvania, in which he suggests that the computer might someday be a useful tool for accountants. After 1960, the ideas and methods were explicitly incorporated into research designs. A pre-1960 paper on cost estimation would suggest that accountants consider using statistical methods, while a post-1960 paper would use a particular method and discuss its properties.

<u>Three Examples</u>.

To provide a flavor of how the character of the literature changed over time, we have summarized the chronological developments of three topics: (1) direct versus absorption costing, (2) cost allocation, and (3) information economics. The issue of direct versus absorption costing received considerable attention from about 1950 to about 1965, but very little after that. The second, cost allocation, has been with us since the beginning of accounting and probably will be until the end. The seminal work in the third topic, information economics, appeared in the post-1960 literature.

<u>Example 1: Direct versus absorption costing</u>. The direct versus absorption cost controversy presents an excellent example of how the literature on a topic would develop quickly into a heated debate, in which the writers would use

argumentative methods to persuade readers about the inherent properties of particular costing methods. We found only one article on the topic before 1951 (Schlatter [1945]); more than twenty between 1951 and 1965; and only a few since 1965. This literature had only three modeling papers and one empirical (field) study. The rest of the literature is based on a priori (i.e., argumentative) methods. Although this literature has provided some definitional groundwork, we learned very little about whether and why firms choose direct and/or absorption costing; and we have made only modest progress in demonstrating decision sensitivity to the choice of costing method (Bailey [1973], Demski [1970], and Ijiri, Jaedicke, and Livingstone [1965] could be considered exceptions).

Example 2: Cost allocation. Although early textbooks gave considerable attention to cost allocation, we were surprised to see how recently the topic was introduced into the research literature. An early article on cost allocation was written by Vatter [1945], who set forth the limitations of cost allocation and called for research in the area. This was followed by several definitional and conceptual articles until 1964, when two modeling papers (Churchill [1964] and Williams and Griffin [1964]) moved the literature from a definitional orientation to one focusing on the application of models.

In recent years, many authors of modeling papers have downplayed the normative tone of the cost allocation literature. As Kaplan [1977] concluded: according to these authors, "We're not telling you to allocate, but if you must, use one of the models describe here" (p. 59). In short, many cost allocation papers are schizophrenic -- on the one hand, they display reasonably sophisticated methods for allocating costs; on the other, there remain reservations about the propriety of allocating costs in the first place. The topic calls for some positive theory (e.g., Zimmerman [1979]) and empirical work that will help us to specify the use of cost allocations in organizations. While we are beginning to understand that the demand for allocation is derived from the properties of decentralized organizations, it is still a mystery why costs, particularly accounting costs, are allocated.

Clearly, we have reached a major turning point in this literature. We appear to have reached the point of diminishing returns to argumentative discussions and modeling and helpful answers to the "why do firms allocate" questions could come from positive economic theory and behavioral research. The potential for breakthrough in this area is exciting.

Example 3: Information Economics: It would be amazing to find that the conditions of supply and demand for accountants' products had not been considered prior to 1968 -- but that is very nearly the case. Some of the early work on cost concepts implicitly considered the usefulness of cost data,[2] but there was no explicit consideration of the value of information in the accounting literature until Feltham [1968] and LaValle and Rappaport [1968]. Information economics became a growth industry in a remarkably short period of time. It is likely that there was a "demand" for an explicit formulation of the value of information in accounting, but the "supply" was not available until the pathbreaking work by von Neumann and Morgenstern [1947] and Savage [1954], among others.

While readers of the information economics literature have come to expect it to consist of abstract modeling, that is not necessarily so (e.g., see Crandell [1969] and Mock [1969]). It is interesting to speculate how the

---

[2]For example, see the passage from Rorem's [1928] article on differential costing quoted earlier.

literature might have differed as to both its character and its application if a significant subset of the early literature had been less abstract.

Summary

We can observe a number of points of inflection in the managerial accounting literature since 1926. Some important ones include the search for principles of cost and managerial accounting in the early 1950s; the application of management science models to managerial accounting in the 1960s; and the development of information economics and agency theory in the accounting literature in the late 1960s and early 1970s. Perhaps the most important change was to a user orientation in the 1960s.

REFERENCES

Bailey, A. (1973), "A Dynamic Programming Approach to the Analysis of Different Costing Methods in Accounting for Inventories," The Accounting Review (July 1973).

Churchill, N. (1964), "Linear Algebra and Cost Allocations: Some Examples," The Accounting Review (October 1964).

Crandall, R. (1969), "Information Economics and Its Implications for the Development of Accounting Theory," The Accounting Review (July 1969).

Demski, J. (1970), "The Decision Implementation Interface: Effects of Alternative Performance Measurement Models," The Accounting Review (January 1970).

Feltham, G. (1968), "The Value of Information," The Accounting Review (October 1968).

Horngren, C. (1975), "Management Accounting: Where are We?" in Management Accounting and Control (Madison: University of Wisconsin, 1975).

Ijiri, Y., R. Jaedicke, and J. Livingstone (1965), "The Effect of Inventory Costing Methods on Full and Direct Costing," Journal of Accounting Research (Spring 1965).

Kaplan, R. (1977), "Application of Quantitative Models in Managerial Accounting: A State of the Art Survey," in Management Accounting - State of the Art (Robert Beyer Lecture Series: University of Wisconsin - Madison, 1977).

LaValle, I. and A. Rappaport (1968), "On the Economics of Acquiring Information of Imperfect Reliability," The Accounting Review (April 1968).

Matz, A. (1946), "Electronics in Accounting," The Accounting Review (October 1946).

Mock, T. (1969), "Comparative Values of Information Structures," Journal of Accounting Research Supplement (1969).

Rorem, C. R. (1928), "Differential Costs," The Accounting Review (December 1928).

Savage, L. J., The Foundation of Statistics (New York: Wiley, 1954).

Schlatter, C., (1945), "Fixed Expense," The Accounting Review (April 1945).

Vatter, W. (1945), "Limitations of Overhead Allocations," The Accounting Review April 1945).

von Neumann, J. and Morgenstern, O., Theory of Games and Economic Behavior, (Princeton, New Jersey: Princeton University Press, 1947).

Williams T. and C. Griffin (1964), "Matrix Theory and Cost Allocations," The Accounting Review (July 1964).

Zimmerman, J. (1979), "The Costs and Benefits of Cost Allocations," The Accounting Review (July 1979).

GENERAL LITERATURE

1. GENERAL LITERATURE (pp. 27-78)

This category includes articles dealing with multiple topics, fundamental concepts about managerial and cost accounting, and articles not easily classified by topic.

This category contains the following subcategories:

1.1 Fundamental Concepts (pp. 28-43).

1.2 Information Economics/Value of Information (pp. 44-51).

1.3 Descriptions of Firm/Industry Practices (pp. 52-57).

1.4 Human Resource Accounting (pp. 58-60).

1.5 International Comparisons (pp. 61-62).

1.6 Systems (pp. 63-67).

1.7 Economics of Internal Organization (pp. 68-71).

1.8 General-Miscellaneous (pp. 72-78).

1.1 FUNDAMENTAL CONCEPTS (pp. 28-43)

The articles in this subcategory deal with fundamental concepts in managerial and cost accounting. They include numerous AAA reports attempting to define "principles of cost/managerial accounting."

Noble, H. S., "Some Cost Accounting Concepts of Wider Application," The Accounting Review (December 1926), pp. 48-54.

(1) Discusses the existence of particular cost accounting "principles" and their extension to selling and administrative expenses and commercial enterprises other than manufacturing. Presents three concepts: 1) the existence of intraorganization transactions, 2) value passes from one account to another without loss, and 3) the operating statement and not the balance sheet is of primary importance. Early expression of the idea of definable cost concepts.

(2) Categories: A. Unspecified B. A Priori C. Fundamental Concepts

* * * * *

Categories: A--Source discipline. B--Method of analysis. C--Topic.

Rorem, C. R., "Similarities of Accounting and Statistical Methods," The Accounting Review (March 1927), pp. 10-18.

(1) Compares accounting to statistics and says both have in common 1) the measurement of phenomena, 2) the classification and summarization of data, and 3) the interpretation and use of data. Accounting focuses on classification and the author calls for more attention on the other two. Has a 1970's-80's perspective of accounting; introduces concepts that were to be discussed in later years.

(2) Categories: A. Unspecified B. A Priori C. Fundamental Concepts

* * * * *

Noble, H. S., "The Relation of Business Organization to Accounting," The Accounting Review (September 1927), pp. 232-236.

(1) Discusses the relationship between an organization's structure and the structure of its accounting system. Discusses internal organization in terms of the various functions performed and argues that knowledge by the accountant of the individuals responsible for various activities will increase accounting's usefulness. One of the earliest discussions of information system choice where the user is explicitly discussed.

(2) Categories: A. Unspecified B. A Priori C. Fundamental Concepts

* * * * *

Peloubet, M. E., "Observations on Cost," The Accounting Review (January 1943), pp. 9-16.

(1) A critical discussion of the government practice of allowable/non-allowable costs in the execution of government contracts. Emphasis is put on the differences between the government and business views of costs and the effects of "proving" rather than reducing costs. Early article related to government influences on cost accounting. One of several articles written on this topic during World War II.

(2) Categories: A. Unspecified B. A Priori C. Fundamental Concepts

* * * * *

Categories: A--Source discipline. B--Method of analysis. C--Topic.

Dixon, R. L., "The Need for a Statement of the Principles Underlying Cost Accounting," The Accounting Review (July 1943), pp. 256-258.

(1) Proposes that several recent developments (e.g., Robinson-Patman Act, NRA, and Cost-Plus Contracts) have made it desirable to attempt a degree of uniformity in cost accounting, at least as to governing principles. Calls for an attempt to state the underlying principles of cost accounting. (The search continues today.)

(2) Categories: A. Unspecified B. A Priori C. Fundamental Concepts

* * * * *

Prickett, A. L., "General Principles of Cost Accounting," The Accounting Review (April 1944), pp. 169-180.

(1) Discusses the search for and setting of generally accepted principles of cost accounting with emphasis on calculating the Cost of Goods Manufactured. Compares various methods of treating costs with the pure theoretical treatment.

(2) Categories: A. Unspecified B. A Priori C. Fundamental Concepts

* * * * *

Crawford, J. R., "Statistical Accounting Procedures," The Accounting Review (July 1944), pp. 266-270.

(1) Describes the decisions made in the installation of a cost accounting control system and how the specifics of the work done in the factory influence the cost accounting system installed. Recognition of the perspective that information systems should be designed specifically for the organization/operation.

(2) Categories: A. Unspecified B. A Priori C. Fundamental Concepts

* * * * *

Rice, W. B., "Statistical Uses of Accounting Data," The Accounting Review (July 1944), pp. 260-266.

(1) Discusses the use of statistics in presenting and analyzing accounting data. An early call for attention to user needs. (The term "statistics" here is not used in the modern sense.)

(2) Categories: A. Mathematics B. A Priori C. Fundamental Concepts

* * * * *

Categories: A--Source discipline. B--Method of analysis. C--Topic.

Garner, S. P., "Historical Development of Cost Accounting," The Accounting Review (October 1947), pp. 385-389.

(1) Short presentation on the background of the development of cost accounting for the work of the "Committee on Cost Principles." It sets the stage for the work of the Committee to follow and shows that many cost accounting developments thought to be of modern origin have their genesis in past decades. Good review.

(2) Categories: A. Unspecified B. A Priori C. Fundamental Concepts--AAA Committee

* * * * *

Read, W. H., C. L. Stanford, H. W. Kendrick and R. L. Dixon, "Report of Committee on Statement of Cost Accounting Concepts," The Accounting Review (January 1948), pp. 28-43.

(1) Report of the committee set up to develop a statement of basic principles in the field of cost accounting. It consists of four sections: introductory remarks by the first author and separate papers by the other three on cost minimization, income determination, and special problems and definitions. First of an ongoing series of reports from this committee in an attempt to define and establish principles of cost accounting.

(2) Categories: A. Unspecified B. A Priori C. Fundamental Concepts--AAA Committee

* * * * *

AAA, "Report of the Committee on Cost Concepts and Standards," The Accounting Review (April 1952), pp. 174-188.

(1) Report of the study on the possibility of setting principles, concepts and standards of cost accounting including a discussion of objectives, cost computations, and definitions and the relationship of cost accounting to financial accounting. Stresses definitions and concepts rather than principles or standards. Second in a series attempting to determine the principles of cost accounting.

(2) Categories: A. Unspecified B. A Priori C. Fundamental Concepts--AAA Committee

* * * * *

Categories: A--Source discipline. B--Method of analysis. C--Topic.

de Swardt, G. D., "A Theory of Cost and Cost Accounting I," Accounting Research (April 1952a), pp. 150-167.

(1) Discusses the various types of costs in an attempt to contribute to a theory of cost with an accounting orientation. Focuses on the costs of the various factors of production including materials, plant and equipment, interest, and labor.

(2) Categories: A. Economics B. A Priori C. Fundamental Concepts

* * * * *

de Swardt, G. D., "A Theory of Cost and Cost Accounting II," Accounting Research (July 1952b), pp. 237-265.

(1) Continues the discussion in de Swardt (1952a) and focuses on the relationship between costs and volume of output and the pricing and overhead allocation decisions. Includes an appendix illustrating an accounting method which takes into consideration the issues raised.

(2) Categories: A. Economics B. A Priori C. Fundamental Concepts

* * * * *

Benninger, L. J., "Development of Cost Accounting Concepts and Principles," The Accounting Review (January 1954), pp. 27-37.

(1) Presents a report from the Committee on Cost Accounting Concepts and Standards on the role of the Committee, its position in the AAA hierarchy, its recent past attempts at developing a statement of principles, and its current objectives. Continuing reports; this one is a discussion by one of the members rather than a formal report.

(2) Categories: A. Unspecified B. A Priori C. Fundamental Concepts--AAA Committee

* * * * *

AAA, "Tentative Statement of Cost Concepts Underlying Reports for Management Purposes," The Accounting Review (April 1956), pp. 182-193.

(1) Presents the concepts of the Committee and discusses the nature of business costs, the classification of costs, and the uses of cost for planning and control. This report provided many concepts and definitions.

(2) Categories: A. Unspecified B. A Priori C. Fundamental Concepts--AAA Committee

* * * * *

Categories: A--Source discipline. B--Method of analysis. C--Topic.

Mattessich, R., "The Constellation of Accountancy and Economics," The Accounting Review (October 1956), pp. 551-564.

(1) Discusses the overlap between economics and accounting, references considerable literature, and suggests how the two fields might be integrated. Speculates that in the future accountants will need comprehensive training in economic analysis and mathematics. An excellent discussion of economics and accounting.

(2) Categories: A. Economics B. A Priori C. Fundamental Concepts

* * * * *

Gregory, R. H. and T. V. V. Atwater, "Cost and Value of Management Information as Functions of Age," Accounting Research (January 1957), pp. 42-69.

(1) Presents an analysis of the effect age of information has on its cost and value. Includes discussion of information interval, reporting delay, and the calculation of optimal cost and age. Interesting analysis of the cost and value of information.

(2) Categories: A. Unspecified B. A Priori C. Fundamental Concepts

* * * * *

Bedford, N. M., "The Nature of Business Costs, General Concepts," The Accounting Review (January 1957), pp. 8-14.

(1) Presents a discussion of the thinking of the Cost Committee in formulating the tentative statement of concepts [AAA (1956)]. The discussion includes the multiple valuations of business cost, the elements of business costs, the Committee's development of a framework, and the various cost definitions within the framework. Provides insight into the workings of the Committee.

(2) Categories: A. Unspecified B. A Priori C. Fundamental Concepts--AAA Committee

* * * * *

Categories: A--Source discipline. B--Method of analysis. C--Topic.

Anthony, R. N., "Cost Concepts for Control," The Accounting Review (April 1957), pp. 229-234.

(1) Discusses the cost framework and details the approach used by the Committee in defining the concepts in the 1956 tentative statement relating to control. The paper begins with a discussion of psychology and motivation and an example illustrates the effect an accounting system can have. This paper by a member of the Committee provides insight as well as an excellent definitional discussion of the motivational aspects of accounting for control.

(2) Categories: A. Unspecified B. A Priori C. Fundamental Concepts--AAA Committee

* * * * *

Wallace, E. L., "Some Comments on the Statement of Planning Costs," The Accounting Review (July 1957), pp. 448-466.

(1) Discusses the planning costs section of the 1956 tentative statement report including the concept of cash equivalents and measurement procedures, including discounting. Includes an example of how these concepts can apply to actual cases. Provides insight into the work of the Committee and includes some good definitions.

(2) Categories: A. Unspecified B. A Priori C. Fundamental Concepts--AAA Committee

* * * * *

Barhydt, D., R. H. Clement, D. W. Lufkin and A. J. Yorke, "Planning Concepts in the 'Tentative Statement of Cost Concepts'," The Accounting Review (October 1957), pp. 593-597.

(1) Discusses the planning portion of the 1956 tentative statement from the perspective of a business manager. Includes discussion of its strengths, weaknesses, and overall effectiveness. Provides a user perspective on a statement of cost accounting principles.

(2) Categories: A. Unspecified B. A Priori C. Fundamental Concepts--AAA Committee

* * * * *

Categories: A--Source discipline. B--Method of analysis. C--Topic.

Perry, K. W., "Accounting and Economics Reciprocally Indebted," The Accounting Review (July 1958), pp. 450-454.

(1) Argues that accounting and economics are closely related since they treat similar material and subjects. Reviews the debts each field owes to the other and calls for recognition of their interdependence. Continues the discussion of economic and accounting concepts and their similarities and differences.

(2) Categories: A. Economics B. A Priori C. Fundamental Concepts

* * * * *

AAA, "Report of the Committee on Management Accounting," The Accounting Review (April 1959), pp. 207-214.

(1) Defines management accounting and discusses the significance and related educational implications of management accounting. Provides a discussion of where management accounting fits in.

(2) Categories: A. Unspecified B. A Priori C. Fundamental Concepts--AAA Committee

* * * * *

AAA, "Report of the Committee on Management Accounting," The Accounting Review (July 1960), pp. 400-404.

(1) Presents an amplification of the 1958 report [AAA (1959)] on the nature and significance of management accounting by defining more explicitly the functions to be performed and the problem areas of management accounting. Organizes the problem areas under production, distribution, and financial management.

(2) Categories: A. Unspecified B. A Priori C. Fundamental Concepts--AAA Committee

* * * * *

Boyd, V. and D. Taylor, "The Magic Words-Managerial Accounting," The Accounting Review (January 1961), pp. 105-112.

(1) Discusses the managerial approach as found in textbooks and courses and defines it as one which places emphasis on the use of accounting data as differentiated from the conventional approach which emphasizes the preparation of accounting reports. While primarily oriented toward teaching accounting this article indicates the shift in perspective from producers of accounting information to users.

(2) Categories: A. Unspecified B. A Priori C. Fundamental Concepts

* * * * *

Categories: A--Source discipline. B--Method of analysis. C--Topic.

Kircher, P., "Theory and Research in Management Accounting," The Accounting Review (January 1961), pp. 43-49.

(1) Describes current management accounting literature as mostly descriptions of actual practices or those thought to be effective and proposes a framework for a field of theory in management accounting. Such a framework would provide a logical structure and show researchers how their efforts are linked. Good critique of the lack of theory behind most of the literature of the day.

(2) Categories: A. Unspecified B. A Priori C. Fundamental Concepts

* * * * *

Singer, F. A., "Management Accounting," The Accounting Review (January 1961), pp. 112-118.

(1) Defines management accounting and discusses many of the current topics in the area including product costing, planning, and control. While primarily oriented toward teaching management accounting this article provides insight into the topics current at that time.

(2) Categories: A. Unspecified B. A Priori C. Fundamental Concepts

* * * * *

AAA, "Report of the Management Accounting Committee," The Accounting Review (July 1962), pp. 523-537.

(1) Discusses the conceptual differences between management accounting and other fields of accounting. Concludes that the concepts and reporting objectives differ and that there is justification for attempting to formulate a separate body of concepts.

(2) Categories: A. Unspecified B. A Priori C. Fundamental Concepts--AAA Committee

* * * * *

Davidson, S., "Old Wine into New Bottles," The Accounting Review (April 1963a). pp. 278-284.

(1) Reviews J. M. Clark's Studies in the Economics of Overhead Costs, points out sections pertinent to cost accounting, criticizes some in light of current standards, and discusses those that have merit but have not yet been implemented. This is the first review of this book in an accounting journal (although not the first by an accountant as pointed out by the author).

(2) Categories: A. Economics B. A Priori C. Fundamental Concepts

* * * * *

Categories: A--Source discipline. B--Method of analysis. C--Topic.

Davidson, S., "The Day of Reckoning: Managerial Analysis and Accounting Theory," Journal of Accounting Research (Autumn 1963b), pp. 117-126.

(1) Discusses the introduction of managerial analysis to accounting theory as a resolution of the apparent conflict between managerial and financial accounting. Includes discussion of areas where the two differ including obsolescence, development costs, inventories, and income taxes. Introduces the idea of incorporating managerial analysis techniques into general accounting practice.

(2) Categories: A. Unspecified B. A Priori C. Fundamental Concepts

* * * * *

Golembiewski, R. T., "Accountancy as a Function of Organization Theory," The Accounting Review (April 1964), pp. 333-341.

(1) Discusses the effect organizational structure has on the management accounting system and illustrates how the organization can be designed to overcome the dysfunctional effects of traditional structure. Early discussion of organization theory and how it could impact the design of organizations and accounting systems.

(2) Categories: A. Psychology-Organization B. A Priori
C. Fundamental Concepts

* * * * *

Willingham, J. J., "The Accounting Entity: A Conceptual Model," The Accounting Review (July 1964), pp. 543-552.

(1) Presents a description of an accounting entity from the theory of social organization. Includes discussion of human interaction, norm, role, position in the organization, and exchange both inside and outside the organization. While not specifically related to management accounting, this article discusses many of the concepts important to an understanding of the functioning of individuals in an organization.

(2) Categories: A. Psychology-Organization B. A Priori
C. Fundamental Concepts

* * * * *

Categories: A--Source discipline. B--Method of analysis. C--Topic.

Benninger, L. J., "Accounting Theory and Cost Accounting," The Accounting Review (July 1965), pp. 547-557.

(1) Discusses recent theory formulations of the AAA and AICPA and how cost accounting fits in. Includes discussion of three problem areas: normal overhead rates, the loss concept, and accounting for marketing costs.

(2) Categories: A. Unspecified B. A Priori C. Fundamental Concepts

* * * * *

Haseman, W. C., "An Interpretive Framework for Cost," The Accounting Review (October 1968), pp. 738-752.

(1) Presents a framework for interpreting the meaning of cost in different situations.

(2) Categories: A. Unspecified B. A Priori C. Fundamental Concepts

* * * * *

Solomons, D. ed., Studies in Cost Analysis, Second Edition (Homewood, IL: Irwin, 1968).

(1) A second edition (the first was called Studies in Costing) presenting a collection of important articles in cost analysis and control. Includes sections on cost concepts, cost behavior, pricing, cost control, and mathematical programming. This "readings" book is included in this bibliography because it contains many research papers that have not appeared elsewhere in the accounting research literature.

(2) Categories: A. Economics/Mathematics B. Multiple C. Fundamental Concepts

* * * * *

Hakansson, N., "An Induced Theory of Accounting Under Risk," The Accounting Review (July 1969), pp. 495-514.

(1) Presents a normative model of the individual's economic decision problem under risk and shows that it provides a basis for the formation and operation of firms and an induced theory of accounting for these firms. An excellent discussion of individual preferences, resources, opportunities, strategies, and decision-relevant information.

(2) Categories: A. Economics B. Modeling C. Fundamental Concepts

* * * * *

Categories: A--Source discipline. B--Method of analysis. C--Topic.

AAA, "Report of the Committee on Managerial Decision Models," <u>The Accounting Review</u> (Supplement 1969), pp. 43-76.

(1) Discusses managerial decision models and the accounting information needed to implement such models. Includes discussion of behavioral factors, the relationship of standards from ASOBAT to information for decision models, and specific models including inventory and capital budgeting. The first in a new series of committee reports.

(2) Categories: A. Unspecified B. A Priori C. Fundamental Concepts--AAA Committee

* * * * *

AAA, "Report of the Committee on Managerial Accounting," <u>The Accounting Review</u> (Supplement 1970), pp. 1-8.

(1) Discusses the data needs of the planning and control functions and the differences and inconsistencies that can arise between the two.

(2) Categories: A. Unspecified B. A Priori C. Fundamental Concepts--AAA Committee

* * * * *

McDonough, J. J., "The Accountant, Data Collection and Social Exchange," <u>The Accounting Review</u> (October 1971), pp. 676-685.

(1) Discusses the theory of social exchange and relates it to the accountant's role as a data collector in an organization. Concludes that awareness of and sensitivity to the social exchange process is important for the accountant. Introduces the theory of social exchange and continues the discussion of the accountant in an organization.

(2) Categories: A. Unspecified B. A Priori C. Fundamental Concepts

* * * * *

AAA, "Report of the Committee on Managerial Accounting, 1969-1971," <u>The Accounting Review</u> (Supplement 1972), pp. 317-335.

(1) Presents a taxonomy of information choice problems in management accounting and a review of the literature in the area using this taxonomy. References considerable literature.

(2) Categories: A. Unspecified B. A Priori C. Fundamental Concepts--AAA Committee

* * * * *

Categories: A--Source discipline. B--Method of analysis. C--Topic.

AAA, "Report of the Committee on Internal Measurement and Reporting," The Accounting Review (Supplement 1973), pp. 209-241.

(1) Discusses the research strategies used in studying the areas of internal measurement and reporting. Includes discussion of the approaches and data collection techniques of historical, experimental, and field study research.

(2) Categories: A. Unspecified B. A Priori C. Fundamental Concepts--AAA Committee

* * * * *

AAA, "Report of the Committee on Concepts and Standards-Internal Planning and Control," The Accounting Review (Supplement 1974), pp. 79-96.

(1) Discusses the alternative approaches to internal accounting system design and the factors that should be considered in implementing one particular approach, the information evaluation approach. Concludes that tradeoffs among desirable factors are possible and illustrates the different rankings that occur under two different decision situations.

(2) Categories: A. Unspecified B. A Priori C. Fundamental Concepts--AAA Committee

* * * * *

Mock, T. J., Measurement and Accounting Information Criteria, Studies in Accounting Research #13 (American Accounting Association, 1976).

(1) Discusses measurement theory and its relationship to accounting and derives a set of accounting information criteria including usefulness, reliability, and validity. Concludes that accountants should emphasize the measurement aspects of data produced by accounting systems. Presents a review and synthesis of measurement theory in accounting. Has some implications for management accounting.

(2) Categories: A. Psychology B. A Priori C. Fundamental Concepts

* * * * *

Categories: A--Source discipline. B--Method of analysis. C--Topic.

Gordon, L. A. and D. Miller, "A Contingency Framework for the Design of Accounting Information Systems," Accounting, Organizations and Society, (June 1976), pp. 59-69.

(1) Discusses the design of accounting information systems within the context of a contingency framework which takes into account the environment, organizational attributes, and managerial decision style. Several hypotheses are developed.

(2) Categories: A. Psychology-Organization B. A Priori C. Fundamental Concepts

* * * * *

Hayes, D. C., "The Contingency Theory of Managerial Accounting," The Accounting Review (January 1977), pp. 22-39.

(1) Proposes a performance evaluation theory which hypothesizes that subunit performance is affected by three major contingency aspects: internal, interdependency, and environmental. The results of an empirical test of this theory are presented which support all three contingencies.

(2) Categories: A. Sociology/Organizational Behavior B. Empirical Test C. Fundamental Concepts

* * * * *

AAA, "Report of the Committee on Concepts and Standards-Managerial Planning and Control," The Accounting Review (Supplement 1977), pp. 55-63.

(1) Discusses a general framework of managerial planning and control and the influence the areas of management science, behavioral science, and management information systems have had on management accounting. The last published committee report in this area.

(2) Categories: A. Unspecified B. A Priori C. Fundamental Concepts--AAA Committee

* * * * *

Categories: A--Source discipline. B--Method of analysis. C--Topic.

Hopwood, A. G., "Towards an Organizational Perspective for the Study of Accounting and Information Systems," Accounting, Organizations and Society (August 1978), pp. 3-13.

(1) Discusses studies with an organizational perspecive toward the design and operation of accounting systems as an introduction to an entire issue of articles on this topic. An interesting review of the area of organizational literature.

(2) Categories: A. Psychology-Organization B. A Priori
C. Fundamental Concepts

* * * * *

Sathe, V., "The Relevance of Modern Organization Theory for Managerial Accounting," Accounting, Organizations and Society (August 1978), pp. 89-92.

(1) Reports on a symposium organized to explore the relevance of recent developments in organization theory to management accounting and discusses the main points contained in papers presented and discussed. Continues the literature on organization theory (ties to Golembiewski [1964]).

(2) Categories: A. Psychology-Organization B. A Priori
C. Fundamental Concepts

* * * * *

Waterhouse, J. H. and P. Tiessen, "A Contingency Framework for Management Accounting System Research," Accounting, Organizations and Society (August 1978), pp. 65-76.

(1) Presents a model for the comparative analysis of organizations based on contingency theory which permits identification of control requirements of various types of organizations. Develops hypotheses on the relationship between organization structure and the design of management accounting systems.

(2) Categories: A. Psychology-Organization B. A Priori
C. Fundamental Concepts

* * * * *

Categories: A--Source discipline. B--Method of analysis. C--Topic.

Otley, D. T., "The Contingency Theory of Management Accounting: Achievement and Prognosis," Accounting, Organizations and Society (December 1980), pp. 413-428.

(1) Reviews the literature on the contingency theory of management accounting and discusses the implications for research. Concludes that while the theory looks promising as a theory of management accounting the realization of such is a long way off.

(2) Categories: A. Psychology-Organization B. A Priori C. Fundamental Concepts

* * * * *

Ewusi-Mensah, K., "The External Organizational Environment and Its Impact on Management Information Systems," Accounting, Organizations and Society (December 1981), pp. 301-316.

(1) Discusses the interaction between organizations and their environments and the approaches organizations can use to collect, process, evaluate, and communicate information about the external environment for use in decision-making.

(2) Categories: A. Unspecified B. A Priori C. Fundamental Concepts

* * * * *

Categories: A--Source discipline. B--Method of analysis. C--Topic.

1.2 INFORMATION ECONOMICS/VALUE OF INFORMATION (pp. 44-51)

This subcategory includes papers dealing explicitly with the value of information. The works listed here are a subset of the total information economics literature, much of which has been published outside of accounting. Other articles related to this topic are included in subcategory 6.4, Principal-Agent (pp. 190-192).

LaValle, I. H. and A. Rappaport, "On the the Economics of Acquiring Information of Imperfect Reliability," The Accounting Review (April 1968), pp. 225-230.

(1) Discusses and illustrates the analysis of the costs and benefits of acquiring information of known, but not perfect, reliabilty. The first article in our list that deals explicitly with the economics of information.

(2) Categories: A. Statistics/Economics B. Modeling C. Information Economics.

* * * * *

Feltham, G. A., "The Value of Information," The Accounting Review. (October 1968), pp. 684-696.

(1) Presents a framework for determining the value of a change in the information system and includes discussion of time horizon, preciseness, and relevance of information. Excellent discussion of the various aspects of the value of information.

(2) Categories: A. Economics/Decision Sciences B. Modeling C. Information Economics

* * * * *

Crandall, R. H., "Information Economics and Its Implications for the Further Development of Accounting Theory," The Accounting Review (July 1969), pp. 457-466.

(1) Discusses the information economics model and the accounting model and whether the theory of the economics of information has any implications for the future development of accounting theory. Although not directly addressing management accounting, this provides an early discussion of information economics.

(2) Categories: A. Economics B. A Priori C. Information Economics

* * * * *

Categories: A--Source discipline. B--Method of analysis. C--Topic.

Mock, T. J., "Comparative Values of Information Structures," Journal of Accounting Research (Supplement 1969), pp. 124-159.

(1) Analyzes and tests the effects of changing the structure of the information system in a game environment. Concludes that the comparative value of timely information can be determined.

(2) Categories: A. Economics B. Laboratory Experiment C. Information Economics

* * * * *

Demski, J. S., "Some Decomposition Results for Information Evaluation," Journal of Accounting Research (Autumn 1970b), pp. 178-198.

(1) Discusses the decomposition approach to information system evaluation as proposed by Feltham and concludes it is possible to control for the error induced when decomposing certain total models.

(2) Categories: A. Economics/Decision Sciences B. Modeling C. Information Economics

* * * * *

Feltham, G. A. and J. S. Demski, "The Use of Models in Information Evaluation," The Accounting Review (October 1970), pp. 623-640.

(1) Describes and presents a model of how information evaluators select the information to be provided to decision makers and compares it to the model used to predict the decision maker's actions and selections.

(2) Categories: A. Economics B. Modeling C. Information Economics

* * * * *

Mock, T. J., "Concepts of Information Value and Accounting," The Accounting Review (October 1971), pp. 765-778.

(1) Discusses the information value of a message including value for decision-making, model improvement, and learning. Several hypotheses relating to information systems design are presented.

(2) Categories: A. Unspecified B. A Priori C. Information Economics

* * * * *

Categories: A--Source discipline. B--Method of analysis. C--Topic.

Butterworth, J. E., "The Accounting System as An Information Function," Journal of Accounting Research (Spring 1972), pp. 1-27.

(1) Describes accounting information as a function of the set of observable effects and discusses the use of this function in analyzing real-world systems.

(2) Categories: A. Operations Research B. Modeling C. Information Economics

* * * * *

Demski, J. S., "Information Improvement Bounds," Journal of Accounting Research (Spring 1972a), pp. 58-76.

(1) Discusses the existence of improvement bounds in the optimal information system decision and analyzes it for a quadratic utility function setting. Techniques for approximating these for more complex utility functions are also discussed.

(2) Categories: A. Economics/Decision Theory B. Modeling C. Information Economics

* * * * *

Mock, T. J., T. L. Estrin and M. A. Vasarhelyi, "Learning Patterns, Decision Approach, and Value of Information," Journal of Accounting Research (Spring 1972), pp. 129-153.

(1) Discusses the findings of Mock (1969) and the relationships between different information structures, learning patterns, and decision approaches.

(2) Categories: A. Unspecified B. A Priori C. Information Economics

* * * * *

Marshall, R. M., "Determining an Optimal Accounting Information System for an Unidentified User," Journal of Accounting Research (Autumn 1972), pp. 286-307.

(1) Presents a decision model for the problem of determining an optimal information system for a rational decision maker whose preferences for different decision outcomes and beliefs are unknown. Discusses the conditions under which such a solution exists.

(2) Categories: A. Economics/Decision Theory B. Modeling C. Information Economics

* * * * *

Categories: A--Source discipline. B--Method of analysis. C--Topic.

Feltham, G. A., Information Evaluation, Studies in Accounting Research #5, (American Accounting Association, 1972).

(1) Discusses the nature of information and presents a multiperiod information evaluation model and applies the model to the notions of relevance, timeliness, and accuracy of the information reported. An example employing the basic inventory model is used throughout to illustrate.

(2) Categories: A. Economics B. Modeling C. Information Economics

* * * * *

Ronen, J. and G. Falk, "Accounting Aggregation and the Entropy Measure: An Experimental Approach," The Accounting Review (October 1973), pp. 696-717.

(1) Reports the results of experiments designed to test the relationship between the information measure of entropy and the perceived value of expected information. The findings cast doubt on the general applicability of entropy measures in accounting. Behavioral studies with implications for the economics of information.

(2) Categories: A. Unspecified B. Experiment C. Information Economics

* * * * *

Baiman, S., "The Evaluation and Choice of Internal Information Systems Within a Multi-person World," Journal of Accounting Research (Spring 1975), pp. 1-15.

(1) Analyzes the optimal choice of internal information systems in a multi-person setting and concludes that under certain condition the choice of information system can affect the actions of the competitor.

(2) Categories: A. Economics B. Modeling C. Information Economics (Also could be classified as an early principal-agent paper.)

* * * * *

Categories: A--Source discipline. B--Method of analysis. C--Topic.

Demski, J. S. and G. A. Feltham, Cost Determination: A Conceptual Approach, (Ames, Iowa: Iowa State University Press, 1976).

(1) Presents a conceptual framework for selecting among cost measurement techniques based upon an information evaluation approach. Takes a resource allocation perspective and includes illustrative examples. Conceptual discussion of the impact various cost measurement methods have on decision-making.

(2) Categories: A. Economics B. Modeling C. Information Economics

* * * * *

Feltham, G. A., "Cost Aggregation: An Information Economic Analysis," Journal of Accounting Research (Spring 1977), pp. 42-70.

(1) Analyzes the payoff consequences of aggregating cost information and predictions and presents the results of a simulation analysis of the extent of loss due to aggregation.

(2) Categories: Economics/Decision Theory B. Modeling and Simulation Analysis C. Information Economics.

* * * * *

Itami, H., Adaptive Behavior: Management Control and Information Analysis, Studies in Accounting Research #15 (American Accounting Association, 1977).

(1) Presents a mathematical analysis of two problems of adaptive behavior: the design of a performance evaluation system that will motivate such behavior, and the analysis of information flows for this behavior. Includes presentation of an adaptive behavior model and a discussion of the results derived from it. It is a rigorous analysis of management control systems. Although, it deals with principal-agent problems, it is not solely an agency manograph.

(2) Categories: A. Economics/Operations Research B. Modeling C. Information Economics (Could also be classified under Principal-Agent models.)

* * * * *

Categories: A--Source discipline. B--Method of analysis. C--Topic.

Uecker, W. C., "A Behavioral Study of Information System Choice," Journal of Accounting Research (Spring 1978), pp. 169-189.

(1) Presents the results of a test of the ability of accountants to apply concepts from the normative theory of information evaluation (Feltham and Demski 1970) to the information system choice decision. The findings indicate such ability is limited. One of a few experiments with implications for information economics.

(2) Categories: A. Psychology B. Laboratory Experiment
C. Information Economics

* * * * *

Mock, T. J. and M. A. Vasarhelyi, "A Synthesis of the Information Economics and Lens Models," Journal of Accounting Research (Autumn 1978), pp. 414-423.

(1) Presents an information processing model that integrates the Brunswick lens model within the information economics model and provides a combined model which considers both normative and descriptive elements. While not directly oriented toward management accounting, this model integrates two of the primary research areas affecting management accounting.

(2) Categories: A. Economics and Psychology B. Modeling
C. Information Economics

* * * * *

Sundem, G. L., "A Game Theory Model of the Information Evaluator and the Decision Maker," Journal of Accounting Research (Spring 1979), pp. 243-261.

(1) Presents a model of the multiperson relationship within an organization between the information evaluator and the decision maker using a game theory approach. Includes coverage of both cooperative and noncooperative solutions.

(2) Categories: A. Economics/Decision Theory B. Modeling
C. Information Economics

* * * * *

Categories: A--Source discipline. B--Method of analysis. C--Topic.

Hilton, R. W., "The Determinants of Cost Information Value: An Illustrative Analysis," Journal of Accounting Research (Autumn 1979), pp. 411-435.

(1) Discusses the value of information and identifies and illustrates in a CVP context the role various factors play in determining the value of information. Specific determinants identified included the nature of the information system, initial uncertainty, and the decision makers' technology environment and preferences.

(2) Categories: A. Economics B. A Priori C. Information Economics

* * * * *

Demski, J. S., Information Analysis, Second Edition, (Reading, Mass.: Addison-Wesley Publishing Company, 1980).

(1) Presents an analysis of the economic aspects of information for a decision-maker under uncertainty. Includes discussion of producer-user separation and information market considerations. The second edition of a classic book on the applications of information economics in accounting.

(2) Categories: A. Economics/Decision Theory B. Modeling
C. Information Economics

* * * * *

Lobo, G. J. and M. W. Maher, Information Economics and Accounting Research (Ann Arbor, Michigan: Division of Research, Graduate School of Business Administration, The University of Michigan, 1980).

(1) Presents lectures, readings, and summarized discussions from a workshop conducted by Joel Demski on the economics of information. Includes applications to both management and financial accounting. Presents a synthesis of the work in this area, including some of the key articles published outside of the accounting literature.

(2) Categories: A. Economics B. Modeling C. Information Economics

* * * * *

Newman, D. P., "Prospect Theory: Implications for Information Evaluation," Accounting, Organizations and Society (July 1980), pp. 217-230.

(1) Discusses and compares expected utility theory and prospect theory in a setting of alternative information system choices. The findings suggest different implications for information evaluation depending on the theory chosen.

(2) Categories: A. Economics B. A Priori C. Information Economics

* * * * *

Categories: A--Source discipline. B--Method of analysis. C--Topic.

Hilton, R. W., R. J. Swieringa, and R. E. Hoskin, "Perception of Accuracy as a Determinant of Information Value," Journal of Accounting Research (Spring 1981), pp. 86-108.

(1) Reports the results of an experiment designed to examine the effect the information evaluators' perception of accuracy has on information value. The findings showed individualistic differences which differed significantly from previous studies.

(2) Categories: A. Psychology B. Laboratory Experiment
C. Information Economics

* * * * *

Hilton, R. W. and R. J. Swieringa, "Perception of Initial Uncertainty as a Determinant of Information Value," Journal of Accounting Research (Spring 1981), pp. 109-119.

(1) Reports the results of an experiment designed to test the effect degree of uncertainty in the prior state probability distribution has on information value. The findings differed somewhat from the findings reported in Hilton, Swieringa and Hoskin (1981).

(2) Categories: A. Unspecified B. Laboratory Experiment
C. Information Economics

* * * * *

Categories: A--Source discipline. B--Method of analysis. C--Topic.

1.3 DESCRIPTIONS OF FIRM/INDUSTRY PRACTICES (pp. 52-57)

The articles in this subcategory are discussions of practices in organizations and industries. They are descriptive, relying mostly on personal observation (presumably by the author). Many are excellent descriptions of "what is" (at that time); however, they are not designed for theory testing.

Rorem, C. R., "Cost Analysis for Hospitals," The Accounting Review (June 1930), pp. 159-161.

(1) Discusses the costs of hospital care and the analysis and classification of the various types of costs as well as the allocation of indirect expenses. Provides an early extension of the concepts developed in a factory setting to the analysis of costs in a not-for-profit organization.

(2) Categories: A. Unspecified B. Personal Observation
C. Description of Firm/Industry Practices

* * * * *

Danford, F., "Some Modern Developments in Accounting for Manufacturing Enterprises," The Accounting Review (June 1933), pp. 119-121.

(1) Discusses the cost accounting features at ARMCO that might be applied in other manufacturing concerns; discusses standard costs and the budget plan and gives variance calculations.

(2) Categories: A. Unspecified B. Personal Observation
C. Description of Firm/Industry Practices

* * * * *

Hungate, T. L., "Unit Costs in Institutions of Higher Education," The Accounting Review (March 1934), pp. 38-43.

(1) Discusses the cost of instruction at the college and university level and the determination of unit costs which should be useful in internal administration. Illustrates the movement of cost accounting techniques to another sector and emphasizes the need to know costs when planning.

(2) Categories: A. Unspecified B. Personal Observation
C. Description of Firm/Industry Practices

* * * * *

Categories: A--Source discipline. B--Method of analysis. C--Topic.

McLean, H. I., "Unit Costs of Instruction at the University of Pennsylvania," The Accounting Review (March 1934), pp. 33-37.

(1) Reports on the accounting system used to provide data for an analysis of instructional costs. The costs are reportedly used to present a picture of each school's situation so that corrective action can be taken if needed. Presents a system described as "satisfactory and which does work and presents the information desired." An extension of cost techniques outside the manufacturing setting.

(2) Categories: A. Unspecified B. Personal Observation
C. Description of Firm/Industry Practices

* * * * *

Lorig, A. N., "Cost Accounting and the Classification of Municipal Expenditures," The Accounting Review (September 1936), pp. 291-295.

(1) Defines municipal cost accounting and outlines its purposes and limitations. Projects a marked acceleration in the introduction of costing schemes into municipal accounting. Concludes by calling for a class of expenditures basic to cost accounting which will coordinate the needs for a system of accounts and for cost information.

(2) Categories: A. Unspecified B. Personal Observation
C. Description of Firm/Industry Practices

* * * * *

Walden, R. E., "Cost Analysis for Electric Utilities," The Accounting Review (July 1942), pp. 257-264.

(1) Discusses the extension of cost analysis beyond cost-per-KWH including the use of flexible budget distribution and allocation of costs. Evaluates the various methods of allocating capacity costs.

(2) Categories: A. Unspecified B. Personal Observation
C. Description of Firm/Industry Practices

* * * * *

Smith, F. P., "Lot Release Cost Accounting in the Aviation Industry," The Accounting Review (January 1947), pp. 68-74.

(1) Discusses lot cost accounting as practiced in the aviation industry during the war and the principal problems involved including start-up costs and the material, labor, and overhead costs.

(2) Categories: A. Unspecified B. Personal Observation
C. Description of Firm/Industry Practices

* * * * *

Categories: A--Source discipline. B--Method of analysis. C--Topic.

Zraick, L. E., "Packing House Accounting," The Accounting Review (July 1947), pp. 299-303.

(1) Describes the accounting and cost control procedures used in the meat packing industry. Provides a chart of accounts.

(2) Categories: A. Unspecified B. Personal Observation
C. Description of Firm/Industry Practices

* * * * *

Judd, F., "Development of Cost Accounting Concepts of Scheduled Airlines," The Accounting Review (January 1949), pp. 61-67.

(1) Reviews the development of airline operations which have determined the industry's approach to cost accounting. Includes a discussion of the allocation of various costs. A specific example of how an industry's operations influences its accounting methods.

(2) Categories: A. Unspecified B. Personal Observation
C. Description of Firm/Industry Practices

* * * * *

Bray, F. S., C. Smith and D. R. B. Smith, "Worsted Spinning Costs: A Specific Application of the General Principles of Standard Costing," Accounting Research (July 1949), pp. 163-204.

(1) Discusses the determination and use of standard costs in the textile industry in the U.K. Includes several illustrated examples and considerable description of actual practices.

(2) Categories: A. Unspecified B. Personal Observation
C. Description of Firm/Industry Practices

* * * * *

Lehnberg, V. B., "Cost Accounting for Motor Freight Lines," The Accounting Review (April 1950), pp. 184-191.

(1) Uses an example to illustrate the use of standards in the trucking industry to permit analysis of shipping costs.

(2) Categories: A. Unspecified B. Personal Observation
C. Description of Firm/Industry Practices

* * * * *

Categories: A--Source discipline. B--Method of analysis. C--Topic.

Osborn, R. C., "The Relative Efficiency of Large, Medium-Sized and Small Business," The Accounting Review (July 1950), pp. 262-273.

(1) Presents statistical data on the relative efficiency of various sized firms as measured on a cost basis. Includes discussion of studies made in the iron and steel industry, the rubber tire industry, the wholesale bread industry, and others. While not directly concerning management accounting, the study does provide a good discussion of efficiency and the use of cost data in measuring efficiency or lack of it.

(2) Categories: A. Unspecified B. Field Studies C. Description of Firm/Industry Practices

* * * * *

Lehnberg, V. B., "Cost Accounting for Motor Freight Terminals," The Accounting Review (April 1952), pp. 215-220.

(1) Extension of a previous analysis of transportation costs [Lehnberg (1950)] to include a consideration of weight groups in showing how the costs of transporting the various classes and groups can be determined.

(2) Categories: A. Unspecified B. Personal Observation C. Description of Firm/Industry Practices

* * * * *

Peacock, R. B., "The Assessment of a Project in the Heavy Chemical Industry," Accounting Research (October 1954), pp. 275-288.

(1) Describes the decision process in the chemical industry for decisions such as level of capacity, make-or-buy, and processing of by products. Includes discussion of costs and volume of output.

(2) Categories: A. Unspecified B. Personal Observation C. Description of Firm/Industry Practices

* * * * *

Categories: A--Source discipline. B--Method of analysis. C--Topic.

Anton, H. R., "The Funds Statement as an Internal Report to Management," The Accounting Review (January 1955), pp. 71-79.

(1) Reports the results of a survey of 500 industrial firms (197 responses) on the uses of the funds statement. Presentation of the results includes use by size of firm, form of data (historical/ projected), form of report, and others. The results indicate the statement is used for managerial planning and control.

(2) Categories: A. Unspecified B. Survey C. Description of Firm/ Industry Practices

* * * * *

Feyerharm, R. W., "Budgetary Accounting Procedures and Accounting Forms for Small Colleges and Universities," The Accounting Review (January 1955), pp. 80-85.

(1) Reports on a survey of the accounting procedures of colleges and universities, presents the results, and makes observations.

(2) Categories: A. Unspecified B. Survey C. Description of Firm/ Industry Practices

* * * * *

Pape, M. E., "Costs and Inventory Values in the Glue Industry," The Accounting Review (January 1959), pp. 52-58.

(1) Presents a discussion of a case illustrating the cost procedures used in a glue plant.

(2) Categories: A. Unspecified B. Personal Observation
C. Description of Firm/Industry Practices

* * * * *

Carlisle, H. M., "Cost Accounting for Advanced Technology Programs, The Accounting Review (January 1966), pp. 115-120.

(1) Discusses internal accounting for high technology/research organizations and presents ten guidelines including several relating to cost codes and the accumulation and classification of costs by organizational unit and by project.

(2) Categories: A. Unspecified B. Personal Observation
C. Description of Firm/Industry Practices

* * * * *

Categories: A--Source discipline. B--Method of analysis. C--Topic.

Vatter, W. J., "The Use of Operations Research in American Companies," The Accounting Review (October 1967), pp. 721-730.

(1) Presents a survey analysis of the use of operations research in 360 firms including type of methods used, organization of the OR unit, and extent of and use of the output. One of a few comprehensive descriptive papers in the literature

(2) Categories: A. Operations Research B. Survey C. Description of Firm/Industry Practices

* * * * *

Categories: A--Source discipline. B--Method of analysis. C--Topic.

1.4 HUMAN RESOURCE ACCOUNTING (pp. 58-60)

This subcategory contains the small set of human resource accounting articles that dealt with management accounting.

Brummet, R. L., E. G. Flamholtz and W. C. Pyle, "Human Resource Measurement - A Challenge for Accountants," The Accounting Review (April 1968), pp. 217-224.

(1) Proposes including the various costs of maintaining a work force in an asset account rather than the current practice of showing no human resources. Includes a discussion of the various measures of human resources. First discussion of human resource accounting.

(2) Categories: A. Unspecified B. A Priori C. Human Resource Accounting

* * * * *

Flamholtz, E. G., "A Model for Human Resource Valuation: A Stochastic Process with Service Rewards," The Accounting Review (April 1971), pp. 253-267.

(1) Presents a model for valuing human resources based on the discounted value of expected future services.

(2) Categories: A. Unspecified B. Modeling C. Human Resource Accounting

* * * * *

Flamholtz, E. G., "Assessing the Validity of a Theory of Human Resource Value: A Field Study," Journal of Accounting Research (Supplement 1972a), pp. 241-282.

(1) Presents the results of a study designed to test the validity of the theory of human resource value and determine whether the set of hypothesized variables is actually used by managers in assessing the value of human resources.

(2) Categories: A. Unspecified B. Field Study C. Human Resource Accounting

* * * * *

Categories: A--Source discipline. B--Method of analysis. C--Topic.

Flamholtz, E. G., "Towards a Theory of Human Resource Value in Formal Organizations," The Accounting Review (October 1972b), pp. 666-676.

(1) Presents a model of the determinants of an individual's value to an organization including a discussion of both individual factors and organizational factors.

(2) Categories: A. Unspecified B. A Priori C. Human Resource Accounting

* * * * *

Dermer, J. and J. P. Siegel, "The Role of Behavioral Measures in Accounting for Human Resources," The Accounting Review (January 1974), pp. 88-97.

(1) Reports the results of an experimental analysis of the role behavioral measures might play in valuing human resources. The findings indicate measurement of behavioral variables is not effective in valuing human resources.

(2) Categories: A. Unspecified B. Experiment C. Human Resource Accounting

* * * * *

Jaggi, B. and H. Lau, "Toward a Model for Human Resource Valuation," The Accounting Review (April 1974), pp. 321-329.

(1) Presents a model for human resource valuation based on actuarial concepts using homogeneous Markov analysis.

(2) Categories: A. Mathematics B. Modeling C. Human Resource Accounting

* * * * *

Tomassini, L. A., "Behavioral Research on Human Resource Accounting: A Contingency Framework," Accounting, Organizations and Society (August 1976), pp. 239-252.

(1) Presents a framework for behavioral research in human resource accounting based on contingency theory. Specific hypotheses related to each dimension of the framework are suggested.

(2) Categories: A. Psychology-Organization B. A Priori C. Human Resource Accounting

* * * * *

Categories: A--Source discipline. B--Method of analysis. C--Topic.

Flamholtz, E. G., "The Impact of Human Resource Valuation on Management Decisions: A Laboratory Experiment," Accounting, Organizations and Society (August 1976), pp. 153-165.

(1) Reports the results of a laboratory experiment designed to test the effect human resource value information has on the staffing decision. The findings indicate nonmonetary information may influence the decisions and the decision-maker's decision set.

(2) Categories: A. Unspecified B. Laboratory Experiment C. Human Resource Accounting

* * * * *

Tomassini, L. A., "Assessing the Impact of Human Resource Accounting: An Experimental Study of Managerial Decision Preferences," The Accounting Review (October 1977), pp. 904-914.

(1) Reports the results of a study designed to examine the effect human resource accounting data has on decision making preferences. The findings indicate support for HRA data causing preference differences.

(2) Categories: A. Psychology-Individual B. Laboratory Experiment C. Human Resource Accounting

* * * * *

Harrell, A. M. and H. D. Klick, "Comparing the Impact of Monetary and Nonmonetary Human Asset Measures on Executive Decision Making," Accounting, Organizations and Society (December 1980), pp. 393-400.

(1) Reports the results of an experiment designed to test the different weights decision makers place on monetary and nonmonetary HRA measures and their effects on decisions made. The findings indicate greater emphasis is placed on monetary measures and different decisions were made with the different measures.

(2) Categories: A. Psychology-Individual B. Laboratory Experiment C. Human Resource Accounting

* * * * *

Categories: A--Source discipline. B--Method of analysis. C--Topic.

1.5 INTERNATIONAL COMPARISONS (pp. 61-62)

The articles in this subcategory are descriptions of practices in foreign countries. They are descriptive and generally based on personal observation.

Noble, H. S., "Cost Accounting in Great Britain," The Accounting Review (June 1929), pp. 88-93.

(1) Presents a discussion of the similarities and differences in U.K. and U.S. practice.

(2) Categories: A. Unspecified B. Personal Observation C. International Comparisons

* * * * *

Matz, A., "Cost Accounting in Germany," The Accounting Review (September 1940), pp. 371-379.

(1) Presents a description based upon the "General Principles of Cost Accounting" of the German Board of Industrial Economy. Includes coverage of the nature and tasks of cost accounting and the principles of construction of a cost accounting system. A description of a statement of principles from another country.

(2) Categories: A. Unspecified B. Personal Observation C. International Comparisons

* * * * *

Mann, E. J., "Management and Industrial Accounting in Western Europe," The Accounting Review (April 1956), pp. 244-252.

(1) Discusses the backgrounds, management, and use of industrial accounting techniques including budgeting and standard costs in western Europe.

(2) Categories: A. Unspecified B. Personal Observation C. International Comparisons

* * * * *

Categories: A--Source discipline. B--Method of analysis. C--Topic.

Wright, W. H., "Observations of an American Cost Accountant Abroad," The Accounting Review (January 1957), pp. 107-111.

(1) Discusses the variety of cost accounting systems and techniques in western Europe including standard costs and the rise of the certification of cost accountants in England.

(2) Categories: A. Unspecified B. Personal Observation C. International Comparisons

* * * * *

Smyth, E. B., "Management Accounting in Australia," The Accounting Review (July 1960), pp. 464-470.

(1) Compares the use of management accounting techniques in Australia with those used in the U.S. and Canada. References surveys on the extent of use in all three countries.

(2) Categories: A. Unspecified B. Survey C. International Comparisons

* * * * *

Mauldon, R. G., H. P. Schapper and D. W. G. Treloar, "A Managerial Accounting System for Australian Agriculture," Abacus (August 1968), pp. 39-50.

(1) Presents a managerial accounting system used in Australia to generate information for managerial uses. The system is established at a university and provides information as a service to local farmers. Interesting discussion of a central system providing managerial information to autonomous farmers rather than subunits.

(2) Categories: A. Unspecified B. Personal Observation C. International Comparisons

* * * * *

Gorelick, G., "Soviet Accounting, Planning and Control," Abacus (June 1974), pp. 13-25.

(1) Describes the central industrial planning and control system of the Soviet Union and the role played by accounting information.

(2) Categories: A. Economics B. Personal Observation C. International Comparisons (Could also be classified under planning and control.)

* * * * *

Categories: A--Source discipline. B--Method of analysis. C--Topic.

1.6 SYSTEMS (pp. 63-67)

The articles in this subcategory discuss management accounting in systems terms, and include those on computer-based systems.

Matz, A., "Problems in Designing an Accounting System," The Accounting Review (April 1945), pp. 216-222.

(1) Discusses the design of a cost system which will produce usable cost reports in light of the requirements, specifications, laws, regulations, and restrictions of the day. Includes coverage of mechanical accounting devices, personnel, internal auditing, and government cost principles. An early article addressing the design from a total system perspective.

(2) Categories: A. Unspecified B. A Priori C. Systems

* * * * *

Matz, A., "Electronics in Accounting," The Accounting Review (October 1946), pp. 371-379.

(1) Traces the development of computing devices up to the invention of the electronic general purpose computer in 1945 and discusses its industrial and accounting implications. Includes discussion of its speed and timeliness capabilities and also its potential to bring to light many unknown factors of costs and production. Earliest discussion of the accounting potential of electronic computers.

(2) Categories: A. Unspecified B. A Priori C. Systems

* * * * *

Zlatkovich, C. T., "Some Principles of Accounting System Design," The Accounting Review (July 1958), pp. 419-422.

(1) Discusses five general principles of systems work which will yield satisfactory results at low cost. Considerable emphasis is placed on tailoring the system to the needs of users.

(2) Categories: A. Unspecified B. A Priori C. Systems

* * * * *

Categories: A--Source discipline. B--Method of analysis. C--Topic.

Pfenning, R. E., "Business Information Systems," The Accounting Review (April 1962), pp. 234-243.

(1) Discusses business information systems in general, the requirements for information, and the factors to consider in designing such a system. Illustrates the information system at General Electric by tracing the flow of information through the various computer runs. Good discussion of user needs and the way the accounting system fits into the overall information system.

(2) Categories: A. Unspecified B. Personal Observation C. Systems

* * * * *

Woods, R. S., "Some Dimensions of Integrated Systems," The Accounting Review (July 1964), pp. 598-614.

(1) Discusses the concept of an integrated system and two problems which arise in its use: the intra- and inter- corporate boundaries of the system and the internal redundancies of subsystems. Relates these concepts to accounting and illustrates with an example.

(2) Categories: A. Unspecified B. A Priori C. Systems

* * * * *

Firmin, P. A. and J. J. Linn, "Information Systems and Managerial Accounting," The Accounting Review (January 1968), pp. 75-82.

(1) Discusses the total management information system of a firm and the part management accounting plays. Concludes the new decision models have a need for forms of data other than that supplied by the traditional accounting system. Continues the discussion of management accounting from a "total systems" perspective.

(2) Categories: A. Systems B. A Priori C. Systems

* * * * *

Field, J. E., "Toward a Multi-Level, Multi-Goal Information System," The Accounting Review (July 1969), pp. 593-599.

(1) Discusses the structure of an organization and its management accounting system in terms of systems theory and includes a discussion of organization goals, information systems, and the meaning of control in such a system. An early discussion of the organization in systems terms in the accounting literature.

(2) Categories: A. Psychology-Organization B. A Priori C. Systems

* * * * *

Categories: A--Source discipline. B--Method of analysis. C--Topic.

Colantoni, C. S., R. P. Manes and A. Whinston, "A Unified Approach to the Theory of Accounting and Information Systems," The Accounting Review (January 1971), pp. 90-102.

(1) Proposes an accounting and information system in which monetary and non-monetary economic events are recorded and in which each item of information is linked to every other item.

(2) Categories: A. Unspecified B. A Priori C. Systems

* * * * *

Godfrey, J. T. and T. R. Prince, "The Accounting Model from an Information Systems Perspective," The Accounting Review (January 1971), pp. 75-89.

(1) Describes a formal computer based information system, compares it to a traditional accounting system, and discusses a system that combines elements of both.

(2) Categories: A. Unspecified B. A Priori C. Systems

* * * * *

Lieberman, A. Z. and A. B. Whinston, "A Structuring of an Events - Accounting Information System," The Accounting Review (April 1975), pp. 246-258.

(1) Proposes a total integrated information system designed to provide all information needed for management decision-making, including that not normally including in accounting systems. Uses the concept of events accounting and includes a data base and user-defined structures and functions.

(2) Categories: A. Unspecified B. A Priori C. Systems

* * * * *

Prakash, P. and A. Rappaport, "Information Interdependencies: System Structure Induced by Accounting Information," The Accounting Review (October 1975), pp. 723-734.

(1) Presents a framework that integrates the accounting roles of providing information for managerial purposes and of linking the firm to its environment. Although this article contains considerable emphasis on external aspects, it continues the discussion of accounting in systems terms.

(2) Categories: A. Unspecified B. A Priori C. Systems

* * * * *

Categories: A--Source discipline. B--Method of analysis. C--Topic.

Lucas, H. C., "The Use of an Accounting Information System, Action and Organizational Performance," The Accounting Review (October 1975), pp. 735-746.

(1) Reports the results of a study designed to test the relationships among the use of accounting information, the action taken, and the performance of the manager. Discusses the findings and the implications for systems design.

(2) Categories: A. Psychology-Organization B. Field Experiment C. Systems

* * * * *

Haseman, W. D. and A. B. Whinston, "Design of a Multidimensional Accounting System," The Accounting Review (January 1976), pp. 65-79.

(1) Discusses the data structure of information systems and describes a model for designing the data structure to be used in a multidimensional accounting system; includes an example.

(2) Categories: A. Unspecified B. A Priori C. Systems

* * * * *

Ansari, S. L., "An Integrated Approach to Control System Design," Accounting, Organizations and Society (June 1977), pp. 101-112.

(1) Discusses the interaction between the structural considerations of control systems design and the behavioral considerations and proposes an open systems approach which takes both into account.

(2) Categories: A. Organization Theory B. A Priori C. Systems

* * * * *

Argyris, C., "Organizational Learning and Management Information Systems," Accounting, Organizations and Society (June 1977), pp. 113-124.

(1) Analyzes the implementation problem of management information systems in light of the theory of organizational learning.

(2) Categories: A. Psychology-Organization B. A Priori C. Systems

* * * * *

Categories: A--Source discipline. B--Method of analysis. C--Topic.

Banbury, J. and J. E. Nahapiet, "Towards a Framework for the Study of the Antecedents and Consequences of Information Systems in Organizations," Accounting, Organizations and Society (February 1980), pp. 163-178.

(1) Presents a framework within which information systems and their interface with their organizational context can be studied and their consequences explained. Discusses the part played by beliefs and expectations of both the developers and users of the information and control systems.

(2) Categories: A. Psychology-Organization B. A Priori C. Systems

* * * * *

Ginzberg, M. J., "An Organizational Contingencies View of Accounting and Information Systems Implementation," Accounting, Organizations and Society (December 1980), pp. 369-383.

(1) Presents a typology of accounting and information systems based on the nature of the task supported by the system; propositions for systems design are developed and a framework for analysis and implementation of information systems is presented.

(2) Categories: A. Unspecified B. A Priori C. Systems

* * * * *

Collins, F., "Managerial Accounting Systems and Organizational Control: A Role Perspective," Accounting, Organizations and Society (May 1982), pp. 107-122.

(1) Discusses the relationship between management accounting systems and organization control including accounting's use in communicating role expectations, its importance to motivation, and its use in communicating climate.

(2) Categories: A Psychology-Organization B. A Priori C. Systems

* * * * *

Categories: A--Source discipline. B--Method of analysis. C--Topic.

1.7 ECONOMICS OF INTERNAL ORGANIZATION (pp. 68-71)

The articles in this subcategory address the economics of internal organization. Nearly all are from the economics literature.

Coase, R. H., "The Nature of the Firm," Economica, (November 1937), pp. 386-405.

(1) Discusses the existence of firms and why they emerge in an exchange economy. Includes discussion of the price mechanism, the costs of the market, and uncertainty as they relate to the nature of firms. Classic economic discussion of the firm. Not an accounting paper, but included here because it is generally regarded as the seminal work in the field.

(2) Categories: A. Economics B. A Priori C. Economics of Internal Organization

* * * * *

Chenault, L. R., "Business Behavior and the Theory of the Firm," The Accounting Review (October 1954), pp. 645-651.

(1) Compares/contrasts economist's views of the firm with accounting practices by discussing the economic theory of the firm, whether these concepts coincide with those in accounting, and the shortcomings of economic theory.

(2) Categories: A. Economics B. A Priori C. Economics of Internal Organization

* * * * *

Cyert, R. M. and J. March, Behavioral Theory of the Firm (Englewood Cliffs, N.J.: Prentice Hall, Inc., 1963).

(1) Presents models, and tests of these models, relating to decision-making within business organizations. Includes discussion of organization goals, choices, and expectations as affected by organizational structure and conventional practice.

(2) Categories: A. Economics B. Modeling C. Economics of Internal Organization

* * * * *

Categories: A--Source discipline. B--Method of analysis. C--Topic.

Alchian, A. A., and H. Demsetz, "Production, Information Costs, and Economic Organization," American Economic Review (December 1972), pp. 777-795.

(1) Discusses the theory of economic organization and in particular the process of team production and why this leads to the organization of firms. Includes discussion of the classical theory of the firm and shirking and concludes that it may be that the flow of information to the employer makes the firm take on the characteristics of an efficient market.

(2) Categories: A. Economics B. A Priori C. Economics of Internal Organization

* * * * *

Williamson, O. E., "Markets and Hierarchies: Some Elementary Considerations," American Economic Review (May 1973), pp. 316-325.

(1) Discusses the factors that cause nonmarket organizations to arise in place of markets and within internal organizations the types of hierarchical relationships that arise. Continues the literature on the economics of internal organization begun by Alchian and Demsetz (1972).

(2) Categories: A. Economics B. A Priori C. Economics of Internal Organization

* * * * *

Arrow, K. J., The Limits of Organization, (New York: W. W. Norton and Co. Inc., 1974).

(1) Discusses the organization of society including the price system, the government, the firm, and moral and ethical principles. Includes discussion of decision making and information flows in an organizational context.

(2) Categories: A. Economics B. A Priori C. Economics of Internal Organization

* * * * *

Categories: A--Source discipline. B--Method of analysis. C--Topic.

Spence, A. M., "The Economics of Internal Organization: An Introduction," <u>The Bell Journal of Economics</u> (Spring 1975), pp. 163-172.

(1) Presents an overview of the economics of internal organization, or as the author points out the economic theory of the firm, and introduces five papers on the subject. The papers all are concerned with information and are written by K. J. Arrow; R. Wilson; R. Radner; S. A. Boorman and O. E. Williamson; and M. L. Wachter and J. E. Harris. These papers continue the works of Coase (1937) and Alchian and Demsetz (1972) on resource allocation in nonmarket settings of constrained information.

(2) Categories: A. Economics B. Modeling C. Economics of Internal Organization

* * * * *

Williamson, O. E., <u>Markets and Hierarchies: Analysis and Antitrust Implications</u> (New York: Free Press, 1975).

(1) Discusses markets and organizations and the conditions under which markets will fail and organization will rise to take their place. Includes discussion of the importance of information and transactions costs as they affect the internal structure of the organization. A potential "classic" book on the economics of internal organization.

(2) Categories: A. Economics/Organization Theory B. A Priori C. Economics of Internal Organization

* * * * *

Jensen, M. C., and W. M. Meckling, "Theory of the Firm: Managerial Behavior, Agency Costs, and Ownership Structure," <u>Journal of Financial Economics</u> (October 1976), pp. 305-360.

(1) Presents a theory of the ownership structure of firms based on the theories of property rights, agency, and finance. Includes discussion of the concept and nature of agency costs and who bears these costs. Continues the literature on the form and structure of organizations although primarily oriented toward finance.

(2) Categories: A. Economics B. A Priori C. Economics of Internal Organization

* * * * *

Categories: A--Source discipline. B--Method of analysis. C--Topic.

Ouchi, W., "A Conceptual Framework for the Design of Organizational Control Mechanisms," Management Science (September, 1979), pp. 833-848.

(1) Discusses the problem of motivating cooperation among the members of a team and describes three mechanisms through which organizations can evaluate and control such members: markets, bureaucracies, and clans. Includes an example of each of the three mechanisms.

(2) Categories: A. Economics/Organization Behavior B. A Priori C. Economics of Internal Organization

* * * * *

Maher, M. W., "Regulation and Controls: Firms' Response to the Foreign Corrupt Practices Act," The Accounting Review (October 1981).

(1) Describes how firms allocated resources in response to the FCPA. Presents research based on the premise that managers make cost/benefit decisions in their self-interest, which predicted (a) no change in controls because of the FCPA, but (b) an expenditure of resources to "demonstrate" compliance with the law.

(2) Categories: A. Economics B. Field Study C. Economics of Internal Organization

* * * * *

Dhaliwal, D. S., G. L. Salamon and E. D. Smith, "The Effect of Owner versus Management Control on the Choice of Accounting Methods," Journal of Accounting and Economics (July 1982), pp. 41-56.

(1) Presents an analysis of the relationship between the ownership status of firms and the selection of depreciation method by their managers. Includes empirical tests of derived hypotheses.

(2) Categories: A. Economics B. Empirical C. Economics of Internal Organization

* * * * *

Categories: A--Source discipline. B--Method of analysis. C--Topic.

1.8 GENERAL-MISCELLANEOUS (pp. 72-78)

This subcategory contains articles otherwise not classified. It includes works on the controller department, methods of designing accounting reports, and the regulation aspects of management accounting.

Taggart, H. F., "The Relation of a Cost Accountant to the NRA Codes," The Accounting Review (June 1934), pp. 149-157.

(1) Discusses the extension of cost accounting from its role as a guide to management in the private sector to its appearance in the public sector because of the cost requirements of the NRA. Speculates that the NRA will do for cost accounting what the tax law did for general accounting but concludes that cost will continue to be most important in furnishing facts for the guidance of internal policies.

(2) Categories: A. Unspecified B. A Priori C. General-Misc.

* * * * *

Taggart, H. F., "Accounting and Code Regulation," The Accounting Review (March 1935), pp. 69-76.

(1) Describes the use of cost data in making and amending codes of the NRA, with particular emphasis on the rule against selling goods below cost. Argues that these developments result in a greater need for cost knowledge and are an explicit sanction by the government for cost accounting. That is, the NRA will encourage cost accounting as it makes industry more cost conscious.

(2) Categories: A. Unspecified B. A Priori C. General-Misc.

* * * * *

Elliott, V. L., "Functions and Activities of the Controller's Department," The Accounting Review (June 1940), pp. 185-190.

(1) Traces the development of the controller and discusses his duties and importance. The discussion emphasizes the annual report and auditing but internal aspects of controllership are also covered.

(2) Categories: A. Unspecified B. Personal Observation C. General-Misc. (Role of the Accountant)

* * * * *

Categories: A--Source discipline. B--Method of analysis. C--Topic.

Taggart, H. F., "Accounting in the National-Defense Program," The Accounting Review (March 1941), pp. 33-40.

(1) Reviews the accounting features of the buildup in national defense including the effects of cost-plus contracts and price stablization. An early piece on a topic that was relevant and important during World War II from a practitioners' viewpoint.

(2) Categories: A. Unspecified B. A Priori C. General-Misc.

* * * * *

Kelley, A. C., "Cost Analysis of a Cost-Plus Contract," The Accounting Review (October 1942), pp. 370-376.

(1) Presents a discussion of the problems of controlling costs when the incentive for personal profit has been eliminated by the use of a cost-plus contract. Concludes that the problem is difficult and that no satisfactory solution is apparent. Early recognition of cost-plus contracts brought on by World War II.

(2) Categories: A. Unspecified B. A Priori/Personal Observation C. General-Misc.

* * * * *

Anderson, D. R., "The Function of Industrial Controllership," The Accounting Review (January 1944), pp. 55-65.

(1) Presents the nature of the controllership function and its place in industry from a controller's perspective. Discusses the functions, organizational problems, and responsibilities of the controller. One of several articles during these years defining and discussing the controllership position.

(2) Categories: A. Unspecified B. Personal Observation C. General-Misc. (Role of the Accountant)

* * * * *

Categories: A--Source discipline. B--Method of analysis. C--Topic.

Nelson, O. S., "Cost Principles in Termination Settlements," The Accounting Review (October 1944), pp. 422-430.

(1) Discusses the "Contract Settlement Act of 1944" and how the government will settle up with contractors once the war is over. Includes coverage of the accounting and cost principles to be used in collecting data for a termination settlement, the costs allowed, and the amount of profit permitted. Provides another discussion and view of the government's effects on cost accounting, foreshadowing the CASB's involvement.

(2) Categories: A. Unspecified B. Personal Observation C. General-Misc.

* * * * *

Kohler, E. L. and W. W. Cooper, "Costs, Prices and Profits: Accounting in the War Program," The Accounting Review (July 1945), pp. 267-308.

(1) Reviews a number of the accounting developments in the war program including price control, contract renegotiation, war procurement, and contract termination. Considers some of the possible long-range effects, particularly the use of accounting in establishing social controls.

(2) Categories: A. Unspecified B. Personal Observation C. General-Misc.

* * * * *

Silverman, O. J., "Pretermination Planning," The Accounting Review (July 1945), pp. 316-320.

(1) Presents some of the major problems facing the textile industry in settling its termination claims with the government after the end of the war. The discussion concerns the pretermination planning that is required and includes discussion of the disposition of raw materials, goods in process, and finished goods inventory and the pricing of each.

(2) Categories: A. Unspecified B. Personal Observation C. General-Misc.

* * * * *

Tiffany, K. C., "Reports for Management," The Accounting Review (April 1950), pp. 142-148.

(1) Reviews some of the principles and practices which can be followed to make accounting reports as helpful and effective as possible to management. The perspective taken is that of a manufacturing company and control of its operations. The principles remain the same for both reporting on performance and planning.

(2) Categories: A. Unspecified B. A Priori C. General-Misc.

Categories: A--Source discipline. B--Method of analysis. C--Topic.

Warriner, P., "How Statistical Analysis Can Serve Accountants," The Accounting Review (July 1951), pp. 362-370.

(1) Examines and discusses the use of statistical methods by accountants in extending and improving their services. Of interest to management accounting is the discussion on the need for statistical measurements of cost-volume relationships and the contributions made by research findings which indicate a simple straight-line relationship for costs. Quotes economic research findings indicating straight-line cost curves rather than the hypothesized curvilinear ones. Also could be classified as a cost-estimation paper.

(2) Categories: A. Statistics/Economics B. A Priori C. General-Misc.

* * * * *

Greer, H. C., "Managerial Accounting - Twenty Years From Now," The Accounting Review (April 1954), pp. 175-185.

(1) Discusses management and the current state of cost accounting with a look forward to the developments which could come about in such areas as budgeting and standards, cost analysis, the relationship between costs and prices, and the timliness and form of financial statements.

(2) Categories: A. Unspecified B. A Priori C. General-Misc.

* * * * *

Trueblood, R. M., and W. W. Cooper, "Research and Practice in Statistical Applications to Accounting, Auditing, and Management Control," The Accounting Review (April 1955), pp. 221-229.

(1) Presents a discussion of a research project studying the application of statistical methods to accounting, auditing, and control. Coverage includes progress of the work to date and possible directions for future work. Examples given are primarily auditing; however, management accounting applications are also presented. Presents the concepts of using statistical methods in recording and controlling costs and in controlling inventories.

(2) Categories: A. Unspecified B. A Priori C. General-Misc.

* * * * *

Edwards, J. D., "Reports to Top Management," The Accounting Review (January 1957), pp. 56-59.

(1) Discussion of the communication of information to top management including the basic criteria for accounting statements. Has an explicit user orientation.

(2) Categories: A. Unspecified B. A Priori C. General-Misc.

Categories: A--Source discipline. B--Method of analysis. C--Topic.

Crossman, P. T., "The Nature of Management Accounting," The Accounting Review (April 1958), pp. 222-227.

(1) Defines management accounting and reviews pertinent landmarks from the last two centuries up through its use in marketing and the use of accounting machines. The author concludes that management accounting is not a new development but rather an evolution of providing operating data for managers.

(2) Categories: A. Unspecified B. A Priori C. General-Misc.

* * * * *

McFarland, W. B., "Research in Management Accounting by the National Association of Accountants," The Accounting Review (January 1961), pp. 21-25.

(1) Reviews the evolution of the NAA and discusses its current research program. Provides a perspective on research going on in NAA.

(2) Categories: A. Unspecified B. Personal Observation C. General-Misc.

* * * * *

Ladin, E., "The Role of the Accountant in Operations Analysis," The Accounting Review (April 1962), pp. 289-294.

(1) Provides a conceptual discussion of operations research and the role that accounting plays. Topics discussed include business management and the methodology and techniques of operations research. Introduces O. R. to accountants and vice-versa.

(2) Categories: A. Mathematics B. A Priori C. General-Misc.

* * * * *

Bierman, H., "Probability, Statistical Decision Theory, and Accounting," The Accounting Review (July 1962), pp. 400-405.

(1) Defines uncertainty and introduces the use of subjective probabilities and the use of a loss function to the decision process. The discussion has applications to financial accounting, auditing and management accounting, including breakeven, inventory control and variance investigation decisions. Introduces statistical decision theory to the accounting literature.

(2) Categories: A. Mathematics/Statistics B. A Priori C. General-Misc.

* * * * *

Categories: A--Source discipline. B--Method of analysis. C--Topic.

Zannetos, Z. S., "Mathematics as a Tool of Accounting Instruction and Research, The Accounting Review (April 1963), pp. 326-335.

(1) Discusses the use of mathematics in accounting as both an operational or optimizing tool and as a tool for building models.

(2) Categories: A. Mathematics B. A Priori C. General-Misc.

* * * * *

Simon, S. I., "Cost Accounting and the Law," The Accounting Review (October 1964), pp. 884-889.

(1) Discusses the view of cost accounting principles and practices held by the legal system as shown by a review of legislation, FTC rulings, and court decisions.

(2) Categories: A. Legal B. A Priori C. General-Misc.

* * * * *

Hartley, R. V., "Operations Research and Its Implications for the Accounting Profession," The Accounting Review (April 1968), pp. 321-332.

(1) Discusses operations research techniques and the information supplied by accountants. Includes discussion of verbal model building, data collection, and solution control.

(2) Categories: A. Operations Research B. A Priori C. General-Misc.

* * * * *

Nichols, A. C. and D. E. Grawig, "Accounting Reports with Time as a Variable," The Accounting Review (October 1968), pp. 631-639.

(1) Discusses the idea of preparing accounting reports on some basis other than time and illustrates by comparing statements prepared on a units sold basis with statements prepared on the traditional time basis. Concludes such an approach can provide information useful for decision making in certain areas. Early discussion of nontraditional reporting methods.

(2) Categories: A. Unspecified B. A Priori C. General-Misc.

* * * * *

Categories: A--Source discipline. B--Method of analysis. C--Topic.

Rosenzweig, K., "An Exploratory Field Study of the Relationships Between the Controller's Department and Overall Organizational Characteristics," Accounting, Organizations and Society (December 1981), pp. 339-354.

(1) Presents the results of a field study designed to explore the relationship between the structure of the controller's department and the characteristics of the organization as a whole. The findings indicate size and unionization of the organization affect the nature of the controller's department.

(2) Categories: A. Unspecified B. Field Study C. General-Misc. (Role of the Accountant)

* * * * *

Categories: A--Source discipline. B--Method of analysis. C--Topic.

PRODUCT COSTING

2. PRODUCT COSTING (pp. 79-99)

This category includes articles dealing with product costing, of which the direct/absorption costing controversy makes up the largest subset. Most of this literature was published before 1965.

This category contains the following subcategories:

2.1 Direct/Absorption Costing (pp. 80-88).

2.2 Distribution Costs (pp. 89-92).

2.3 Product Costing--General (pp. 93-99).

2.1 DIRECT/ABSORPTION COSTING (pp. 80-88)

This topic dominated the managerial accounting literature during the 1950's and early 1960's.

Schlatter, C. F., "Fixed Expense," The Accounting Review (April 1945), pp. 156-163.

(1) Discusses the consequences of fixed costs in inventory. Includes an example showing the differences between considering fixed overhead a cost and considering it an expense. An early discussion of the concept of absorption versus variable costing.

(2) Categories: A. Unspecified B. A Priori C. Direct/Absorption Costing.

* * * * *

Gordon, M. J., "Cost Allocations and the Design of Accounting Systems for Control," The Accounting Review (April 1951), pp. 209-220.

(1) Argues that collecting costs for product costing does not provide information appropriate for control purposes. Proposes the use of a system in which direct costs only are carried into inventory thereby providing information for both purposes. Earliest explicit call for direct costing in the academic literature.

(2) Categories: A. Unspecified B. A Priori C. Direct/Absorption Costing.

* * * * *

Categories: A--Source discipline. B--Method of analysis. C--Topic.

Raun, D. L., "The Problem of Fixed Charges," The Accounting Review (July 1951), pp. 338-346.

(1) Illustrates by examples the problems caused by fixed costs and the inaccuracies that may result in determining profit and selling prices. Proposes the alternative that only variable costs be taken to the inventory accounts which would eliminate over/under absorbed overhead and assign only controllable (variable) costs to cost centers.

(2) Categories: A. Unspecified B. A Priori C. Direct/Absorption Costing.

* * * * *

Neilsen, O., "Direct Costing--The Case 'For'," The Accounting Review (January 1954), pp. 89-93.

(1) Comparison piece to Hepworth (1954) presenting arguments in favor of direct costing including the elimination of allocation problems, an emphasis on cost analysis rather than inventory determination, and the simplicity of computations.

(2) Categories: A. Unspecified B. A Priori C. Direct/Absorption Costing.

* * * * *

Hepworth, S. R., "Direct Costing--The Case 'Against'," The Accounting Review (January 1954), pp. 94-99.

(1) Companion piece to Neilsen (1954) presenting the argument that direct costing is too radical a departure from traditional cost accounting methods to be worth adopting. Includes a discussion of such claimed advantages as simplicity and conservative inventory valuation and its usefulness for marginal and controllable cost analyses. Part of the argument over direct costing; includes references to the economics literature when discussing marginal analysis.

(2) Categories: A. Economics B. A Priori C. Direct/Absorption Costing.

* * * * *

Categories: A--Source discipline. B--Method of analysis. C--Topic.

Amerman, G., "Facts About Direct Costing for Profit Determination," Accounting Research (April 1954b), pp. 154-166.

(1) Presents an analysis of the use of absorption and direct costing for profit determination and an analysis of their use for break-even analysis. Recommends a contribution margin income statement with either total fixed costs or the absorption cost increment being used for income determination. Notes that break-even analysis is greatly simplified with the use of direct costing.

(2) Categories: A. Unspecified B. A Priori C. Direct/Absorption Costing.

* * * * *

Marple, R. P., "Direct Costing and the Uses of Cost Data," The Accounting Review (July 1955), pp. 430-438.

(1) Discusses direct costing in light of the purposes for which cost data are collected. Includes coverage of cost classifications, direct versus absorption costing, comparison of income statements, appraisal of segment performance, and reporting to external users.

(2) Categories: A. Unspecified B. A Priori C. Direct/Absorption Costing.

* * * * *

Brummet, R. L., "Direct Costing - Should It Be a Controversial Issue?" The Accounting Review (July 1955), pp. 439-443.

(1) Discusses the term "direct costing" and whether it provides 1) information for decision-making and 2) a basis for accurate income measurement and reasonable inventory valuation. Concludes that it can be used for internal decision-making but not for external reporting.

(2) Categories: A. Unspecified B. A Priori C. Direct/Absorption Costing.

* * * * *

Categories: A--Source discipline. B--Method of analysis. C--Topic.

Moss, M. F. and W. C. Haseman, "Some Comments on the Applicability of Direct Costing to Decision Making," The Accounting Review (April 1957), pp. 184-193.

(1) Discusses certain aspects of direct (variable) costing as an aid to management decision-making, compares and contrasts it with marginal costing, and discusses opportunity costs. Coverage also includes its use and limitations in pricing, joint product, and oligopoly situations. Excellant discussion of direct costing in an economic theory framework.

(2) Categories: A. Economics B. A Priori C. Direct/Absorption Costing.

* * * * *

Edwards, J. D., "This New Costing Concept - Direct Costing?" The Accounting Review (October 1958), pp. 561-567.

(1) Discusses product costing and in particular the accounting for fixed costs including short-run and long-run considerations and compares conventional costing with direct costing.

(2) Categories: A. Unspecified B. A Priori C. Direct/Absorption Costing.

* * * * *

Seiler, R. E., "Improvements in External Reporting by Use of Direct Costing," The Accounting Review (January 1959), pp. 59-66.

(1) Discusses GAAP, traces the historical development of direct costing, compares direct and absorption costing, and discusses the effects direct costing would have on the balance sheet and income statement and its usefulness to stockholders and the general public.

(2) Categories: A. Unspecified B. A Priori C. Direct/Absorption Costing.

* * * * *

Categories: A--Source discipline. B--Method of analysis. C--Topic.

Ferrara, W. L., "Idle Capacity as a Loss - Fact or Fiction," The Accounting Review (July 1960), pp. 490-496.

(1) Sets forth the view that there is no such thing as a loss due to idle capacity for purposes of income measurement. Instead capacity costs should be allocated so that there is no excess (e.g., units of production depreciation). Includes discussion of fixed and semi-variable capacity costs and various measures of capacity. (Also see Ferrara, 1961).

(2) Categories: A. Unspecified B. A Priori C. Direct/Absorption Costing.

* * * * *

Ferrara, W. L., "Overhead Costs and Income Measurement," The Accounting Review (January 1961), pp. 63-70.

(1) Discusses the allocation of fixed and variable costs to production for income measurement purposes and proposes an allocation scheme which eliminates over or under absorbed overhead. This results in unit cost of production fluctuating with volume of production. Continues Ferrara (1960).

(2) Categories: A. Unspecified B. A Priori C. Direct/Absorption Costing.

* * * * *

Horngren, C. T. and G. H. Sorter, "'Direct' Costing for External Reporting," The Accounting Review (January 1961), pp. 84-93.

(1) Examines the suitability of variable costing for external reporting by analyzing the assumptions underlying variable costing and their relationship to existing accounting theory. The authors conclude variable costing is more in line with GAAP and it provides more useful information for external users than does absorption costing.

(2) Categories: A. Unspecified B. A Priori C. Direct/Absorption Costing.

* * * * *

Weinwurm, E. H., "The Importance of Idle Capacity Costs," The Accounting Review (July 1961), pp. 418-421.

(1) Discusses the issues raised by Ferrara (1960) and concludes managers do experience idle capacity. Distinguishes between theoretical models and ones designed to be used in practice and notes the differences between them are causing the differing interpretations.

(2) Categories: A. Unspecified B. A Priori C. Direct/Absorption Costing.

* * * * *

Categories: A--Source discipline. B--Method of analysis. C--Topic.

Fess, P. E., "The Theory of Manufacturing Costs," The Accounting Review (July 1961), pp. 446-453.

(1) Discusses the nature of production costs and direct and absorption costing from the perspective of accounting principles and other theoretical considerations. Concludes that direct costing for external reporting is not in accord with generally accepted theory and that different purposes require different costs.

(2) Categories: A. Unspecified B. A Priori C. Direct/Absorption Costing.

* * * * *

Fess, P. E. and W. L. Ferrara, "The Period Cost Concept for Income Measurement - Can It be Defended?" The Accounting Review (October 1961), pp. 598-602.

(1) Discusses period versus product costs, income measurement, and value added. Concludes that the period cost concept is not appropriate for purposes of income measurement and that matching is most important.

(2) Categories: A. Unspecified B. A Priori C. Direct/Absorption Costing.

* * * * *

Fremgen, J. M., "Variable Costing for External Reporting - A Reconsideration," The Accounting Review (January 1962), pp. 76-81.

(1) Presents a critique of Horngren and Sorter (1961) and a general argument against the use of variable costing for income determination. Disagreement is based primarily on different definitions of "service potential."

(2) Categories: A. Unspecified B. A Priori C. Direct/Absorption Costing.

* * * * *

Sorter, G. H. and C. T. Horngren, "Asset Recognition and Economic Attributes - The Relevant Costing Approach," The Accounting Review (July 1962), pp. 391-399.

(1) Discusses the problem of asset versus expense and examines the assumptions made by accountants in this area. They then illustrate how their approach, relevant costing, is different from other approaches. Introduces relevant costing (a cost is carried forward only if it has a favorable economic effect on expected future costs or revenues) as an alternative to either direct or absorption costing.

(2) Categories: A. Unspecified B. A Priori C. Direct/Absorption Costing.

Categories: A--Source discipline. B--Method of analysis. C--Topic.

Staubus, G. J., "Direct, Relevant or Absorption Costing?" The Accounting Review (January 1963), pp. 64-74.

(1) Discusses product costing and concludes direct costing is unsatisfactory for external reporting. Includes a postscript on Sorter and Horngren (1962) and their reply.

(2) Categories: A. Unspecified B. A Priori C. Direct/Absorption Costing.

* * * * *

Ferrara, W. L., "Relevant Costing - Two Points of View," The Accounting Review (October 1963), pp. 719-722.

(1) Discusses the positions advanced in Sorter and Horngren (1962) and Fess and Ferrara (1961) to clear up the possible misinterpretation of thoughts and ideas.

(2) Categories: A. Unspecified B. A Priori C. Direct/Absorption Costing.

* * * * *

Fess, P. E., "The Relevant Costing Concept for Income Measurement-Can it Be Defended," The Accounting Review (October 1963), pp. 723-732.

(1) Critically examines the concept of relevant costing and whether it should be used in reporting to external users and contrasts its short term decision-making usefulness with the needs of external users.

(2) Categories: A. Unspecified B. A Priori C. Direct/Absorption Costing.

* * * * *

Fremgen, J. M., "The Direct Costing Controversy - An Identification of the Issues," The Accounting Review (January 1964), pp. 43-51.

(1) Reviews the arguments for and against direct costing and attempts to identify the principal issues in the discussion of its use for external reporting.

(2) Categories: A. Unspecified B. A Priori C. Direct/Absorption Costing.

* * * * *

Categories: A--Source discipline. B--Method of analysis. C--Topic.

Lentilhon, R. W., "Direct Costing - Either ... Or?" The Accounting Review (October 1964), pp. 880-883.

(1) Discusses standard cost as a third alternative in the direct versus absorption costing controversy. Includes an illustrated example.

(2) Categories: A. Unspecified B. A Priori C. Direct/Absorption Costing.

* * * * *

Hirschman, R. W., "Direct Costing and the Law," The Accounting Review (January 1965), pp. 176-183.

(1) Discusses the legal implications of direct costing with respect to taxation, securities regulations, antitrust legislation, and other legislation.

(2) Categories: A. Legal B. A Priori C. Direct/Absorption Costing.

* * * * *

Ijiri, Y., R. K. Jaedicke and J. L. Livingstone, "The Effect of Inventory Costing Methods on Full and Direct Costing," Journal of Accounting Research (Spring 1965), pp. 63-74.

(1) Analytically investigates the differences between full and direct cost profit due to the impact of the various inventory cost flow assumptions and due to differences in profit variance patterns. One of a few articles modeling the direct/absorption costing controversy.

(2) Categories: A. Unspecified B. Modeling C. Direct/Absorption Costing.

* * * * *

Langholm, O., "Cost Structure and Costing Method: An Empirical Study," Journal of Accounting Research (Autumn 1965), pp. 218-227.

(1) Reports the results of a study concerning the effect a firm's cost structure has on whether it uses full, direct, or variable costing. Includes graphical and mathematical analyses and concludes it does not.

(2) Categories: A. Unspecified B. Field Study C. Direct/Absorption Costing.

* * * * *

Categories: A--Source discipline. B--Method of analysis. C--Topic.

Fekrat, M. A., "The Conceptual Foundations of Absorption Costing," The Accounting Review (April 1972), pp. 351-355.

(1) Discusses the relationships of direct and absorption costing to the microeconomic theory of the firm. Concludes that direct costing is not compatible with the modern theory of the firm whereas absorption costing is (contrast with Largay (1973)).

(2) Categories: A. Economics B. A Priori C. Direct/Absorption Costing.

* * * * *

Largay, J. A., "Microeconomic Foundations of Variable Costing," The Accounting Review (January 1973), pp. 115-119.

(1) Discusses direct costing and the microeconomic theory of the firm and finds economic theory supports the time period view of fixed costs (contrast with Fekrat (1972)). Concludes the issue of appropriateness of a costing method is an empirical issue.

(2) Categories: A. Unspecified B. A Priori C. Direct/Absorption Costing.

* * * * *

Gordon, L. A. and H. Cook, "Absorption Costing and Fixed Factors of Production," The Accounting Review (January 1973), pp. 128-129.

(1) Discusses the concept of fixed factors of production used by Fekrat (1972) in his microeconomic analysis of absorption costing.

(2) Categories: A. Unspecified B. A Priori C. Direct/Absorption Costing.

* * * * *

Bailey, A. D., "A Dynamic Programming Approach to the Analysis of Different Costing Methods in Accounting for Inventory," The Accounting Review (July 1973), pp. 560-574.

(1) Analyzes the viability of using dynamic programming in considering alternative accounting methods and in particular the effects of variable versus absorption costing on management decisions. Includes an appendix on the techniques of dynamic programming.

(2) Categories: A. Mathematics/Operations Research B. Modeling/ Simulation C. Direct/Absorption Costing

* * * * *

Categories: A--Source discipline. B--Method of analysis. C--Topic.

2.2. DISTRIBUTION COSTS (pp. 89-92)

This subcategory contains articles on distribution costs. Most deal with the short-lived controversy over the inclusion of distribution costs in product costs.

Castenholz, W. B., "The Proper Treatment of Distribution Costs." The Accounting Review (March 1927), pp. 19-27.

(1) Argues for applying distribution cost to the cost of manufactured goods as an extension of cost accounting principles to the whole of commercial costs. Such a perspective would view distribution costs as adding value and therefore a "proper" cost of inventory. An early discussion of applying a value added principle to all costs of such a nature.

(2) Categories: A. Unspecified B. A Priori C. Product Costing--Distribution Costs

* * * * *

Woodbury, N. F., "A Treatment of Distribution Cost," The Accounting Review (June 1927), pp. 124-128.

(1) Discusses the inventorying of distribution costs rather than expensing and describes how it is done in a specific firm. Mentions statistics which are being gathered by different firms that appear to show the large magnitude of distribution cost so it is the earliest management accounting article to refer to empirical data.

(2) Categories: A. Unspecified B. Personal Observation C. Product Costing--Distribution Costs

* * * * *

Paton, W. A., "Distribution Costs and Inventory Values," The Accounting Review (September 1927), pp. 246-253.

(1) Continues the argument for including in inventory and deferring until sale the cost of distributing the product when such costs increase the value of the product. The idea was well argued but apparently waned shortly after this although interest in general in distribution costs (primarily control of) continued to be a popular topic through the 1940's.

(2) Categories: A. Unspecified B. A Priori C. Product Costing--Distribution Costs

* * * * *

Categories: A--Source discipline. B--Method of analysis. C--Topic.

Harris, G. L., "An Application of Standard Costs in the Field of Distribution," The Accounting Review (June 1931), pp. 118-124.

(1) Discusses an actual case of applying standard costs outside the field of production. Presents the operationalization of a system designed to set standards for and provide incentives to reduce distribution costs while at the same time maintaining incentives to sell. A combination of two popular topics at this time: standard costs and control of distribution costs.

(2) Categories: A. Unspecified B. Personal Observation C. Product Costing--Distribution Costs

* * * * *

Castenholz, W. B., "Selling and Administrative Expense as a Basis for Sales Control and Cost Reduction," The Accounting Review (June 1931), pp. 125-130.

(1) Discusses the application of cost techniques to the area of sales control. Argues that expense analysis must extend to all facets of the business with the goal of such analysis being the setting of standards. Calls for standard distribution costs.

(2) Categories: A. Unspecified B. A Priori C. Product Costing--Distribution Costs

* * * * *

Lowles, D. C., "Some Results of Cost Analysis in Industrial Distribution," The Accounting Review (June 1931), pp. 131-135.

(1) Quotes the results of a survey of manufacturers relating to whether it is practical to set up accounting procedures for distribution costs that will result in better control and aid in setting selling prices. Argues that analysis rather than technical classification or allocation is what provides the data which can result in economies of distribution. First management accounting article actually citing empirical data.

(2) Categories: A. Unspecified B. Survey C. Product Costing--Distribution Costs

* * * * *

Categories: A--Source discipline. B--Method of analysis. C--Topic.

Greer, H. C., "The Technique of Distribution Cost Accounting," The Accounting Review (June 1931), pp. 136-139.

(1) Discusses the distribution of products and the costs of such distribution. Greer provides a functional classification of these costs as opposed to the traditional objects-of-expenditure classification.

(2) Categories: A. Unspecified B. A Priori C. Product Costing--Distribution Costs

* * * * *

Ostlund, H. J., "Cost Research in the Field of Distribution," The Accounting Review (March 1932), pp. 48-53.

(1) From his viewpoint of collecting and analyzing cost data for a wholesale association the author discuses the behavior of costs and draws generalizations that are tentatively supported by data from his cost studies. His findings include the importance of differential and opportunity costs and the futility of extensive and minute allocations. An early use of empirical data although the data are not presented.

(2) Categories: A. Unspecified B. Field Study C. Product Costing--Distribution Costs

* * * * *

White, W. L., "Problems in Determining Total Costs of Distribution," The Accounting Review (March 1934), pp. 15-22.

(1) Discusses the objectives, various methods, and the problems connected with distribution cost analysis. The author notes a need for common and uniform procedures and calls for further study of the problem.

(2) Categories: A. Unspecified B. A Priori C. Product Costing--Distribution Costs

* * * * *

Atwood, P. W., "The Manufacturer Looks at His Cost of Distribution," The Accounting Review (March 1934), pp. 23-28.

(1) Presents a report on a study done for an association of advertisers attempting to answer how the costs of distribution compare across manufacturing firms. This article references some of the figures from the total report and is presented as a factfinding survey with no attempt to explain variations in the cost patterns observed.

(2) Categories: A. Unspecified B. Survey C. Product Costing--Distribution Costs

* * * * *

Categories: A--Source discipline. B--Method of analysis. C--Topic.

Schaefer, H. P., "The Distribution Cost Problem," The Accounting Review (October 1958), pp. 625-631.

(1) Discusses distribution costs, their definition, and their methods of analysis including by natural expense, by function, and by manner of distribution effort. This article is unique in this section in that it goes beyond product costing issues.

(2) Categories: A. Unspecified B. A Priori C. Product Costing--Distribution Costs

* * * * *

Categories: A--Source discipline. B--Method of analysis. C--Topic.

2.3. PRODUCT COSTING - GENERAL (pp. 93-99)

This subcategory contains those product costing articles not otherwise categorized.

Bennett, G. E., "Some Observations on the Application of Manufacturing Expense to Production," The Accounting Review (March 1926), pp. 1-7.

(1) Discusses the application of manufacturing cost to products and the decision of what base to use in setting the application rate. Provides an early discussion of the place of standardization in accounting and whether the function of the accountant is merely to provide facts or to act as a guide in their interpretation.

(2) Categories: A. Unspecified B. A Priori C. Product Costing - General

* * * * *

Cox, C. E., "What is Cost?" The Accounting Review (December 1930), pp. 288-297.

(1) Provides a presentation of the economic concept of the cost of production followed by a discussion of the accounting concept for comparison. The accounting perspective is one of return to the owner but the discussion is somewhat relevant from the management accounting point of view. This is an example of the continuing attempt during this time period to integrate economic concepts into accounting.

(2) Categories: A. Economics B. A Priori C. Product Costing—General

* * * * *

Canning, J. B., "Cost of Production and Market Price," The Accounting Review (September 1931), pp. 161-164.

(1) Discusses the relationship between the cost of production and selling price within the economic concepts of cost and future prices and the divergence between the economic notion and the accountant's cost figure. Presents another attempt to integrate economics with accounting.

(2) Categories: A. Economics B. A Priori C. Product Costing—General

* * * * *

Categories: A--Source discipline. B--Method of analysis. C--Topic.

Prickett, A. L., "Labor Turnover Rate and Cost," The Accounting Review (December 1931), pp. 261-276.

(1) Discusses the cost of unemployment and turnover, whether these costs are known or used, and some plans to reduce the problem. Reports the results of a questionnaire survey and other studies in presenting the costs of turnover and unemployment in various industries. Provides one of the first empirical studies in the management accounting literature designed as such.

(2) Categories: A. Unspecified B. Survey C. Product Costing-General

* * * * *

Rorem, C. R., "The Costs of Medical Care," The Accounting Review (March 1932), pp. 38-41.

(1) Discusses an ongoing study by the Committee on the Costs of Medical Care, whose purpose is to determine the amount and distribution of such costs and to suggest methods by which they may be reduced.

(2) Categories: A. Unspecified B. Field Study C. Product Costing-General

* * * * *

Balch, J., "Some Aspects of Standard Costs," The Accounting Review (March 1934), pp. 29-32.

(1) Discusses the implementation of a standard cost system including standard material, labor, and overhead costs. Emphasizes the need for practicalness and usefulness in the data to be presented to decision-makers.

(2) Categories: A. Unspecified B. A Priori C. Product Costing-General

* * * * *

McFarland, W. B., "The Basic Theory of Standard Costs," The Accounting Review (June 1939), pp. 151-158.

(1) Presents a summarization of the many ideas put forth on standard costs with the idea that in a generalized form the basic principles of standard costs will be more accessible and better understood. Emphasizes the need to bring cost accounting into accord with modern management methods and broaden the usefulness of its data.

(2) Categories: A. Unspecified B. A Priori C. Product Costing-General

* * * * *

Categories: A—Source discipline. B--Method of analysis. C—Topic.

McFarland, W. B., "The Economics of Business Costs," The Accounting Review (June 1940), pp. 196-205.

(1) Discusses several cost concepts significant to business management including controllable/noncontrollable, fixed/variable, direct/ indirect, and incremental. Explains that the definition of cost must be appropriate for the problem at hand and that no single cost concept can be made to serve all needs of business.

(2) Categories: A. Unspecified B. A Priori C. Product Costing-General

* * * * *

Dixon, R. L., "Fixed and Variable Costs," The Accounting Review (June 1940), pp. 218-222.

(1) Advocates dividing operating expenses into fixed and variable categories on the income statement for external reporting. One of the first specific references to the idea of presenting a contribution income statement for external use.

(2) Categories: A. Unspecified B. A Priori C. Product Costing-General

* * * * *

Whittaker, E., "Realism and Cost Accounting," The Accounting Review (January 1946), pp. 13-19.

(1) Presents a comparison of the economic definition of cost with the ideology of cost accounting. Includes a discussion of fixed and variable costs, the problem of joint costs, and the method of inventory valuation.

(2) Categories: A. Economics B. A Priori C. Product Costing-General

* * * * *

Goliger, J., "Analysis of Semi-Variable Expenses," The Accounting Review (July 1949), pp. 308-310.

(1) Illustrates the segregation of semivariable costs into fixed and variable components by the use of an algebraic method. Presents the formulas for such calculations.

(2) Categories: A. Unspecified B. Modeling C. Product Costing-General

* * * * *

Categories: A—Source discipline. B—Method of analysis. C—Topic.

Benninger, L. J., "The Traditional vs. the Cost Accounting Concept of Cost," The Accounting Review (October 1949), pp. 387-391.

(1) Characterizes the traditional accounting concept of cost as being in terms of monetary outlays and compares this to the cost accounting concept which distinguishes product costs on a unit basis from period costs.

(2) Categories: A. Unspecified B. A Priori C. Product Costing-General

* * * * *

Benninger, L. J., "A Proposed Reconciliation of Standard and Current Material Costs," The Accounting Review (April 1950a), pp. 156-160.

(1) Presents a suggested solution to the problem of reconciling standard costs with current replacement cost of material and illustrates with an example how such a combined replacement-standard cost system would work.

(2) Categories: A. Unspecified B. A Priori C. Product Costing-General

* * * * *

Benninger, L. J., "Standard Costs for Income Determination, Control, and Special Studies," The Accounting Review (October 1950b), pp. 378-383.

(1) Discusses the integration of standard costs used for management purposes with the established financial accounts to provide data not only for cost control but also for income determination and special cost analyses. Presents an early call for the introduction of standard costs into the accounts.

(2) Categories: A. Unspecified B. A Priori C. Product Costing-General

* * * * *

Lemke, B. C., "Is Manufacturing Cost an Objective Concept?" The Accounting Review (January 1951), pp. 77-79.

(1) Discusses the attributes of an objective cost and whether production costs under cost accounting techniques provide such a cost. Includes coverage of the concepts of lowest unit cost and the cost of maintaining flexible capacity.

(2) Categories: A. Unspecified B. A Priori C. Product Costing-General

* * * * *

Categories: A--Source discipline. B--Method of analysis. C--Topic.

Albery, M., "Analysis Versus Interpretation of Cost," The Accounting Review (July 1953), pp. 425-430.

(1) Defines and discusses "analysis" and "interpretation" and provides a list of the mental steps followed in analyzing and interpreting a cost problem.

(2) Categories: A. Unspecified B. A Priori C. Product Costing-General

* * * * *

Luttrell, W. F., "Some Problems of Inter-Plant Cost Comparisons," Accounting Research (April 1954), pp. 107-120.

(1) Discusses the problems faced by firms attempting to make cost comparisons across branches which have a variety of record-systems from the perspective of having recently completed a study on the problem. Concludes with a discussion of the record requirements needed for such comparisons to be useful.

(2) Categories: A. Unspecified B. Personal Observation C. Product Costing-General

* * * * *

Paddock, H. E., "Production Waste - Its Nature and Its Accounting," The Accounting Review (January 1958), pp. 50-55.

(1) Discusses accounting for waste and distinguishes between avoidable and unavoidable waste. Concludes that a waste accounting system should distinguish between these, assigning avoidable waste to the appropriate departments and unavoidable waste to current income. Continues the discussion of what is properly inventoriable as a cost of production.

(2) Categories: A. Unspecified B. A Priori C. Product Costing-General

* * * * *

Gibbs, G., "New Cost Accounting Concepts," The Accounting Review (January 1958), pp. 96-101.

(1) Discusses cost concepts within the requirements of management and government agencies and identifies the purposes of cost accounting. Also discusses marginal cost analysis and the relationships between the economist's cost curves and direct and differential costing.

(2) Categories: A. Economics B. A Priori C. Product Costing-General

* * * * *

Categories: A--Source discipline. B--Method of analysis. C--Topic.

Castenholz, W. B., "What Constitutes Material Cost of Production," The Accounting Review (October 1958), pp. 650-653.

(1) Discusses the costs to be included in the cost of materials including transportation, insurance, storage, and the variable expenses of the purchasing and receiving departments.

(2) Categories: A. Unspecified B. A Priori C. Product Costing-General

* * * * *

Koch, A. P., "A Fallacy in Accounting for Spoiled Goods," The Accounting Review (July 1960), pp. 501-502.

(1) Distinguishes between normal and abnormal spoilage and uses a problem to illustrate the effect of absorbing spoilage loss into all jobs by charging it to manufacturing overhead. Discuss the results and implications.

(2) Categories: A. Unspecified B. A Priori C. Product Costing-General

* * * * *

Wiener, J., "Separation of Fixed and Variable Costs," The Accounting Review (October 1960), pp. 686-690.

(1) Discusses the allocation of manufacturing costs into fixed and variable categories and suggests a method of eliminating the fixed component from semi-variable costs. Could also be classified in Cost Estimation or CVP.

(2) Categories: A. Unspecified B. A Priori C. Product Costing-General

* * * * *

Berkow, W. F., "Need for Engineering Influence Upon Accounting Procedures," The Accounting Review (April 1964), pp. 377-386.

(1) Discusses accounting procedures from the perspective of a plant engineer and offers suggestions as to how accounting could better reflect the work and viewpoint of engineers. Includes discussion of product tolerances, repair costs, and labor costs. First mention of recording certain labor costs (e.g., hiring) as assets.

(2) Categories: A. Unspecified B. A Priori C. Product Costing-General

* * * * *

Categories: A--Source discipline. B--Method of analysis. C--Topic.

Purdy, C. R., "Industry Patterns of Capacity or Volume Choice: Their Existence and Rationale," Journal of Accounting Research (Autumn 1965), pp. 228-241.

(1) Reports the results of a study designed to test whether or not there exist industry patterns in the selection of measures of capacity. Some evidence of industry pattern is shown. An early empirical study of the effect environment has on accountng practices.

(2) Categories: A. Economics B. Survey C. Product Costing-General

* * * * *

Skinner, R. C., "Process Costing," Abacus (December 1978), pp. 160-170.

(1) Presents the results of a field survey on the accounting practices of firms engaged in continuous process manufacturing. The results indicate such firms do not use process costing but rather use operation costing (process costing with no work in process).

(2) Categories: A. Unspecified B. Field Survey (interviews) C. Product Costing-General

* * * * *

Categories: A—Source discipline. B--Method of analysis. C—Topic.

COST ALLOCATION

3. COST ALLOCATION (pp. 100-112)

This category is comprised of works on cost allocation, including overhead allocation and joint cost allocation. Articles on the allocation of fixed and variable costs are included in subcategory 2.1, Direct/Absorption Costing (pp. 80-88).

Vatter, W. J., "Limitations of Overhead Allocation," The Accounting Review (April 1945), pp. 163-176.

(1) Provides an indepth discussion of joint costs, the procedures used to assign them to costing units, and the conflicts that arise because of the various objectives of cost calculations. Discusses inventory, pricing, and control and concludes with a call for research on cost allocation. Good review of the area of joint cost allocation.

(2) Categories: A. Unspecified B. A Priori C. Cost Allocation--Joint Costs

* * * * *

Avery, H. G., "Accounting for Joint Costs," The Accounting Review (April 1951), pp. 232-238.

(1) Illustrates by means of examples the problems and procedures of accounting for by- and joint-products including allocation by weight and sales value and no allocation. Concludes that allocation techniques need to be improved and in the end the basic criterion is that revenue must cover the total costs of production.

(2) Categories: A. Unspecified B. A Priori C. Cost Allocation--Joint Costs

* * * * *

Beckett, J. A., "A Study of the Principles of Allocating Costs," The Accounting Review (July 1951), pp. 327-333.

(1) Distinguishes among three methods of assigning costs: 1) direct application, 2) allocation, and 3) proration and discusses whether accountants should assign all costs or just apply direct costs. Concludes that there is no firm rule concerning allocation and proration and each proves useful in some contexts and not useful in others.

(2) Categories: A. Unspecified B. A Priori C. Cost Allocation

* * * * *

Categories: A--Source discipline. B--Method of analysis. C--Topic.

Lorig, A. N., "Joint Cost Analysis as an Aid to Management," The Accounting Review (October 1955), pp. 634-637.

(1) Illustrates the use of joint cost allocation in making the decision to process further beyond the split-off point. Introduces a specific analysis procedure for joint costs.

(2) Categories: A. Unspecified B. A Priori C. Cost Allocation--Joint Costs

* * * * *

Burke, W. L., "Cost Allocation and Distribution - Merchandise Accounting," The Accounting Review (October 1963), pp. 802-812.

(1) Discusses the allocation of costs to departments, product lines, and individual items within retail firms. Includes examples and accounts used. Description of a real-world cost system for cost allocation.

(2) Categories: A. Unspecified B. A Priori C. Cost Allocation

* * * * *

Williams, T. H., and C. H. Griffin, "Matrix Theory and Cost Allocation," The Accounting Review (July 1964), pp. 671-678.

(1) Discusses the allocation of costs and the problems in arithmetically distributing the costs. Proposes a method based on matrix theory which will allocate reciprocally related costs and illustrates the technique with an example. Introduces the matrix method of reciprocal cost allocation.

(2) Categories: A. Mathematics B. Modeling C. Cost Allocation

* * * * *

Churchill, N., "Linear Algebra and Cost Allocations: Some Examples," The Accounting Review (October 1964), pp. 894-904.

(1) Illustrates the use of linear algebra for several cost problems including cost allocation, analysis of process costs, analysis of cost center balances, and analysis of product costs as examples of the use of mathematical analysis in accounting.

(2) Categories: A. Mathematics B. Modeling C. Cost Allocation

* * * * *

Categories: A—Source discipline. B—Method of analysis. C—Topic.

Manes, R. P. and V. L. Smith, "Economic Joint Cost Theory and Accounting Practice," The Accounting Review (January 1965), pp. 31-35.

(1) Discusses the relationship between accounting for joint costs and economic theory. Includes discussion of two different models and their second order conditions for optimality. Sophisticated economic analysis of the joint cost problem.

(2) Categories: A. Economics B. Modeling C. Cost Allocation--Joint Costs

* * * * *

Wright, H. W., "Allocation of General and Administrative Expenses," The Accounting Review (October 1966), pp. 626-633.

(1) Discusses the conceptual problem of allocating general and administrative expenses including discussion of cost pools, distribution bases, and year's activity. Includes recommendations for changes.

(2) Categories: A. Unspecified B. A Priori C. Cost Allocation

* * * * *

Chiu, J. S. and D. T. DeCoster, "Multiple Product Costing by Multiple Correlation Analysis," The Accounting Review (October 1966), pp. 673-681.

(1) Discusses the problems of accounting for the costs of products produced from a joint or multiple process and illustrates the application of multiple correlation analysis to the problem.

(2) Categories: A. Economics/Statistics B. Modeling C. Cost Allocation--Joint Costs

* * * * *

Bierman, H., "Inventory Valuation: The Use of Market Prices," The Accounting Review (October 1967), pp. 731-737.

(1) Discusses the use of market price to value inventory and its appropriateness for different market and production conditions. Includes a discussion of marginal analysis and the allocation of joint costs.

(2) Categories: A. Economics B. A Priori C. Cost Allocation--Joint Costs

* * * * *

Categories: A—Source discipline. B—Method of analysis. C—Topic.

Livingstone, J. L., "Matrix Algebra and Cost Allocation," The Accounting Review (July 1968), pp. 503-508.

(1) Discusses the different cost allocation models based on matrix algebra and shows that the models are not different but rather are alternate ways of expressing the same general model.

(2) Categories: A. Unspecified B. Modeling C. Cost Allocation

* * * * *

Brief, R. P. and J. Owen, "A Least Squares Allocation Model," Journal of Accounting Research (Autumn 1968).

(1) Presents a mathematical allocation model based on the generalized least squares model. Includes a mathematical appendix.

(2) Categories: A. Mathematics B. Modeling C. Cost Allocation

* * * * *

Weil, R. L., "Allocating Joint Costs," American Economic Review (December 1968), p. 1342-1345.

(1) Discusses joint cost allocations as marginal revenues and the usefulness of allocations based on constrained optimization, Lagrange multipliers, and Kuhn-Tucker theory in decision-making.

(2) Categories: A. Economics B. Modeling C. Cost Allocation--Joint Costs

* * * * *

Thomas, A. L., The Allocation Problem, Studies in Accounting Research #3 (American Accounting Association, 1969).

(1) Discusses the allocation of nonmonetary inputs including the theoretical justifications for allocation, specific approaches to the problem, and evaluation of certain of the approaches given the theoretical justifications. Concludes all such allocations are arbitrary and no solution exists to the problem within the present framework. Although not directly aimed at the allocation problem in management accounting this article is a classic in the area.

(2) Categories: A. Unspecified B. A Priori C. Cost Allocation

* * * * *

Categories: A--Source discipline. B--Method of analysis. C--Topic.

Kaplan, R. S., and G. Thompson, "Overhead Allocation via Mathematical Programming Models," The Accounting Review (April 1971), pp. 352-364.

(1) Proposes a cost allocation procedure based on a linear programming model of the firm which has the advantage over traditional methods of taking into account the relative profitability of the products and their sales and production interdependencies. Continues the literature on cost allocation, but is a substantial change from the overhead allocation disputes a la direct/absorption costing.

(2) Categories: A. Operations Research B. Modeling C. Cost Allocation

* * * * *

Hartley, R. V., "Decision Making When Joint Products are Involved," The Accounting Review (October 1971), pp. 746-755.

(1) Discusses and illustrates the use of linear programming in deciding whether to process beyond the split-off point of a joint product.

(2) Categories: A. Unspecified B. Modeling C. Cost Allocation--Joint Costs

* * * * *

Minch, R., and E. Petri, "Matrix Models of Reciprocal Service Cost Allocation," The Accounting Review (July 1972), pp. 576-80.

(1) Discusses previous matrix algebra approaches to cost allocation and proposes a new matrix method, relating it to those previously presented. The differences are in the placement in the model of credits for services performed.

(2) Categories: A. Unspecified B. Modeling C. Cost Allocation

* * * * *

Kaplan, R. S., "Variable and Self-Service Costs in Reciprocal Allocation Models," The Accounting Review (October 1973), pp. 738-748.

(1) Analyzes two properties of the different matrix algebra cost allocation models: calculation of the marginal cost of supplying additional output from each service department and calculations involving service to own department. Concludes that the model advanced by Williams and Griffin (1964) and later expanded allocates costs consistent with the underlying economics of the situation.

(2) Categories: A. Mathematics B. Modeling C. Cost Allocation

* * * * *

Categories: A--Source discipline. B--Method of analysis. C--Topic.

Jensen, D. L., "The Role of Cost in Pricing Joint Products: A Case of Production in Fixed Proportions," The Accounting Review (July 1974), pp. 465-476.

(1) Discusses the information requirements of the pricing decision for joint production in fixed proportions. Extends the Manes and Smith (1965) analysis.

(2) Categories: A. Economics B. Modeling C. Cost Allocation--Joint Costs

* * * * *

Kaplan, R. S., and U. P. Welam, "Overhead Allocation with Imperfect Markets and Nonlinear Technology," The Accounting Review (July 1974), pp. 477-484.

(1) Presents a discussion of a generalized linear programming model for cost allocation with a nonlinear objective function and nonlinear constraints. Nonlinear production functions are also discussed. Extends Kaplan and Thompson (1971) and continues the literature on overhead allocation.

(2) Categories: A. Operations Research B. Modeling C. Cost Allocation

* * * * *

Thomas, A. L., The Allocation Problem: Part Two, Studies in Accounting Research #9 (American Accounting Association, 1974).

(1) Continues and expands the arguments in Thomas (1969) concerning the allocation of costs. Includes discussion of the utilities of allocations, empirical research in the area, and allocation-free statements. Concludes that accounting's allocation assertions are ambiguous and incorrigible but they can possess purpose-utility under some circumstances. Classic discussion of the allocation problem, albeit from a financial accounting perspective (with some managerial implications).

(2) Categories: A. Unspecified B. A Priori C. Cost Allocation

* * * * *

Categories: A—Source discipline. B—Method of analysis. C—Topic.

Moriarity, S., "Another Approach to Allocating Joint Costs," Accounting Review (October 1975), pp. 791-795.

(1) Discusses the cost allocation problem and proposes a new computational procedure based on the savings realized by acquiring the services jointly instead of independently.

(2) Categories: A. Unspecified B. Modeling C. Cost Allocation--Joint Costs

* * * * *

Eckel, L. G., "Arbitrary and Incorrigible Allocations," The Accounting Review (October 1976), pp. 764-777.

(1) Reviews and analyzes AAA Studies in Accounting Research #3 and #9 on the allocation problem and discusses whether the deficiencies of cost allocation noted and the conclusions of those studies are warranted.

(2) Categories: A. Unspecified B. A Priori C. Cost Allocation

* * * * *

Hamlen, S. S., W. A. Hamlen, and J. T. Tschirhart, "The Use of Core Theory in Evaluating Joint Cost Allocation Schemes," Accounting Review (July 1977), pp. 616-627.

(1) Discusses several joint cost allocation schemes and evaluates four of them using the concept of the core from game theory. Such an approach considers the possibility of suboptimal decisions and provides several criteria for evaluating allocation schemes.

(2) Categories: A. Game Theory B. Modeling C. Cost Allocation--Joint Costs

* * * * *

Jensen, D. L., "A Class of Mutually Satisfactory Allocations," The Accounting Review (October 1977), pp. 842-856.

(1) Presents a class of allocations that results from a list of axioms from the economics literature and discusses the reduced forms of the model that result when certain cost functions are assumed.

(2) Categories: A. Economics B. Modeling C. Cost Allocation

* * * * *

Categories: A—Source discipline. B—Method of analysis. C—Topic.

Bodnar, G. and E. J. Lusk, "Motivational Considerations in Cost Allocation Systems: A Conditioning Theory Approach," The Accounting Review (October 1977), pp. 857-868.

(1) Analyzes the motivational aspects of the cost allocation problem in the context of conditioning theory and illustrates a proposed model that calculates cost allocations in a manner sensitive to behavioral considerations.

(2) Categories: A. Psychology B. Modeling C. Cost Allocation

* * * * *

Callen, J., "Financial Cost Allocation: A Game Theoretic Approach," The Accounting Review (April 1978), pp. 303-308.

(1) Discusses the use of the game-theoretic Shapley technique for allocating time-dependent financial cost allocations. While not addressing managerial cost allocation, this piece continues the discussion of cost allocation via the Shapley technique (see Hamlen et al. 1977 and Jensen 1977).

(2) Categories: A. Operations Research B. Modeling C. Cost Allocation

* * * * *

Zimmerman, J. L., "The Costs and Benefits of Cost Allocations," The Accounting Review (July 1979), pp. 504-521.

(1) Presents a positive analysis of why organizations allocate costs for internal reporting purposes and illustrates that such allocations can serve as a tax which reduces management's consumption of perquisites and as a proxy for difficult-to-observe costs.

(2) Categories: A. Economics B. A Priori C. Cost Allocation

* * * * *

Baker, K. R. and R. E. Taylor, "A Linear Programming Framework for Cost Allocation and External Acquisition When Reciprocal Services Exist," The Accounting Review (October 1979), pp. 784-790.

(1) Proposes a linear programming model for the acquisition of external services which uses the simultaneous equation relationships of the reciprocal service allocation model. The model also provides cost allocations.

(2) Categories: A. Mathematical Programming B. Modeling C. Cost Allocation

* * * * *

Categories: A--Source discipline. B--Method of analysis. C--Topic.

Roth, A., and R. E. Verrecchia, "The Shapley Value as Applied to Cost Allocation: A Reinterpretation," Journal of Accounting Research (Spring 1979), pp. 295-303.

(1) Presents a discussion of the use of the Shapley value in cost allocation, a game theoretic formulation of the problem, and the normative assumptions behind the model. As formulated the value provides a costless surrogate for a bargained solution to the problem.

(2) Categories: A. Operations Research/Game Theory B. Modeling C. Cost Allocation

* * * * *

Hughes, J. and J. Scheiner, "Efficiency Properties of Mutually Satisfactory Allocations," The Accounting Review (January 1980), pp. 85-95.

(1) Analyzes the efficiency conditions of the game-theoretic schemes described in the accounting literature for allocating common costs in a multidivision firm. Concludes that these schemes do not in general lead to efficient solutions.

(2) Categories: A. Operations Research B. Modeling C. Cost Allocation

* * * * *

Hamlen, S. S., W. A. Hamlen and J. T. Tschirhart, "The Use of the Generalized Shapley Allocation in Joint Cost Allocation," The Accounting Review (April 1980), pp. 269-287.

(1) Discusses the use of the simple Shapley model for cost allocation and its limitations and proposes a generalized Shapley which maintains the favorable properties of the simple model while removing the identified weaknesses.

(2) Categories: A. Economics B. Modeling C. Cost Allocation--Joint Costs

* * * * *

Categories: A--Source discipline. B--Method of analysis. C--Topic.

Thomas, A. L., A Behavioral Analysis of Joint-Cost Allocation and Transfer Pricing (Champaign, Illinois: Stipes Publishing Company, 1980).

(1) Continues the work in Thomas (1969, 1974) and presents a comparison among the joint-cost allocation and transfer pricing techniques found in the literature on their behavioral congruence properties. Presents a review and discussion of the methods of both joint-cost allocation and transfer pricing.

(2) Categories: A. Unspecified B. A Priori C. Cost Allocation

* * * * *

Balachandran, B. and R. Ramakrishnan, "Joint Cost Allocation: A Unified Approach," The Accounting Review (January 1981), pp. 85-96.

(1) Discusses joint cost allocation schemes in the literature and the weaknesses and desirable properties of two. Using the desirable properties of these two a modified Shapley Value scheme is proposed.

(2) Categories: A. Economics B. Modeling C. Cost Allocation--Joint Costs

* * * * *

Billera, L. J., D. C. Heath and R. E. Verrecchia, "A Unique Procedure for Allocating Common Costs from a Production Process," Journal of Accounting Research (Spring 1981), pp. 185-196.

(1) Discusses the cost allocation problem in a multiple product setting and presents a decomposed set of properties that a cost allocation scheme would exhibit if the costs were separable. These properties then imply a unique procedure for allocating common costs.

(2) Categories: A. Mathematics/OR B. Modeling C. Cost Allocation--Joint Costs

* * * * *

Gangolly, J. S., "On Joint Cost Allocation: Independent Cost Proportional Scheme (ICPS) and Its Properties," Journal of Accounting Research (Autumn 1981), pp. 299-312.

(1) Presents a scheme for the allocation of joint costs in which cost savings are distributed in proportion to independent costs. An example is included and ICPS properties and their significance are discussed.

(2) Categories: A. OR/Game Theory B. Modeling C. Cost Allocation--Joint Costs

* * * * *

Categories: A--Source discipline. B--Method of analysis. C--Topic.

Cohen, S. I. and M. Loeb, "Public Goods, Common Inputs, and the Efficiency of Full Cost Allocations," The Accounting Review (April 1982), pp. 336-347.

(1) Discusses the cost allocation problem as analogous to the problem of providing a public good and presents a general model for allocating common inputs (public goods). Includes discussion of the free-rider problem and allocation of mixed (public and private) inputs.

(2) Categories: A. Economics B. Modeling C. Cost Allocation

* * * * *

Moriarity, S., ed., Joint Cost Allocation, Proceedings of the University of Oklahoma Conference on Cost Allocations (Center for Economic and Management Research, Norman OK, 1981).

(1) Presents the papers and proceedings of a conference on joint cost allocation held at the University of Oklahoma.

(2) Categories: A. Economics/Decision Theory B. Multiple Methods C. Cost Allocation

* * * * *

Verrecchia, R. E., "An Analysis of Two Cost Allocation Cases," The Accounting Review (July 1982), pp. 579-593.

(1) Discusses two cases appealing reimbursement for allocated costs from the government under Cost Accounting Standard 403. Includes discussion of CAS 403, the seven allocation schemes proposed by the parties, and the appeal board's reasoning and decision.

(2) Categories: A. Unspecified B. A Priori C. Cost Allocation

* * * * *

Manes, R. P., S. H. Park and R. Jensen, "Relevant Costs of Intermediate Goods and Services," The Accounting Review (July 1982), pp. 594-606.

(1) Discusses the reciprocal services allocation model proposed by Baker and Taylor (1979) and by means of an example extends it to include relevant nonvariable service costs and converts the model into a profit-maximization model.

(2) Categories: A. Unspecified B. Modeling C. Cost Allocation

* * * * *

Categories: A--Source discipline. B--Method of analysis. C--Topic.

Thomas, A. L., "Goals for Joint-Cost Allocation: An Incompatibility in the Literature," Abacus (December 1982), pp. 166-174.

(1) Presents arguments that core membership of a cost allocation scheme (Hamlen, Hamlen and Tschirhart (1977, 1980)) and allocative efficiency are not always compatible. Discusses implications this has for the use of cost allocations.

(2) Categories: A. Unspecified B. A Priori C. Cost Allocation

* * * * *

Categories: A—Source discipline. B—Method of analysis. C—Topic.

COST ESTIMATION

4. COST ESTIMATION (pp. 113-117)

This category contains works on cost estimation, including those incorporating learning curves in the estimate. The majority of articles deal with statistical methods in cost estimation. The CVP section, subcategory 5.1 (pp. 119-127), also contains articles relating to cost estimation.

Bornemann, A., "Empirical Cost Study and Economic Theory," The Accounting Review (July 1945), pp. 327-331.

(1) Discusses empirical cost studies from the economics literature and how they relate to economic theory. Includes discussion of marginal cost, variable and fixed costs, the use of accounting records as data sources for the studies, and the difficulties likely to be encountered in such studies. Quotes a number of economics articles listing problems and offering explanations for the empirical linear curves rather than the theoretical U-shaped curves. Provides a discussion of economic concepts relevant to cost accountants.

(2) Categories: A. Economics B. A Priori C. Cost Estimation

* * * * *

Avery, H. G. and M. Pollack, "Cost and Output Relationships," The Accounting Review (October 1946), pp. 419-424.

(1) Discusses the relationship between unit costs and the amount of output and presents formulas for unit cost calculation. Three problems with solutions are presented to illustrate the effect on unit cost of various changes in total cost and units produced. An analytical example of the changing nature of cost.

(2) Categories: A. Unspecified B. A Priori C. Cost Estimation

* * * * *

Wasserman, M. J., "Costs and Volume in the Milk Pasteurizing Industry," The Accounting Review (October 1946), pp. 425-429.

(1) Presents the results of a study on the relationship between costs and volume in the milk industry. The data support the general partitioning of costs into fixed and variable categories. An early true empirical study with statistical analysis of the data (coefficient of correlation).

(2) Categories: A. Economics B. Field Study C. Cost Estimation

* * * * *

Categories: A--Source discipline. B--Method of analysis. C--Topic.

Field, J. E., "Inventory Valuation and the Short-Run Cost Function," The Accounting Review (January 1960), pp. 104-110.

(1) Discussion of cost accounting incorporating economic concepts of inventory valuation. The objective is to restate accounting information in a relevant form for management use. Uses regression to relate cost and sales. Concludes that inventory should be valued at marginal cost. A rather sophisticated continuation of the discussion of economics, accounting, and costs.

(2) Categories: A. Economics B. A Priori C. Cost Estimation

* * * * *

McClenon, P. R., "Cost Finding Through Multiple Correlation Analysis," The Accounting Review (July 1963), pp. 540-548.

(1) Proposes multiple correlation analysis as a method of developing cost estimates not determinable by other means, presents an example, and describes the analytical process. Includes a technical appendix.

(2) Categories: A. Statistics B. Modeling C. Cost Estimation

* * * * *

Thompson, W. W. and E. L. Kemper, "Probability Measures for Estimated Data," The Accounting Review (July 1965), pp. 574-578.

(1) Discusses the use of subjective estimates and illustrates the use of probability concepts and variance estimates in forecasting sales data.

(2) Categories: A. Statistics B. A Priori C. Cost Estimation

* * * * *

Comiskey, E. E., "Cost Control by Regression Analysis," The Accounting Review (April 1966), pp. 235-238.

(1) Describes the implementation of a cost control model which uses multiple regression to forecast various cost levels. Comparison of actual costs with these forecast costs results in "variances" which are investigated.

(2) Categories: A. Statistics B. Modeling C. Cost Estimation

* * * * *

Categories: A—Source discipline. B--Method of analysis. C—Topic.

Benston, G. J., "Multiple Regression Analysis of Cost Behavior," The Accounting Review (October 1966), pp. 657-672.

(1) Discusses the analysis of costs and the use of multiple regression techniques in such analysis. Includes considerable discussion of the technical requirements of regression and the implications these have for the amount and form of the cost data recorded in the accounts. Also includes an illustrated example.

(2) Categories: A. Statistics B. A Priori C. Cost Estimation

* * * * *

Jensen, R. E., "A Multiple Regression Model for Cost Control: Assumptions and Limitations," The Accounting Review (April 1967), pp. 265-273.

(1) Discusses the assumptions of the multiple regression model and the limitations of this type of analysis on cost data. Violations of model assumptions likely to be made by cost data include heteroscedasticity, multicollinearity, lack of independence, and autocorrelation. An excellent review of regression and discussion of the statistical problems with management cost data.

(2) Categories: A. Statistics B. A Priori C. Cost Estimation

* * * * *

Baloff, N. and J. W. Kennelly, "Accounting Implications of Product and Process Start-Ups," Journal of Accounting Research (Autumn 1967), pp. 131-143.

(1) Discusses start-ups and the learning curve and the implications of these for both internal and external reporting purposes. First discussion of learning curves in the academic accounting literature although it references earlier articles.

(2) Categories: A. Economics B. A Priori C. Cost Estimation--Learning Curves

* * * * *

Jensen, R. E., and C. T. Thomsen, "Statistical Analysis in Cost Measurement and Control," The Accounting Review (January 1968), pp. 83-93.

(1) Discusses the use of statistical sampling techniques in measuring and controlling costs not otherwise found in the accounts or too expensive to collect. Applies sampling theory to management accounting.

(2) Categories: A. Unspecified B. A Priori C. Cost Estimation

* * * * *

Categories: A—Source discipline. B—Method of analysis. C—Topic.

Morse, W. J., "Reporting Production Costs That Follow the Learning Curve Phenomenon," The Accounting Review (October 1972), pp. 761-773.

(1) Presents a cost allocation model that incorporates the learning curve phenomenon with the objective of achieving a better matching of costs and revenues. Includes discussion of economic income, learning curves, and an example.

(2) Categories: A. Mathematics B. Modeling C. Cost Estimation--Learning Curves

* * * * *

Buzby, S., "Extending the Applicability of Probabilistic Management Planning and Control Models," The Accounting Review (January 1974), pp. 42-49.

(1) Proposes the use of Tchebycheff inequalities in overcoming the problem of lack of knowledge about the probability distribution of a variable of interest. Illustrates the proposed technique with a CVP example. Continues the discussion of the statistical distributions in accounting and the estimation of cost parameters. Could also be classified in Planning and Control or CVP.

(2) Categories: A. Statistics B. Modeling C. Cost Estimation

* * * * *

Categories: A--Source discipline. B--Method of analysis. C--Topic.

DECISION MAKING

5. DECISION MAKING (pp. 119-155)

This category includes articles with a definite decision making perspective. Specific sections deal with CVP analysis and capital budgeting; all behavioral articles are included in one section; and all other articles are included in the general subcategory.

This category contains the following subcategories:

5.1 Cost-Volume-Profit (pp. 119-127)

5.2 Capital Budgeting (pp. 128-136)

5.3 Decision Making-Behavioral (pp. 137-144)

5.4 Decision Making-General (pp. 145-155)

5.1. COST-VOLUME-PROFIT (pp. 119-127)

The articles in this category address CVP analysis. The majority of the articles present CVP models that incorporate uncertainty or multiple production constraints. Some papers in the Cost Estimation category (pp. 113-117) use CVP examples.

Brush, L. F., "Graphic Analysis of Expense," The Accounting Review (October 1943), pp. 331-338.

(1) Explains the Break-Even chart and fixed, variable, and mixed costs and discusses its use for plotting and analyzing costs. Introduces the Break Even analysis of costs to the academic accounting literature.

(2) Categories: A. Economics B. A Priori C. CVP

* * * * *

Fill, W. L., "The Break-Even Chart," The Accounting Review (April 1952), pp. 202-209.

(1) Illustrates and describes the use of the break-even chart including scatter plot analysis of costs and the various ways of showing costs on the chart. An elaborate discussion of the break-even chart and its uses in management and accounting.

(2) Categories: A. Economics B. A Priori C. CVP

* * * * *

Categories: A--Source discipline. B--Method of analysis. C--Topic.

Banerjee, K. C., "Cost, Price, Profit and Volume Reactions," Accounting Research (October 1954), pp. 343-362.

(1) Presents an analysis of the effect changes in the various factors have on the P/V ratio. Primary focus is on increases in the number of units sold and decreases in the ratio of variable costs to sales price.

(2) Categories: A. Unspecified B. A Priori C. CVP

* * * * *

Patrick, A. W., "Some Observations on the Breakeven Chart," The Accounting Review (October 1958), pp. 573-580.

(1) Discusses the assumptions and characteristics of the breakeven chart and provides a detailed example in explaining it. The focus is on the computation of the conventional breakeven point under absorption costing when there is a divergence between production and sales.

(2) Categories: A. Unspecified B. A Priori C. CVP

* * * * *

Vickers, D., "On the Economics of Breakeven," The Accounting Review (July 1960), pp. 405-412.

(1) Discusses the economic and accounting views toward breakeven analysis and provides suggestions for improving both the analysis and the application of the technique. The discussion reviews cost definitions, the breakeven chart, how it fits with the economic theory of the firm, and empirical evidence.

(2) Categories: A. Economics B. A Priori C. CVP

* * * * *

Jaedicke, R. K., "Improving Break-Even Analysis by Linear Programming Techniques," NAA Bulletin (March 1961), pp. 5-12.

(1) Discusses the relationships between linear programming and break-even analysis and proposes the use of linear programming as an extension of BE analysis. Illustrates with a product mix problem in a multiple constraint setting.

(2) Categories: A Unspecified B. Modeling C. CVP

Categories: A—Source discipline. B—Method of analysis. C—Topic.

Stettler, H. F., "Breakeven Analysis: Its Uses and Misuses," The Accounting Review (July 1962), pp. 460-463.

(1) Discusses breakeven analysis and its usefulness for various actions and suggests new significant uses of this tool, including planning and the evaluation of new proposals.

(2) Categories: A. Unspecified B. A Priori C. CVP

* * * * *

Wiener, J., "The Cost Structure of the Industrial Enterprise: Pattern of Analysis," The Accounting Review (July 1962), pp. 438-451.

(1) Discusses the analysis of the cost structure of firms and illustrates how labor costs vary with different combinations of its elements (regular work, additional work, and combined work). Illustrates using the cost-volume-profit relationship.

(2) Categories: A. Unspecified B. A Priori C. CVP

* * * * *

Dopuch, N., "Mathematical Programming and Accounting Approaches to Incremental Cost Analysis," The Accounting Review (October 1963).

(1) Discusses the similarities of the mathematical programming and accounting approaches to incremental cost analysis and illustrates a linear programming problem. A sophisticated discussion of mathematical modeling and its use in accounting problems.

(2) Categories: A. Mathematics/Operations Research B. Modeling C. CVP

* * * * *

Jaedicke, R. K., and A. A. Robichek, "Cost-Volume-Profit Analysis Under Conditions of Uncertainty," The Accounting Review (October 1964), pp. 917-926.

(1) Discusses the use of cost-volume-profit analysis when the volume of product is unknown and a probability distribution for the volume is used. The technique is illustrated using both an actual distribution and a general distribution (normal). Introduces uncertainty to C-V-P analysis (a landmark piece).

(2) Categories: A. Mathematics/Statistics B. Modeling C. CVP

* * * * *

Categories: A--Source discipline. B--Method of analysis. C--Topic.

Raun, D. L., "The Limitations of Profit Graphs, Breakeven Analysis, and Budgets," The Accounting Review (October 1964), pp. 927-945.

(1) Discusses profit graphs, scattergraphs, and regression analysis as applied to budgeting and breakeven analysis. Presents a good review of profit graphs and regression topics.

(2) Categories: A. Mathematics/Statistics B. A Priori C. CVP

* * * * *

Goggans, T. P., "Breakeven Analysis with Curvilinear Functions," The Accounting Review (October 1965), pp. 867-871.

(1) Discusses the calculation of breakeven amounts when the cost and/or revenue curves are nonlinear. Illustrates with an example the calculation of breakeven for curivilinear cost-linear revenue and curvilinear cost-curivilinear revenue.

(2) Categories: A. Mathematics/Economics B. A Priori C. CVP

* * * * *

Givens, H. R., "An Application of Curvilinear Break-Even Analysis," The Accounting Review (January 1966), pp. 141-143.

(1) Discusses and illustrates the derivation of curvilinear cost and revenue functions and their use in breakeven analysis. A teaching note but a good explanation.

(2) Categories: A. Unspecified B. A Priori C. CVP

* * * * *

Manes, R. P., "A New Dimension to Break Even Analysis," Journal of Accounting Research (Spring 1966), pp. 87-100.

(1) Proposes the integration of breakeven analysis and capital budgeting by incorporating the cost of capital in the breakeven formula. Also could be classified under capital budgeting.

(2) Categories: A. Economics B. Modeling C. CVP

* * * * *

Categories: A--Source discipline. B--Method of analysis. C--Topic.

Solomons, D., "Breakeven Analysis Under Absorption Costing," The Accounting Review (July 1968), pp. 447-452.

(1) Discusses breakeven analysis and the differences in applying the technique under direct and absorption costing. Provides a model for determining breakeven under absorption costing.

(2) Categories: A. Unspecified B. Modeling C. CVP

* * * * *

Jensen, R. E., "Sensitivity Analysis and Integer Linear Programming," The Accounting Review (July 1968), pp. 425-446.

(1) Discusses the use of sensitivity analysis in integer programming models and compares it to its use in continuous models.

(2) Categories: A. Mathematics B. A Priori C. CVP

* * * * *

Morrison, T. A., and E. Kaczka, "A New Application of Calculus and Risk Analysis to Cost-Volume-Profit Changes," The Accounting Review (April 1969), pp. 330-343.

(1) Discusses the use of cost-volume-profit analysis under conditions of nonlinear revenue functions, the use of probabilistic estimates in C-V-P analysis, and the use of constraints and opportunity costs in C-V-P analysis. These analyses are performed using differential calculus.

(2) Categories: A. Unspecified B. Modeling C. CVP

* * * * *

Colantoni, C. S., R. P. Manes and A. Whinston, "Programming, Profit Rates and Pricing Decisions," The Accounting Review (July 1969), pp. 467-481.

(1) Discusses the use of mathematical programming when the manager is a price-fixer rather than a price-taker and analyzes various aspects of the programming approach under this assumption. Analyzes linear, integer, and quadratic forms of programming.

(2) Categories: A. Mathematics/Operations Research B. Modeling C. CVP

* * * * *

Categories: A--Source discipline. B--Method of analysis. C--Topic.

Johnson, G. L. and S. S. Simik, "Multiproduct C-V-P Analysis Under Uncertainty," Journal of Accounting Research (Autumn 1971), pp. 278-286.

(1) Presents a C-V-P model under uncertainty which uses multivariate analysis to take care of interdependencies among product demands in a multiproduct setting. Using this model, probabilities of various breakeven and profit amounts are calculated.

(2) Categories: A. Statistics B. Modeling C. CVP

* * * * *

Ferrara, W. L., J. C. Hayya and D. A. Nachman, "Normalcy of Profit in the Jaedicke-Robichek Model," The Accounting Review (April 1972), pp. 299-307.

(1) Presents the results of a simulation experiment designed to test the assumption concerning the normality of the product of two normally distributed random variables. The findings indicate this assumption holds only when the coefficients of variation of the variables are close to zero. Continues the discussion of C-V-P under uncertainty (specifically the Jaedicke-Robichek Model (1964)).

(2) Categories: A. Statistics B. Simulation C. CVP

* * * * *

Ijiri, Y. and H. Itami, "Quadratic Cost-volume Relationship and Timing of Demand Information," The Accounting Review (October 1973), pp. 724-737.

(1) Presents an analysis of the effect the timing of perfect information has on the costs of a firm and how a quadratic cost-volume relationship can be used to evaluate cost performance. Addresses topics of interest in information economics.

(2) Categories: A. Unspecified B. Modeling C. CVP

* * * * *

Johnson, G. L. and S. S. Simik, "The Use of Probability Inequalities in Multiproduct C-V-P Analysis Under Uncertainty," Journal of Accounting Research (Spring 1974), pp. 67-79.

(1) Presents a C-V-P model that does not require knowledge of the probability density function of sales volume for use under conditions of uncertainty and multiple products.

(2) Categories: A. Mathematics B. Modeling C. CVP

* * * * *

Categories: A—Source discipline. B—Method of analysis. C—Topic.

Dickinson, J. P., "Cost-Volume-Profit Analysis Under Uncertainty," Journal of Accounting Research (Spring 1974), pp. 182-187.

(1) Discusses the use of historical data in estimating the parameters of the probability distribution of sales for use in C-V-P analyis under uncertainty and the reliability of a sampling approach to such estimation.

(2) Categories: A. Unspecified B. Modeling C. CVP

* * * * *

Hilliard, J. E. and R. A. Leitch, "Cost-Volume-Profit Analysis Under Uncertainty: A Log Normal Approach," The Accounting Review (January 1975), pp. 69-80.

(1) Presents a model of C-V-P analysis under uncertainty which uses a log normal distribution for sales and contribution to profit.

(2) Categories: A. Mathematics/Statistics B. Modeling C. CVP

* * * * *

Nash, J. F., "A Note on Cost-Volume-Profit Analysis and Price Elasticity," The Accounting Review (April 1975), pp. 384-386.

(1) Discusses and illustrates the use of market demand elasticity in CVP analysis for decisions involving price changes.

(2) Categories: A. Unspecified B. Modeling C. CVP

* * * * *

Liao, M., "Model Sampling: A Stochastic Cost-Volume-Profit Analysis," The Accounting Review (October 1975), pp. 780-790.

(1) Presents a CVP model based on model sampling, a sampling technique which uses multiple trials to determine a probability distribution, and a curve-fitting technique. The model overcomes certain differences noted in other models in the literature. Continues the literature on CVP (see Jaedicke-Robichek (1964); Ferrara et al. (1972) introduces the model sampling technique).

(2) Categories: A. Mathematics B. Modeling C. CVP

* * * * *

Categories: A—Source discipline. B—Method of analysis. C—Topic.

Magee, R. P., "Cost-Volume-Profit Analysis, Uncertainty and Capital Market Equilibrium," Journal of Accounting Research (Autumn 1975), pp. 257-266.

(1) Proposes a new model of CVP analysis under uncertainty using capital asset pricing model theory to show that the appropriate measure of risk is not the variance of profits but rather the covariance of profits with return to the market.

(2) Categories: A. Economics/OR B. Modeling C. CVP

* * * * *

Adar, Z., A. Barnea and B. Lev, "A Comprehensive Cost-Volume-Profit Analysis Under Uncertainty," The Accounting Review (January 1977), pp. 137-149.

(1) Presents an approach for CVP analysis under uncertainty using economic models of the firm's optimal output decision modified within the mean-standard deviation framework.

(2) Categories: A. Economics B. Modeling C. CVP

* * * * *

Kottas, J. F., A. H. Lau and H. Lau, "A General Approach to Stochastic Management Planning Models: An Overview," The Accounting Review (April 1978), pp. 389-401.

(1) Presents a general framework for handling stochastic management planning models. Includes numerical examples of CVP and present-value analysis.

(2) Categories: A. Unspecified B. Modeling C. CVP

* * * * *

Kottas, J. F. and H. Lau, "Direct Simulation in Stochastic CVP Analysis," The Accounting Review (July 1978), pp. 698-707.

(1) Discusses stochastic CVP analysis and presents the results of a comparison of a "strong" CVP approach, model sampling (Liao 1975), with a direct simulation approach. The findings indicate simulation is a useful and inexpensive approach to stochastic CVP analysis. Continues the literature on CVP analysis (see in particular Ferrara et al. (1972), Hilliard and Leitch (1975), Jaedicke and Robichek (1964), and Liao (1975)).

(2) Categories: A. Mathematics/OR B. Simulation C. CVP

* * * * *

Categories: A--Source discipline. B--Method of analysis. C--Topic.

Shih, W., "A General Decision Model for Cost-Volume-Profit Analysis Under Uncertainty," The Accounting Review (October 1979), pp. 687-706.

(1) Proposes a model for CVP analysis under uncertainty which takes into account random demand and level of production in determining sales and profits.

(2) Categories: A. Mathematics/Statistics B. Modeling C. CVP

* * * * *

Categories: A--Source discipline. B--Method of analysis. C--Topic.

5.2. CAPITAL BUDGETING (pp. 128-136)

The articles in this subcategory deal with capital budgeting. Most discuss its use in various contexts of uncertainty and resource constraints; there are also experimental, field, and simulation studies.

McFarland, W. B., "Cost Analysis for Equipment Replacement," The Accounting Review (January 1947), pp. 58-64.

(1) Examines the different formulas and methods for computing and comparing costs in the equipment replacement decision and presents a new approach. Includes a discussion of future costs and opportunity costs.

(2) Categories: A. Unspecified B. A Priori C. Capital Budgeting (Replacement)

* * * * *

Christensen, C., "Construction of Present Value Tables for Use in Evaluation of Capital Investment Opportunities," The Accounting Review (October 1955), pp. 666-672.

(1) Illustrates and discusses the construction of a present value table so that calculations need not be repeated for every decision. Introduces the present value table for discounted cash flow calculations.

(2) Categories: A. Mathematics B. A Priori C. Capital Budgeting

* * * * *

Mayer, R. R., "The Role of the Accountant in Equipment Replacement Analyses," The Accounting Review (October 1958), pp. 637-644.

(1) Presents the prerequisites for an equipment policy and continues with a determination of what accountants can supply in this area. Concludes the accountant can contribute in the areas of capital costs and operating data but must be careful in using past data to predict the future.

(2) Categories: A. Unspecified B. A Priori C. Capital Budgeting

* * * * *

Categories: A--Source discipline. B--Method of analysis. C--Topic.

Coughlan, J., "Industrial Accounting," The Accounting Review (July 1959), pp. 415-428.

(1) Discusses industrial accounting and differentiates it from mercantile accounting in a time period orientation. Provides a long illustrative discussion where forward estimates of cash receipts replace assets on the balance sheet when taking the industrial perspective. Provides an explicit recognition of future cash receipts and recommends the use of economic criteria in accounting for capital expenditures.

(2) Categories: A. Unspecified B. A Priori C. Capital Budgeting

* * * * *

Brown, V. H., "Rate of Return: Some Comments on Its Applicability in Capital Budgeting," The Accounting Review (January 1961), pp. 50-62.

(1) Discusses the use of discounted cash flow in making capital expenditure decisions including reinvestment, unequal investments, uncertainty, the investment mix problem, and administrative considerations.

(2) Categories: A. Unspecified B. A Priori C. Capital Budgeting

* * * * *

Bodenhorn, D., "An Economist Looks at Industrial Accounting and Depreciation," The Accounting Review (October 1961), pp. 583-588.

(1) Proposes that the balance sheet be brought nearer economic reality by reflecting the present value of expected receipts rather than cost. Further proposes that the cost of capital be used to discount the future earnings of a project rather than one selected so present value will equal cost (proposed by Coughlan (1959)). Argument concerning cost of capital is most relevant.

(2) Categories: A. Economics B. A Priori C. Capital Budgeting

* * * * *

Categories: A--Source discipline. B--Method of analysis. C--Topic.

Gregory, J. C., "Capital Expenditure Evaluation by Direct Discounting," The Accounting Review (April 1962), pp. 308-314.

(1) Discusses capital budgeting and proposes that it is easier and more useful to discount all projects at the cost of capital rather than solving each for its rate of return. Includes discussion of projects which are dependent, those which are independent, and those with multiple rates of return.

(2) Categories: A. Unspecified B. A Priori C. Capital Budgeting

* * * * *

Wright, F. K., "Measuring Project Profitability: Rate of Return or Present Value," The Accounting Review (July 1962), pp. 433-437.

(1) Discusses the relative merits of both methods and argues that there is a place for each in evaluating investment proposals. An integrated approach using both is presented based on the concept of opportunity cost.

(2) Categories: A. Unspecified B. A Priori C. Capital Budgeting

* * * * *

Moore, C., "The Concepts of the P/V Graph Applied to Capital Investment Planning," The Accounting Review (October 1962), pp. 721-729.

(1) Presents a graph similar in concept to the conventional cost-volume-profit graph which can be used in capital investment planning. Discusses its usefulness in analyses of complex situations such as different time lines and varying cash flows.

(2) Categories: A. Unspecified B. A Priori C. Capital Budgeting

* * * * *

Weingartner, H., "The Excess Present Value Index-A Theoretical Basis and Critique," Journal of Accounting Research (Autumn 1963).

(1) Discusses the excess present value index, its theoretical support, and the limitations of its use in capital budgeting decision-making.

(2) Categories: A. Mathematics B. A Priori C. Capital Budgeting

* * * * *

Categories: A—Source discipline. B—Method of analysis. C—Topic.

Heebink, D. V., "The Optimum Capital Budget," The Accounting Review (January 1964), pp. 90-93.

(1) Discusses the economic theory behind the supply of and demand for capital investment projects. Includes discussion of the conceptual model and some real-world considerations. Excellent review of the theory behind investments.

(2) Categories: A. Economics B. A Priori C. Capital Budgeting

* * * * *

Paine, N. R., "Uncertainty and Capital Budgeting," The Accounting Review (April 1964), pp. 330-332.

(1) Discusses the capital budgeting decision of a portfolio of investments under conditions of uncertainty. Includes discussion of the variance of returns as well as the expected value of the return. Introduces portfolio theory to the capital budgeting literature.

(2) Categories: A. Economics/Finance B. A Priori C. Capital Budgeting

* * * * *

Taussig, R., "Information Requirements of Replacement Models," Journal of Accounting Research (Spring 1964), pp. 67-69.

(1) Discusses the use of replacement models and the accounting information needed for such models.

(2) Categories: A. Mathematics B. A Priori C. Capital Budgeting (Replacement)

* * * * *

Beranek, W., "A Note on the Equivalence of Certain Capital Budgeting Criteria," The Accounting Review (October 1964), pp. 914-916.

(1) Discusses the conditions under which the ranking of proposed capital investments projects under various capital budgeting techniques will be the same and when they will not.

(2) Categories: A. Unspecified B. A Priori C. Capital Budgeting

* * * * *

Categories: A—Source discipline. B—Method of analysis. C—Topic.

Sussman, M. R., "Present-Value Shortcuts," The Accounting Review (April 1965). pp. 407-413.

(1) Discusses present value calculations, provides short cut calculation methods for different cash flow patterns, and discusses their limitations.

(2) Categories: A. Mathematics B. A Priori C. Capital Budgeting

* * * * *

Duvall, R. M. and J. Bullock, "Adjusting Rate of Return and Present-Value for Price Level Changes," The Accounting Review (July 1965), pp. 569-573.

(1) Discusses the effect changing price levels have on rate of return and present-value calculations and provides equations which must be used to adjust these calculations for such changes.

(2) Categories: A. Unspecified B. A Priori C. Capital Budgeting

* * * * *

Luneski, C., "Continuous Versus Discrete Compounding for Capital Budgeting Decisions," The Accounting Review (October 1967), pp. 767-771.

(1) Discusses the differences between the discrete and continuous method of compounding the time value of money.

(2) Categories: A. Unspecified B. A Priori C. Capital Budgeting

* * * * *

Byrne, R., A. Charnes, W. W. Cooper and K. Kortanek, "Some New Approaches to Risk," The Accounting Review (January 1968), pp. 18-37.

(1) Discusses various approaches to the evaluation of risk including the use of decision trees and stochastic linear programming.

(2) Categories: A. Mathematics/Decision Theory/OR B. A Priori
C. Capital Budgeting

* * * * *

Categories: A--Source discipline. B--Method of analysis. C—Topic.

Ma, R., "Project Appraisal in a Divisionalized Company," Abacus (December 1969), pp. 132-142.

(1) Discusses the problems in making capital budgeting decisions in a firm with several divisions. Includes discussion of rate of return to be used for each division and the apprasial of common service projects.

(2) Categories: A. Economics B. A Priori C. Capital Budgeting

* * * * *

Greer, W. R., "Capital Budgeting Analysis with the Timing of Events Uncertain," The Accounting Review (January 1970), pp. 103-114.

(1) Describes the use of probability estimates generated from the beta distribution in performing capital budgeting calculations when the time period of the cash flows is uncertain.

(2) Categories: A. Statistics B. Modeling C. Capital Budgeting

* * * * *

Huefner, R. J., "Analyzing and Reporting Sensitivity Data," The Accounting Review (October 1971), pp. 717-732.

(1) Discusses the use of sensitivity analysis in capital budgeting and the way the data can be presented. Illustrates the use of isoquants for presenting such data.

(2) Categories: A. Unspecified B. Modeling C. Capital Budgeting

* * * * *

Folger, H. R., "Ranking Techniques and Capital Budgeting," The Accounting Review (January 1972), pp. 134-143.

(1) Discusses the relative effectiveness of various ranking techniques in the evaluation of capital investment decisions and relates the ranking process to mathematical models.

(2) Categories: A. Unspecified B. A Priori C. Capital Budgeting

* * * * *

Categories: A—Source discipline. B--Method of analysis. C—Topic.

Lusk, E. J., "Discriminant Analysis as Applied to the Resource Allocation Decision," The Accounting Review (July 1972), pp. 567-575.

(1) Discusses the use of discriminant analysis in evaluating capital investment projects. Project proposals from prior periods both those accepted and those rejected are analyzed to determine priority coefficients which are used to assess future proposals.

(2) Categories: A. Unspecified B. Modeling C. Capital Budgeting

* * * * *

Klammer, T., "The Association of Capital Budgeting Techniques with Firm Performance," The Accounting Review (April 1973), pp. 353-364.

(1) Reports the results of a study on the association between firm performance and its use of capital budgeting. The findings indicate no association and the author concludes this may indicate mere adoption of analytical tools is not sufficient to assure high performance.

(2) Categories: A. Unspecified B. Field Study C. Capital Budgeting

* * * * *

Brief, R. P. and J. Owen, "Present Value Models and the Multi-Asset Problem," The Accounting Review (October 1973), pp. 690-695.

(1) Discusses the interrelationship among revenues in a multi-asset setting and proposes the use of a firm approach in making capital investment decisions rather than the traditional IRR approach on separated revenues.

(2) Categories: A. Unspecified B. Modeling C. Capital Budgeting

* * * * *

Finn, F. J., "Integer Programming, Linear Programming and Capital Budgeting," Abacus (December 1973), pp. 180-192.

(1) Discusses the constrained capital budgeting decision and compares and contrasts the use of integer and linear programming in solution of the problem. Includes discussion of capital constraints, other restrictions, and fractional projects.

(2) Categories: A. Mathematics B. A Priori C. Capital Budgeting

* * * * *

Categories: A--Source discipline. B--Method of analysis. C--Topic.

Sundem, G. L., "Evaluating Simplified Capital Budgeting Models Using a Time-State Preference Metric," The Accounting Review (April 1974), pp. 306-320.

(1) Reports the results of a simulation experiment comparing capital investment decisions from simplified capital budgeting models with the decisions from more sophisticated models. The findings indicate payback improves decisions made with the NPV model in an uncertain environment and different discount rates for different risk classes improves the performance of simple models.

(2) Categories: A. Unspecified B. Modeling C. Capital Budgeting

* * * * *

Harvey, D. W., "Financial Planning Information for Production Start-ups," The Accounting Review (October 1976), pp. 838-845.

(1) Discusses the use of learning models in analyzing production start-ups and extends two such models. Explores their use in planning and in the analysis of capital expenditures. Includes an analysis of the sensitivity of the model to volume, cash flows, and IRR and an example.

(2) Categories: A. Unspecified B. Modeling C. Capital Budgeting (Could also be under Planning and Control.)

* * * * *

Ferrara, W. L., "Probabilistic Approaches to Return on Investment and Residual Income," The Accounting Review (July 1977), pp. 597-604.

(1) Discusses and analyzes various probabilistic approaches to ROI and RI proceeding from those assuming normality for the basic variables through models assuming an ability to simulate the interaction to those requiring alternative approaches. The results indicate RI is more versatile.

(2) Categories: A. Unspecified B. A Priori C. Capital Budgeting

* * * * *

Ma, R., P. Pandey and M. Scott, "Capital Budgeting and Discounted Cash Equivalents," Abacus (December 1978), pp. 180-187.

(1) Discusses a capital budgeting technique advanced by Chambers which uses discounted cash equivalent flows rather than discounted cash flows. Includes discussion of uncertainty and technological improvement and concludes this new model is no improvement over the conventional model.

(2) Categories: A. Unspecified B. A Priori C. Capital Budgeting

* * * * *

Categories: A—Source discipline. B—Method of analysis. C—Topic.

Blocher, E. and C. Stickney, "Duration and Risk Assessments in Capital Budgeting," The Accounting Review (January 1979), pp. 180-188.

(1) Discusses the definition and attributes of duration, a measure of the average maturity of a stream of payments, and its potential use in risk assessments in capital budgeting decisions.

(2) Categories: A. Economics B. Modeling C. Capital Budgeting

* * * * *

Keane, S. M., "The Internal Rate of Return and the Reinvestment Fallacy," Abacus (June 1979), pp. 48-55.

(1) Discusses the reinvestment rate and its effect on IRR and NPV calculations and their relative rankings of investment projects. Concludes the reinvestment rate is irrelevant to the choice of investment model and further that IRR is not a valid investment decision aid.

(2) Categories: A. Unspecified (Finance) B. A Priori C. Capital Budgeting

* * * * *

Peasnell, K. V., "On Capital Budgeting and Income Measurement," Abacus (June 1981), pp. 52-67.

(1) Continues the discussion in Ma, Pandy and Scott (1978) concerning the use of discounted cash flows and discounted incomes in making investment decisions. Includes a discussion of uncertainty and a numerical example.

(2) Categories: A. Unspecified B. A Priori C. Capital Budgeting

* * * * *

Larcker, D. F., "The Perceived Importance of Selected Information Characteristics for Strategic Capital Budgeting Decisions," The Accounting Review (July 1981), pp. 519-538.

(1) Reports the results of a study designed to determine whether decision-makers have similar preferences for information in the capital budgeting decision. The findings indicate similar preferences exist and that differences depend upon the stage of the decision.

(2) Categories: A. Psychology/Decision Theory B. Field Experiment C. Capital Budgeting

* * * * *

Categories: A—Source discipline. B--Method of analysis. C—Topic.

5.3. DECISION MAKING-BEHAVIORAL (pp. 137-144)

This subcategory contains articles reporting laboratory experiments, simulations, and discussions dealing with behavioral aspects of decision making.

Dyckman, T. R., "The Effects of Alternative Accounting Techniques on Certain Management Decisions," Journal of Accounting Research (Spring 1964), pp. 91-107.

(1) Reports the results of a study designed to test whether different inventory cost flow assumptions affect the decision made by managers. The results indicate that the periodic method is less useful than the perpetual method. An early behavioral experiment in decision making.

(2) Categories: A. Unspecified B. Laboratory Experiment C. Decision Making-- Behavioral

* * * * *

Bruns, W. J., "Inventory Valuation and Management Decisions," The Accounting Review (April 1965), pp. 345-357.

(1) Reports the results of a behavioral experiment designed to test the effects inventory valuation methods have on decisions made by managers. The principal hypothesis of no effect could not be rejected. An early behavioral experiment on the effect of accounting on decision making.

(2) Categories: A. Unspecified B. Laboratory Experiment C. Decision Making--Behavioral

* * * * *

Bruns, W. J., "The Accounting Period and Its Effect Upon Management Decisions," Journal of Accounting Research (Supplement 1966), pp. 1-20.

(1) Reports the results of a laboratory experiment designed to test whether the frequency with which information is reported affects the decision made by management. The results were inconclusive.

(2) Categories: A. Unspecified B. Laboratory Experiment C. Decision Making--Behavioral

* * * * *

Categories: A--Source discipline. B--Method of analysis. C--Topic.

Birnberg, J. G. and R. Nath, "Implications of Behavioral Science for Management Accounting," The Accounting Review (July 1967), pp. 468-479.

(1) Discusses the behavioral science literature which is relevant to management accounting and includes specific consideration of the capital budgeting and control processes.

(2) Categories: A. Psychology B. A Priori C. Decision Making--Behavioral

* * * * *

Bruns, W. J., "Accounting Information and Decision Making: Some Behavioral Hypotheses," The Accounting Review (July 1968), pp. 469-480.

(1) Develops and discusses several hypotheses concerning management accounting and decision-making, including the effect of the accounting information on choice of decision model and the effect of other types of information.

(2) Categories: A. Unspecified B. A Priori C. Decision Making--Behavioral

* * * * *

Barton, R. F., "An Experimental Study of the Impact of Competitive Pressures on Overhead Allocation Bids," Journal of Accounting Research (Spring 1969), pp. 116-122.

(1) Reports the results of a study designed to test the effect of competitive pressure and overhead allocations on pricing decisions in an oligopolistic setting. The findings indicated competitive pressure was a stronger determinant than allocated overhead.

(2) Categories: A. Unspecified B. Laboratory Experiment C. Decision Making--Behavioral

* * * * *

Dalton, F. E. and J. B. Miner, "The Role of Accounting Training in Top Management Decision Making," The Accounting Review (January 1970), pp. 134-139.

(1) Reports the results of two experiments designed to test the effect training in accounting has on decision making. In both studies those subjects majoring in accounting were more successful in making decisions.

(2) Categories: A. Unspecified B. Laboratory Experiment C. Decision Making--Behavioral

* * * * *

Categories: A--Source discipline. B--Method of analysis. C--Topic.

Ronen, J., "Some Effects of Sequential Aggregation in Accounting on Decision Making," Journal of Accounting Research (Autumn 1971), pp. 307-332.

(1) Discusses the effects different sequences of aggregation have on decision-making for planning and control, including the aggregation of probabilistic information.

(2) Categories: A. Unspecified B. Laboratory Experiment C. Decision Making--Behavioral

* * * * *

Barefield, R. M., "The Effect of Aggregation on Decision Making Success: A Laboratory Study," Journal of Accounting Research (Autumn 1972), pp. 229-242.

(1) Reports the results of a study designed to test the effect aggregation of data has on decision-making. The findings indicate those receiving disaggregated data performed better than those receiving aggregated data.

(2) Categories: A. Unspecified B. Laboratory Experiment C. Decision Making--Behavioral

* * * * *

Dermer, J. D., "Cognitive Characteristics and the Perceived Importance of Information," The Accounting Review (July 1973), pp. 511-519.

(1) Reports the results of an experiment designed to study the effects cognitive characteristics of the subject have on decision-making behavior and in particular the perceived importance of information.

(2) Categories: A. Unspecified B. Laboratory Experiment C. Decision Making--Behavioral

* * * * *

Dopuch, N. and J. Ronen, "The Effects of Alternative Inventory Valuation Methods," Journal of Accounting Research (Autumn 1973), pp. 191-211.

(1) Reports the result of an experiment designed to test the effect LIFO and FIFO differences have on the resource allocation decision. This behavioral study, while not specifically oriented at management accounting, extends earlier behavioral studies on management decision-making (Dyckman (1964) and Bruns (1965)).

(2) Categories: A. Unspecified B. Laboratory Experiment C. Decision Making--Behavioral

* * * * *

Categories: A--Source discipline. B--Method of analysis. C--Topic.

Becker, S. W., J. Ronen and G. H. Sorter, "Opportunity Costs--An Experimental Approach," Journal of Accounting Research (Autumn 1974), pp. 317-329.

(1) Reports the results of an experiment designed to test whether opportunity costs are used in making decisions and whether opportunity cost information should be produced by the accounting process.

(2) Categories: A. Unspecified B. Laboratory Experiment C. Decision Making--Behavioral

* * * * *

Driver, M. J. and T. J. Mock, "Human Information Processing, Decision Style Theory, and Accounting Information Systems," The Accounting Review (July 1975), pp. 490-508.

(1) Reviews accounting and psychology research in human information processing and reports the results of an experiment designed to test the effect that the subject's decision style has on the information required for decision making.

(2) Categories: A. Psychology--Individual B. Laboratory Experiment C. Decision Making--Behavioral

* * * * *

Swieringa, R. J., M. Gibbins, L. Larsson, and J. L. Sweeney, "Experiments in the Heuristics of Human Information Processing," Journal of Accounting Research (Supplement 1976), pp. 159-187.

(1) Reports the results of experiments designed to test individuals' use of the representative heuristic in making judgments of subjective probability. While not specifically oriented to management accounting, this article address the use of Bayesian decision theory.

(2) Categories: A. Psychology--Individual B. Laboratory Experiment C. Decision Making--Behavioral

* * * * *

Categories: A--Source discipline. B--Method of analysis. C--Topic.

Vasarhelyi, M., "Man-Machine Planning Systems: A Cognitive Style Examination of Interactive Decision Making," Journal of Accounting Research (Spring 1977), pp. 138-153.

(1) Reports the results of an experiment designed to test the impact behavioral factors have on the decision making process. Includes hypotheses relating to behavioral cognition and man-machine interfare.

(2) Categories: A. Psychology--Individual B. Laboratory Experiment
C. Decision Making--Behavioral

* * * * *

Savich, R. S., "The Use of Accounting Information in Decision Making," The Accounting Review (July 1977), pp. 642-652.

(1) Discusses decision style and decision modeling techniques and presents the results of an experiment which attempts to relate the two fields. The findings indicate mixed support for the hypothesized relationships.

(2) Categories: A. Psychology--Individual B. Laboratory Experiment
C. Decision Making--Behavioral

* * * * *

Harrell, A. M., "The Decision-Making Behavior of Air Force Officers and the Management Control Process," The Accounting Review (October 1977), pp. 833-841.

(1) Presents the results of a study designed to test the effect organizational goals have on control decisions in a nonprofit, public sector military organization. The findings indicate support for the control process described by Anthony as consisting of strategic planning, management control, and operational control.

(2) Categories: A. Psychology--Organization B. Field Study
C. Decision Making--Behavioral

* * * * *

Categories: A--Source discipline. B--Method of analysis. C--Topic.

Hirsch, M., "Disaggregated Probabilistic Accounting Information: The Effect of Sequential Events on Expected Value Maximization Decisions," Journal of Accounting Research (Autumn 1978), pp. 254-269.

(1) Reports the results of a study designed to extend the results of Ronen (1971) by incorporating more variables and manipulations in a study on user reaction to disaggregated probabilistic information.

(2) Categories: A. Psychology B. Field Experiment C. Decision Making--Behavioral

* * * * *

Neuman, B. R. and L. A. Friedman, "Opportunity Costs: Further Evidence Through an Experimental Replication," Journal of Accounting Research (Autumn 1978), pp. 400-410.

(1) Reports the results of a study designed to replicate the study by Becker et al. (1974) on the use of opportunity costs in managerial decision making. The findings are inconsistent with those of the previous study and indicate subjects do use opportunity cost information.

(2) Categories: A. Unspecified B. Laboratory Experiment C. Decision Making--Behavioral

* * * * *

Moriarity, S., "Communicating Financial Information Through Multidimensional Graphics," Journal of Accounting Research (Spring 1979), pp. 205-224.

(1) Presents an information display technique which includes many variables in one graphic using cartoon faces whose features represent various aspects of the information set. Such a display allows users to see relationships among the variables and react to a decision task more quickly than if one had to search all items individually. Introduces the area of information display as a subject for research.

(2) Categories: A. Psychology B. Modeling C. Decision Making--Behavioral

* * * * *

Categories: A--Source discipline. B--Method of analysis. C--Topic.

Lusk, E. J., "A Test of Differential Performance Peaking for a Disembedding Task," Journal of Accounting Research (Spring 1979), pp. 286-294.

(1) Presents the results of an experiment designed to test whether there is a difference in performance between groups formed on different levels of disembedding skills. The findings indicate no differential performance due to different disembedding skills and the conclusion is drawn that individualized information systems cannot be rationalized on inherent performance differentials between individuals.

(2) Categories: A. Psychology B. Laboratory Experiment C. Decision Making--Behavioral

* * * * *

Uecker, W. C., "The Effects of Knowledge of the User's Decision Model in Simplified Information Evaluation," Journal of Accounting Research (Spring 1980), pp. 191-213.

(1) Reports the results of a study designed to assess the effect knowledge of the user's decision model has on the quality of the evaluators' information decisions. The findings indicated the performance of those subjects with knowledge of the decision model did not differ from the performance of the subjects without knowledge.

(2) Categories: A. Psychology--Individual B. Laboratory Experiment C. Decision Making--Behavioral

* * * * *

Friedman, L. A. and B. R. Neuman, "The Effects of Opportunity Costs on Project Investment Decisions: A Replication and Extension," Journal of Accounting Research (Autumn 1980), pp. 407-419.

(1) Reports the results of an experiment designed to extend and replicate previous studies on the use of opportunity costs in decision making. The findings indicate subjects do request and use opportunity cost information but they do not attempt to impute opportunity costs when they are not explicitly available. Continues the literature on opportunity costs (see Becker, Ronen and Sorter (1974) and Neumann and Friedman (1978)).

(2) Categories: A. Economics/Psychology--Individual B. Laboratory/Field Experiment (students and CPAs) C. Decision Making--Behavioral

* * * * *

Categories: A--Source discipline. B--Method of analysis. C--Topic.

Ashton, R. H., "A Descriptive Study of Information Evaluation," Journal of Accounting Research (Spring 1981), pp. 42-61.

(1) Reports the results of an experiment designed to test the effect predictability and feedback have on the ability of information evaluators to acquire knowledge about the decision model used and apply that knowledge consistently in their own decision making. The findings indicated support for the hypotheses related to predictability but not for those related to feedback.

(2) Categories: A. Psychology--Individual B. Laboratory Experiment C. Decision Making--Behavioral

* * * * *

Benbasat, I. and A. S. Dexter, "Individual Differences in the Use of Decision Support Aids," Journal of Accounting Research (Spring 1982), p. 1-11.

(1) Reports the results of an experiment designed to test the effect a computer simulation model has on the decision-making ability of individuals with different cognitive styles. The results indicate that cognitive style affects performance and that the decision aid increased the performance of the low-analytic group but not that of the high-analytic group.

(2) Categories: A. Psychology B. Laboratory Experiment C. Decision Making--Behavioral

* * * * *

Otley, D. T. and F. J. B. Dias, "Accounting Aggregation and Decision-Making Performance: An Experimental Investigation," Journal of Accounting Research (Spring 1982), pp. 171-188.

(1) Reports the results of an experiment designed to assess the effect data aggregation has on decision quality and provides weak support for a hypothesized curvilinear relationship.

(2) Categories: A. Psychology B. Laboratory Experiment C. Decision Making--Behavioral

* * * * *

Categories: A--Source discipline. B--Method of analysis. C--Topic.

5.4. DECISION MAKING-GENERAL (pp. 145-155)

This subcategory contains articles on decision making not otherwise classified. Included are articles on opportunity and differential costing, EOQ, pricing, and product mix decisions.

Clark, J. M., Studies in the Economics of Overhead Costs (University of Chicago Press, 1923).

(1) Discusses overhead costs, different classes of costs each of which is valid for some purposes and not for others, and the typical problems which require different definitions of costs for their solutions. Introduces the concept of different costs for different purposes.

(2) Categories: A. Economics B. A Priori C. Decision Making

* * * * *

Mason, P., "The Use of Costs in Setting Selling Prices," The Accounting Review (June 1926), pp. 72-76.

(1) Provides an analysis and statement of the relationship between costs and selling prices. This is an early distinction made between the use of cost to "set" prices and the use of cost to evaluate whether a price can be accepted and a profit made.

(2) Categories: A. Unspecified B. A Priori C. Decision Making (Pricing)

* * * * *

Rorem, C. R., "Differential Costs," The Accounting Review (December 1928), pp. 333-341.

(1) Discusses the analysis of business problems by the examination of differential costs, those costs expected to be incurred to implement a decision without regard to costs previously incurred. First appearance in the accounting literature of the concept introduced by J. M. Clark (1923) which was later accepted and evolved into the concept of differential (relevant) costing. One of the first Accounting Review articles to reference other literature.

(2) Categories: A. Economics B. A Priori C. Decision Making (Differential Costs)

* * * * *

Categories: A--Source discipline. B--Method of analysis. C--Topic.

Sanders, T. H., "The Uses of Differential Costs," The Accounting Review (March 1929), pp. 9-12.

(1) Discusses the relationship of differential costs to other economic concepts and presents a survey of the economic theory of the subject of differential costs. The author considers some practical applications of the concept such as its use in accepting a special order. An early discussion of cost concepts from economics and how they may be applied to accounting.

(2) Categories: A. Economics B. A Priori C. Decision Making (Differential Costs)

* * * * *

Saliers, E. A., "Differential Costs," The Accounting Review (October 1943), pp. 338-340.

(1) Presents a discussion of the theory underlying differential costs and procedures for determining them. Outlines practical procedures for the accumulation of costs including the making of statistical forecasts of costs at various anticipated levels of production.

(2) Categories: A. Economics B. A Priori C. Decision Making (Differential Costs)

* * * * *

Lawrence, W. B., "Cost Accounting versus the Pricing System," The Accounting Review (April 1945), pp. 177-182.

(1) Discusses cost accounting and its application to the problems of management, focusing on the pricing problem. The author contrasts the economics and accounting views and distinguishes between differential costs and out-of-pocket costs. Concludes that cost accounting is important to management and the pricing decision.

(2) Categories: A. Economics B. A Priori C. Decision Making (Pricing)

* * * * *

Doyle, L. A., "Uses of Cost Data for Production and Investment Policies," The Accounting Review (July 1950), pp. 274-282.

(1) Reviews the accumulation and analysis of cost data for production and investment decisions in both single and multi-product plants. An early recognition of a decision-making orientation.

(2) Categories: A. Unspecified B. A Priori C. Decision Making

* * * * *

Categories: A—Source discipline. B—Method of analysis. C—Topic.

Devine, C. T., "Cost Accounting and Pricing Policies," The Accounting Review (October 1950), pp. 384-389.

(1) Discusses the economic and accounting concepts of a firm's pricing policy under competition, oligopoly, and joint cost/multi-process production. Concludes that costs are a partial determinant of price and that pricing should be done on total unit costs.

(2) Categories: A. Economics B. A Priori C. Decision Making (Pricing)

* * * * *

Spruce, W. E., "The Integration of Standard and Current Cost for Profit Measurement," Accounting Research (October 1951), pp. 362-398.

(1) Discusses the use of an accounting system which would integrate standard and current costs for both internal and external reporting purposes. Includes discussion of variances, budgeting, and marginal and total costs.

(2) Categories: A. Unspecified B. A Priori C. Decision Making

* * * * *

Whitin, T. M., "Some Business Applications of Marginal Analysis with Particular Reference to Inventory Control," Accounting Research (July 1952), pp. 205-219.

(1) Discusses the use of marginal analysis in the inventory control problem. Includes discussion of EOQ, safety allowances, and the inventory-sales ratio.

(2) Categories: A. Economics B. Modeling C. Decision Making (Inventory)

* * * * *

Kopta, W. A., "Managerial Utility of Accounting in a Period of Adjustment," The Accounting Review (July 1954), pp. 369-372.

(1) Discusses areas of business management in which accounting can provide information of particular need during periods of economic fluctuation. Such areas include break-even analysis, distribution costs and inventory analysis, and budgeting.

(2) Categories: A. Unspecified B. A Priori C. Decision Making

* * * * *

Categories: A--Source discipline. B--Method of analysis. C--Topic.

Ilersic, A. R., "The Theory and Practice of Stock Control," Accounting Research (April 1955), pp. 123-132.

(1) Discusses the use of economic theory in the control of inventories. Includes discussion of EOQ and the determination of optimum inventory level under uncertainty.

(2) Categories: A. Economics B. A Priori C. Decision Making (Inventory)

* * * * *

Beer, S., "Operational Research and Financial Management," Accounting Research (January 1957), pp. 1-13.

(1) Discusses the application of OR techniques to decision making problems and illustrates the use of linear programming in the profit maximization decision, taking into account the opportunity cost of lost sales. Introduces linear programming to the accounting literature.

(2) Categories: A. Mathematics/OR B. Modeling C. Decision Making

* * * * *

Jaedicke, R. K., "Some Notes on Product-Combination Decisions," The Accounting Review (October 1958), pp. 596-601.

(1) Discusses the multiple-product production decision and introduces a model which uses iso-revenue lines and cost curves to determine the optimum production point. A sophisticated application of marginal analysis to a decision problem.

(2) Categories: A. Economics B. Modeling C. Decision Making (Product Mix)

* * * * *

Lewis, R. B., "The Role of Accounting in Decision Making," The Accounting Review (January 1960), pp. 37-44.

(1) Discusses financial analysis, the common mistakes made, ways of avoiding these, and suggestions for better analysis. Coverage includes use of the incremental approach and writing off nonrecurring losses or expenses.

(2) Categories: A. Unspecified B. A Priori C. Decision Making

* * * * *

Categories: A--Source discipline. B--Method of analysis. C--Topic.

Raun, D. L., "Accounting for Decisions," The Accounting Review (July 1961), pp. 460-471.

(1) Discusses the decision-making process, the relationship between accounting and decision-making, and the correlation between accounting practice and the requirements of the decision process. Includes an illustrative example.

(2) Categories: A. Unspecified B. A Priori C. Decision Making

* * * * *

Davidson, H. J. and R. M. Trueblood, "Accounting for Decision-Making," The Accounting Review (October 1961), pp. 577-582.

(1) Discusses accounting for decision-making and the problems of providing information for both routine and special decisions, including the problems of too much or untimely information. Calls for a definite decision-making perspective away from the traditional fiduciary/stewardship view.

(2) Categories: A. Unspecified B. A Priori C. Decision Making

* * * * *

Mellman, M., "Marketing Cost Analysis - Development and Current Practice," The Accounting Review (January 1963), pp. 118-123.

(1) Reports the results of a survey of 28 firms in several industries on the extent of their use of cost reports in marketing decision-making. The findings indicate little use of such reports.

(2) Categories: A. Unspecified B. Survey C. Decision Making

* * * * *

Shillinglaw, G., "The Concept of Attributable Cost," Journal of Accounting Research (Spring 1963), pp. 73-85.

(1) Discusses the cost information needed for quantitative decisions and concludes a new concept of cost, attributable cost, is required for this type of decision.

(2) Categories: A. Unspecified B. A Priori C. Decision Making

* * * * *

Categories: A--Source discipline. B--Method of analysis. C--Topic.

Gibson, J. L., "Accounting in the Decision-Making Process," The Accounting Review (July 1963), pp. 492-500.

(1) Reports the results of research into management's use of accounting in decision-making, discusses the findings, and concludes with implications for practice. The report emphasizes the description of how managers use accounting data.

(2) Categories: A. Unspecified B. Field Study C. Decision Making

* * * * *

Raun, D. L., "The Application of Monte Carlo Analysis to an Inventory Problem." The Accounting Review (October 1963), pp. 751-758.

(1) Introduces the application of the Monte Carlo method to inventory problems involving uncertain demand and/or lead time. Illustrates with an example the generation of demand and calculation of the optimum order point.

(2) Categories: A. Mathematics/Operations Research B. Modeling C. Decision Making (Inventory)

* * * * *

Samuels, J. M., "Opportunity Costing: An Application of Mathematical Programming," Journal of Accounting Research (Autumn 1965), pp. 182-191.

(1) Discusses the use of mathematical programming in providing marginal and opportunity cost data for decision-making. Includes an example using transfer prices based on shadow prices from a mathematical programming optimization.

(2) Categories: A. Mathematics B. Modeling C. Decision Making (Opportunity Costs) (Could also be classified under Planning and Control.)

* * * * *

Davis, P. M., "Marginal Analysis of Credit Sales," The Accounting Review (January 1966), pp. 121-126.

(1) Discusses the use of economic analysis in helping management decide the amount of credit sales by determining the point at which marginal revenue of the sale equals the marginal cost (including bad-debt cost).

(2) Categories: A. Economics B. Modeling C. Decision Making

* * * * *

Categories: A--Source discipline. B--Method of analysis. C--Topic.

Gross, H., "Make or Buy Decisions in Growing Firms," The Accounting Review (October 1966), pp. 745-753.

(1) Discusses the make or buy decision for a growing firm and lists several factors which enter into the analysis including quantitative factors, qualitative factors, and combined factors.

(2) Categories: A. Unspecified B. A Priori C. Decision Making

* * * * *

Rappaport, A., "Sensitivity Analysis for Decision Making," The Accounting Review (July 1967), pp. 441-456.

(1) Discusses the use of sensitivity analysis in evaluating the effects changes in parameters will have on the outcome of a decision model. Includes discussion of both operating decisions and information decisions. Introduces sensitivity analysis to accounting.

(2) Categories: A. Unspecified B. A Priori C. Decision Making

* * * * *

Bernhard, R. H., "Some Problems in Applying Mathematical Programming to Opportunity Costing," Journal of Accounting Research (Spring 1968), pp. 143-148.

(1) Discusses the problems likely to be encountered in operationalizing an opportunity cost programming model (see Samuels (1965)).

(2) Categories: A. Mathematics/Operations Research B. A Priori C. Decision Making (Opportunity Costs)

* * * * *

Rappaport, A., "Integer Programming and Managerial Analysis," The Accounting Review (April 1969), pp. 297-299.

(1) Discusses the managerial implications of using integer programming under conditions of uncertainty rather than the linear programming models.

(2) Categories: A. Economics/Mathematics/OR B. A Priori C. Decision Making

* * * * *

Categories: A--Source discipline. B--Method of analysis. C--Topic.

Glover, F., "Management Decision and Integer Programming," The Accounting Review (April 1969), pp. 300-303.

(1) Discusses the use of integer programming versus linear programming for managerial decision-making and when each may be appropriate.

(2) Categories: A. Mathematics/Operations Research B. A Priori C. Decision Making

* * * * *

Hartley, R. V., "Some Extensions of Sensitivity Analysis," The Accounting Review (April 1970), pp. 223-234.

(1) Discusses the use of sensitivity analysis in a linear programming model and presents examples of the use of sensitivity analysis when factors in the objective model are changed.

(2) Categories: A. Some Operations Research B. Modeling C. Decision Making

* * * * *

McRae, T. W., "Opportunity and Incremental Cost: An Attempt to Define in Systems Terms," The Accounting Review (April 1970), pp. 315-321.

(1) Discusses the concepts of opportunity and incremental costs and defines each: opportunity cost is defined as an output measure of cost and incremental cost is defined as an input measure.

(2) Categories: A. Unspecified B. A Priori C. Decision Making (Opportunity Costs)

* * * * *

Groves, R., R. Manes and R. Sorensen, "The Application of the Hirsch-Dantzig 'Fixed Charge' Algorithm to Profit Planning: A Formal Statement of Product Profitability Analysis," The Accounting Review (July 1970), pp. 481-489.

(1) Describes the use of the Hirsch-Dantzig integer programming model in computing the optimum product mix when fixed costs are affected by the mix choice. Includes an example.

(2) Categories: A. Mathematics/Operations Research B. Modeling C. Decision Making (Product Mix)

* * * * *

Categories: A--Source discipline. B--Method of analysis. C--Topic.

Hansen, P., "An Operational Cost Information Model," Abacus (December 1970), pp. 154-168.

(1) Presents and discusses a cost information model which uses only unit costs and capacity costs to supply management's decision-making needs.

(2) Categories: A. Unspecified B. A Priori C. Decision Making

* * * * *

Charnes, A., C. Colantoni, W. W. Cooper and K. O. Kortanek, "Economic, Social, and Enterprise Accounting and Mathematical Models," The Accounting Review (January 1972), pp. 85-108.

(1) Discusses mathematical models in the literature, their interrelationships, and their applications. Includes input-output, transportation, and goal programming models.

(2) Categories: A. Mathematics/OR B. Modeling C. Decision Making

* * * * *

Lea, R. B., "A Note on the Definition of Cost Coefficients in a Linear Programming Model," The Accounting Review (April 1972), pp. 346-350.

(1) Discusses the definition of cost which is most appropriate for use in linear programming models. Concludes that opportunity cost is not necessarily the most appropriate and recommends instead entry price.

(2) Categories: A. Operations Research B. Modeling C. Decision Making

* * * * *

Heimann, S. R. and E. J. Lusk, "Decision Flexibility: An Alternative Evaluation Criterion," The Accounting Review (January 1976), pp. 51-64.

(1) Proposes a flexibility model which maximizes the probability of achieving a selected output cutoff for alternative selection decisions in an uncertain setting as an alternative to the traditional maximized expected payoff model. Includes an illustrated example.

(2) Categories: A. Psychology/OR B. Modeling C. Decision Making

* * * * *

Categories: A--Source discipline. B--Method of analysis. C--Topic.

Yetton, P. W., "The Interaction Between a Standard Time Incentive Payment Scheme and a Simple Accounting Information System," Accounting, Organizations and Society (June 1976), pp. 81-87.

(1) Presents a simulation study of the interaction between a standard time incentive payment scheme and a traditional job order cost system to determine the extent of any biases introduced and the implications for the organization.

(2) Categories: A. Sociology B. Simulation C. Decision Making--Behavioral

* * * * *

Dillon, R. D. and J. F. Nash, "The True Relevance of Relevant Costs," The Accounting Review (January 1978), pp. 11-17.

(1) Discusses relevant costs and the incremental approach to decision making and describes conditions under which irrelevant items can become relevant when the decision is based on maximization of utility equivalents.

(2) Categories: A. Economics B. Modeling C. Decision Making (Differential Costs)

* * * * *

Gordon, L. A., D. F. Larcker and F. D. Tuggle, "Strategic Decision Processes and the Design of Accounting Information Systems: Conceptual Linkages," Accounting, Organizations and Society (May 1979), pp. 203-214.

(1) Analyzes the conceptual links between the strategic decision process and the information needed to facilitate such a process and develops and presents design criteria for accounting information systems. Addresses the ways in which accounting can aid the decision process (rather than the traditional input/output view).

(2) Categories: A. Unspecified B. A Priori C. Decision Making

* * * * *

Categories: A--Source discipline. B--Method of analysis. C--Topic.

Cohen, M. A. and R. Halperin, "Optimal Inventory Order Policy for a Firm Using the LIFO Inventory Costing Method," Journal of Accounting Research (Autumn 1980), pp. 375-389.

(1) Discusses the effect LIFO has on the cost of holding inventory, formulates a cost minimizing decision model, and analyzes the model by running data-based information from the annual report of a company. The results indicate the effects of LIFO on optimal inventory decisions.

(2) Categories: A. Unspecified B. Modeling C. Decision Making (Inventory)

* * * * *

Categories: A--Source discipline. B--Method of analysis. C--Topic.

PLANNING AND CONTROL

6. PLANNING AND CONTROL (pp. 156-212)

This category includes articles dealing with the various aspects of planning and control. Specific subcategories are used for budgeting, variance analysis and investigation, transfer pricing, and the principal-agent aspects of planning and control. Certain works in subcategory 1.2, Information Economics, are also related to planning and control.

The category contains the following subcategories:

6.1 Budgeting (pp. 157-170)

6.2 Variance Analysis and Investigation (pp. 171-183)

6.3 Transfer Pricing (pp. 184-189)

6.4 Principal-Agent (pp. 190-192)

6.5 Planning and Control-General (pp. 193-212)

6.1 BUDGETING (pp. 157-170)

The articles in this subcategory deal with budgeting; they include modeling and discussion pieces and laboratory and field studies.

Drucker, A. P. R., "Budgeting and the Sales Quota," The Accounting Review (September 1929), pp. 175-180.

(1) Discusses setting the budget by beginning with an accurate forecast of the sales quota rather than guesses. Argues for the use of salesmen's estimates and such "statistical work" as the secular trend, seasonal variations, business cycle fluctuations, regression forecasts, and prior years' averages as inputs to the sales forecast. A very modern treatment of sales forecasting and its place in budgeting.

(2) Categories: A. Unspecified B. A Priori C. Budgeting

* * * * *

Categories: A--Source discipline. B--Method of analysis. C--Topic.

Drucker, A. P. R., "Factory Production Under Budgetary Control," The Accounting Review (December 1930), pp. 301-304.

(1) Continues a series on budgeting and explains further the development of the budget after the sales estimate has been approved. Calls for more standardization of method in dealing with manufacturing expenses and notes a need for a scientific basis for the distribution of production costs over the products manufactured.

(2) Categories: A. Unspecified B. A Priori C. Budgeting

* * * * *

Drucker, A. P. R., "Budgeting and Control of Machinery," The Accounting Review (September 1931), pp. 192-196.

(1) Discusses the budgeting of machinery on a life time rather than yearly basis. Proposes that increasing yearly maintenance costs cause straight-line or units-of-output depreciation to charge higher costs to production in later years. Instead, the author calls for a total-life budget for machines wherein all costs associated with its use could be included in the base amount and equal charges per unit of output could be made.

(2) Categories: A. Unspecified B. A Priori C. Budgeting

* * * * *

Theiss, E. L., "Budgetary Procedure as a Means of Administrative Control," The Accounting Review (March 1932), pp. 11-21.

(1) Gives a brief review of the early origins of budgeting, discusses the accounting control type of budgeting procedure, and proposes that accountants can contribute to the development of budgets. Includes a discussion of conditions existing at that time with facts drawn from surveys and classifies budgeting procedures according to the objectives aimed at by management. An early reference to empirical data and the importance of budgeting to accounting.

(2) Categories: A. Unspecified B. A Priori C. Budgeting

* * * * *

Categories: A--Source discipline. B--Method of analysis. C--Topic.

Donner, F. G., "General Motors Budgetary Control," The Accounting Review (March 1932), pp. 22-30.

(1) Discusses industrial budgeting as distinct from governmental budgeting and sets out General Motors' budgetary control system.

(2) Categories: A. Unspecified B. A Priori/Personnel Observation C. Budgeting (Could also be classified in Description of Firm/Industry Practices.)

* * * * *

Dohr, J. L., "Budgetary Control and Standard Costs in Industrial Accounting," The Accounting Review (March 1932), pp. 31-33.

(1) Discusses the coordination of the budgetary and standard cost aspects of industrial accounting. Describes how budgets are set on the basis of standard costs and are prepared for varying amounts of output to estimate expected variances for the coming period. Early recognition of the meshing of budgeting and standard costs and of flexible budgeting in the literature.

(2) Categories: A. Unspecified B. A Priori C. Budgeting

* * * * *

Hanson, A. W., "The Relation of Cost Accounting to the Budgetary Control Problem," The Accounting Review (March 1932), pp. 34-37.

(1) Discusses the importance of budgets and the interrelationship of the budget and cost accounting: past cost experience provides a good input to the budget, the budget indicates the information that will be needed from the cost accounts.

(2) Categories: A. Unspecified B. A Priori C. Budgeting

* * * * *

Theiss, E. L., "Accounting and Budgeting," The Accounting Review (June 1935), pp. 156-161.

(1) Discusses the role of accounting data in the budgetary process. Suggests that budgeting should take its place alongside the other services provided by accountants.

(2) Categories: A. Unspecified B. A Priori C. Budgeting

* * * * *

Categories: A--Source discipline. B--Method of analysis. C--Topic.

Blocker, J. G., "Budgeting in Relation to Standard Costs," The Accounting Review (June 1936), pp. 117-124.

(1) Discusses standard costs and the success with which it has been applied to all elements of business. Presents the various quantity and price standards and the problems encountered in establishing them. States that budgeting and standard costs go hand in hand and are inseparable. Early recognition of the relationship between budgeting and standard costs.

(2) Categories: A. Unspecified B. A Priori C. Budgeting

* * * * *

Theiss, E. L., "The Beginnings of Business Budgeting," The Accounting Review (March 1937), pp. 43-55.

(1) Traces the major stages of development through which budgeting has passed in its evolution, from its use in the English government through its adoption and use in U.S. business to its spread to other countries and back to England.

(2) Categories: A. Unspecified B. A Priori C. Budgeting

* * * * *

Marple, R. P. "Combining the Forecast and Flexible Budgets," The Accounting Review (April 1946), pp. 140-148.

(1) Discusses the flexible budget and the forecast budget and the strengths of each for planning, coordination, and control. Proposes a method of combining the two so that they complement each other.

(2) Categories: A. Unspecified B. A Priori C. Budgeting

* * * * *

Millians, P. M., "Profit Planning and Budgetary Control," The Accounting Review (January 1947), pp. 65-68.

(1) Discusses the budget as a master plan and outlines several aspects of its value as an aid to management.

(2) Categories: A. Unspecified B. A Priori C. Budgeting

* * * * *

Categories: A--Source discipline. B--Method of analysis. C--Topic.

Argyris, C., The Impact of Budgets on People (The Controllership Foundation, 1952).

(1) Discusses and reports the results of a field study on the perception supervisors and financial personnel have regarding budgets and each other. Includes an analysis of the impact budgets have on people and suggestions for action. An early recognition of the behavioral implications of accounting techniques.

(2) Categories: A. Organization Theory B. Field Study C. Budgeting

* * * * *

Stedry, A., Budget Control and Cost Behavior (Prentice-Hall, 1960).

(1) Presents an analytical model for budget planning. The discussion covers supporting literature and the study reports the results of an experiment. Discusses budgetary control from the perspective of economics, psychology, organization theory, mathematics, and accounting.

(2) Categories: A. Economics/Psychology/Mathematics B. Modeling/ Experimental C. Budgeting

* * * * *

Mattessich, R., "Budgeting Models and System Simulation," The Accounting Review (July 1961), pp. 384-397.

(1) Defines and discusses simulation and constrained optimization and presents a formal budgeting model. An example is presented. This is an early application of simulation to budgeting.

(2) Categories: A. Operations Research B. Modeling C. Budgeting

* * * * *

Becker, S. W. and D. Green, "Budgeting and Employee Behavior," Journal of Business (October 1962), pp. 392-402.

(1) Discusses budgeting and the motivational reactions it elicits from employees with particular emphasis on the participative budget. Concludes that revision of a budget in a participative setting could serve as an important motivator.

(2) Categories: A. Psychology B. A Priori C. Budgeting

* * * * *

Categories: A—Source discipline. B—Method of analysis. C—Topic.

Hanson, E. I., "The Budgetary Control Function," The Accounting Review (April 1966), pp. 239-243.

(1) Discusses the budgetary control function and the role played by budget-setting in control. Includes discussion of authority, attainability, and participation in the budget-setting process in expanding the traditional concept of the budget. An early discussion of the effect the budget has on subordinates and of participative budgeting.

(2) Categories: A. Unspecified B. A Priori C. Budgeting

* * * * *

Ijiri, Y., J. Kinard and F. Putney, "An Integrated Evaluation System for Budget Forecasting and Operating Performance with a Classfied Budgeting Bibliography," Journal of Accounting Research (Spring 1968), pp. 1-28.

(1) Discusses forecasting and presents a performance measurement system designed to motivate accurate forecasts and operating efficiency.

(2) Categories: A. Unspecified B. Modeling C. Budgeting

* * * * *

DeCoster, D. T. and J. P. Fertakis, "Budget-Induced Pressure and Its Relationship to Supervisory Behavior," Journal of Accounting Research (Autumn 1968), pp. 237-246.

(1) Reports the results of a study designed to test the effects different budget procedures have on leadership behavior. Early behavioral study on the effects of budgets.

(2) Categories: A. Unspecified B. Laboratory Study C. Budgeting

* * * * *

Ijiri, Y. and G. L. Thompson, "Applications of Mathematical Control Theory to Accounting and Budgeting (The Continuous Wheat Trading Model)," The Accounting Review (April 1970), pp. 246-258.

(1) Discusses the application of mathematical control theory to accounting and illustrates the use of the technique in a wheat trading firm.

(2) Categories: A. Mathematics B. Modeling C. Budgeting

* * * * *

Categories: A--Source discipline. B--Method of analysis. C--Topic.

Schiff, M. and A. Y. Lewin, "The Impact of People on Budgets," The Accounting Review (April 1970), pp. 259-268.

(1) Discusses the impact individuals have on the budget and in particular the existence of slack in the budgetary process and the steps organizations can take to remove slack.

(2) Categories: A. Unspecified B. A Priori C. Budgeting

* * * * *

Ferrara, W. L. and J. C. Hayya, "Toward Probabilistic Profit Budgets," Management Accounting (October 1970), pp. 23-28.

(1) Illustrates how income budgets can be made more informative by the use of probability techniques. Three specific methods are presented, each one illustrating a different level of mathematical sophistication. Introduces probability concepts to the profit budget.

(2) Categories: A. Mathematics/OR B. A Priori C. Budgeting

* * * * *

Revsine, L., "Change in Budget Pressure and Its Impact on Supervisor Behavior," Journal of Accounting Research (Autumn 1970), pp. 290-292.

(1) Provides a reassessment of the literature in this area with particular discussion of the Decoster and Fertakis (1968) laboratory study. Hypothesizes their results may have been consistent with prior findings had their measure of budget pressure been higher.

(2) Categories: A. Unspecified B. A Priori C. Budgeting

* * * * *

Holstrum, G. L., "The Effect of Budget Adaptiveness and Tightness on Managerial Decision Behavior," Journal of Accounting Research (Autumn 1971), pp. 268-277.

(1) Reports the results of an experiment designed to measure and compare the effects of adaptiveness and tightness on a budget's response to random shocks and environmental changes. The findings indicated no differences in responsiveness for either tightness or adaptiveness.

(2) Categories: A. Unspecified B. Laboratory Experiment
C. Budgeting

* * * * *

Categories: A--Source discipline. B--Method of analysis. C--Topic.

Swieringa, R. J. and R. H. Moncur, "The Relationship Between Managers' Budget-Oriented Behavior and Selected Attitude, Position, Size, and Performance Measures," Journal of Accounting Research (Supplement 1972), pp. 194-209.

(1) Reports the results of a study designed to test the extent to which budget-oriented behavior is related to various attitude, position, size, and performance measures.

(2) Categories: A. Psychology-Organization B. Field Study
C. Budgeting

* * * * *

Mock, T. J., "The Value of Budget Information," The Accounting Review (July 1973), pp. 520-534.

(1) Reports the results of an experiment designed to test the impact budget feedback and the budgetary process have on decisions and performance. The findings indicate budget feedback is conducive to the learning process.

(2) Categories: A. Unspecified B. Laboratory Experiment
C. Budgeting

* * * * *

Onsi, M., "Factor Analysis of Behavioral Variables Affecting Budgeting Slack," The Accounting Review (July 1973), pp. 535-550.

(1) Reports the results of a factor analysis of variables affecting budgetary slack in an organization. Six factors were identified and included manager's attitude, participation, and uses of the budget.

(2) Categories: A. Unspecified B. Field Study C. Budgeting

* * * * *

Cherrington, D. J. and J. O. Cherrington, "Appropriate Reinforcement Contingencies in the Budgeting Process," Journal of Accounting Research (Supplement 1973), pp. 225-253.

(1) Reports the results of an experiment designed to test the effects budgetary control and reward contingencies have on job performance and satisfaction.

(2) Categories: A. Psychology B. Laboratory Experiment C. Budgeting

* * * * *

Categories: A--Source discipline. B--Method of analysis. C--Topic.

Foran, M. F. and D. T. DeCoster, "An Experimental Study of the Effects of Participation, Authoritarianism, and Feedback on Cognitive Dissonance in a Standard Setting Situtation," The Accounting Review (October 1974), pp. 751-763.

(1) Reports the results of a laboratory study on the effects participation, authoritarianism, and feedback have on an individual's cognitive dissonance. The findings indicated support for the feedback hypotheses but not for those relating to participation and authoritarianism.

(2) Categories: A. Psychology B. Laboratory Experiment C. Budgeting

* * * * *

Milani, K., "The Relationship of Participation in Budget-Setting to Industrial Supervisor Performance and Attitudes: A Field Study," The Accounting Review (April 1975), pp. 274-284.

(1) Reports the results of an empirical study designed to test the relationship between participation and foreman performance, attitudes toward the job, and attitude toward the company.

(2) Categories: A. Psychology B. Field Study C. Budgeting

* * * * *

Livingstone, J. L., "Organization Goals and the Budget Process," Abacus (June 1975), pp. 37-48.

(1) Discusses the interrelationships among managerial goals, the budget process, and the measurement and evaluation of organizational performance. Concludes that all three are related and the accountant is an active participant rather than a passive scorekeeper.

(2) Categories: A. Psychology--Organization B. A Priori C. Budgeting

* * * * *

Ronen, J. and J. L. Livingstone, "An Expectancy Theory Approach to the Motivational Impacts of Budgets," The Accounting Review (October 1975), pp. 671-685.

(1) Discusses the motivational impact of budgets in the context of expectancy theory and how this framework reconciles previous apparent contradictions in the literature.

(2) Categories: A. Psychology B. A Priori C. Budgeting

* * * * *

Categories: A--Source discipline. B--Method of analysis. C--Topic.

Bruns, W. J., and J. Waterhouse, "Budgetary Control and Organization Structure," _Journal of Accounting Research_ (Autumn 1975), pp. 177-203.

(1) Present the results of a study of 25 organizations designed to explore the interaction and relationships between organization structure and the use of budgets by managers. The findings indicate clear relationships between the two.

(2) Categories: A. Psychology--Organization B. Field Study C. Budgeting

* * * * *

Swieringa, R. J. and R. H. Moncur, _Some Effects of Participative Budgeting on Managerial Behavior_ (NAA, 1975).

(1) Presents a theoretical model of the linkages between a company's use of participative budgeting and the behavior of its managers and a factor analytic study of the descriptive and normative measures of management's budget behavior. Includes an analysis of the relationships between these identified measures and predictor and attitude variables. A good methodology discussion of theoretical and empirical work in the area of budgeting.

(2) Categories: A. Psychology--Organization B. Field Study C. Budgeting

* * * * *

Zimmerman, J. L., "Budget Uncertainty and the Allocation Decision in a Nonprofit Organization," _Journal of Accounting Research_ (Autumn 1976), pp. 301-319.

(1) Analyzes the effect uncertain budgets have on the spending problem decision faced by a nonprofit agency with a fixed budget. Empirical data which is consistent with the predictions of the model developed from the analysis is also presented.

(2) Categories: A. Economics B. Field Study C. Budgeting

* * * * *

Categories: A--Source discipline. B--Method of analysis. C--Topic.

Ashton, R. H., "Deviation-Amplifying Feedback and Unintended Consequences of Management Accounting Systems," Accounting, Organizations and Society (November 1976), pp. 289-300.

(1) Introduces the concept of deviation-amplifying feedback and discusses its use in assessing the potential unintended consequences of management accounting systems, specifically budgetary control systems.

(2) Categories: A. Sociology B. A Priori/General descriptive modeling C. Budgeting

* * * * *

Searfoss, D. G., "Some Behavioral Aspects of Budgeting for Control: An Empirical Study," Accounting, Organizations and Society (November 1976), pp. 375-385.

(1) Reports the results of a study evaluating the relationships between perceived budget participation, perceived reward contingency on budget performance, and perceived goal attainability. The findings identified two dimensions of budget motivation: goal-directing effort, related to participation, and evaluative effort, related to reward contingency.

(2) Categories: A. Psychology B. Field Study C. Budgeting

* * * * *

Rockness, H. O., "Expectancy Theory in a Budgeting Setting: An Experimental Examination," The Accounting Review (October 1977), pp. 893-903.

(1) Reports the results of a study designed to test the validity of an expectancy model that includes a multiple-goal, multiple-outcome setting. The findings indicate support for the model.

(2) Categories: A. Psychology B. Laboratory Experiment C. Budgeting

* * * * *

Collins, F., "The Interaction of Budget Characteristics and Personality Variables with Budgetary Response Attitudes," The Accounting Review (April 1978), pp. 324-335.

(1) Reports the results of a study designed to test the effect personality, perceived budget characteristics, and the subjects' attitudes toward these characteristics have on budgeting response attitudes. Additionally, the effect age, tenure, and status have on response attitudes was tested.

(2) Categories: A. Psychology--Organization B. Field Experiment

C. Budgeting

* * * * *

Categories: A--Source discipline. B--Method of analysis. C--Topic.

Kenis, I., "Effects of Budgetary Goal Characteristics on Managerial Attitudes and Performance," The Accounting Review (October 1979), pp. 707-721.

(1) Reports the results of a study designed to test the effects participation, clarity, feedback, evaluation, and difficulty have on job and budget attitudes and managerial performance. The findings indicate participation and goal clarity have the most significant effects.

(2) Categories: A. Psychology B. Field Experiment C. Budgeting

* * * * *

Ansari, S. L., "Towards an Open Systems Approach to Budgeting," Accounting, Organizations and Society (February 1980), pp. 149-162.

(1) Discusses the difference between the open systems and the closed systems approaches to budget variances and concludes the open systems view is more appropriate. Uses the calculation of budget variances to illustrate its usefulness.

(2) Categories: A. Psychology--Organization B. A Priori C. Budgeting

* * * * *

Williams, J. J., "Zero-base Budgeting: Prospects for Developing a Semi-Confusing Budgeting Information System," Accounting, Organizations and Society (August 1981), pp. 153-164.

(1) Discusses the characteristics of a semi-confusing information system and compares these to the characteristics of a zero-base budgeting system. Concludes that ZBB is a destabilizing process which may combine with stablizing traditional budgeting systems to produce a semi-confusing budgeting information system.

(2) Categories: A. Unspecified B. A Priori C. Budgeting

* * * * *

Merchant, K. A., "The Design of the Corporate Budgeting System: Influences on Managerial Behavior and Performance," The Accounting Review (October 1981), pp. 813-829.

(1) Presents and tests a model designed to relate differences in corporate-level budgeting systems to corporate size, diversity and degree of decentralization and how different choices in system design are related to organizational performance and managerial behavior.

(2) Categories: A. Unspecified B. Field Study C. Budgeting

* * * * *

Categories: A--Source discipline. B--Method of analysis. C--Topic.

Brownell, P., "Participation in Budgeting, Locus of Control, and Organizational Effectiveness," The Accounting Review (October 1981), pp. 844-860.

(1) Reports the results of a study designed to test the effect participation, with locus of control as a moderating variable, has on operating performance. The findings indicate participation has a positive effect on those with a high internal locus of control and a negative effect on those with a high external locus.

(2) Categories: A. Psychology--Organization B. Laboratory Experiment C. Budgeting

* * * * *

Ashton, A. H., "An Emprical Study of Budget-Related Predictions of Corporate Executives," Journal of Accounting Research (Autumn 1982), pp. 440-449.

(1) Reports the results of a study designed to test executive decision-making in a budgeting context. The study used Brunswick's lens model as a framework. The results indicate composite predictions and linear predictions are more accurate than executive predictions.

(2) Categories: A. Psychology B. Field Experiment C. Budgeting

* * * * *

Brownell, P., "A Field Study Examination of Budgetary Participation and Locus of Control," The Accounting Review (October 1982), pp. 766-777.

(1) Reports the results of a field study designed to validate the experimental results reported in Brownell (1981) on locus-of-control and performance and extend the previous study to include job satisfaction.

(2) Categories: A. Psychology B. Field Experiment C. Budgeting

* * * * *

Jonsson, S., "Budgetary Behavior in Local Government--A Case Study Over 3 Years," Accounting, Organizations and Society (December 1982), pp. 287-304.

(1) Presents a case study analysis of the budgetary behavior of governmental officials in a setting characterized by confrontation.

(2) Categories: A. Psychology-Organization B. Field Study C. Budgeting

* * * * *

Categories: A--Source discipline. B--Method of analysis. C--Topic.

Seiler, R. E. and R. W. Bartlett, "Personality Variables as Predictors of Budget System Characteristics," Accounting, Organizations and Society (December 1982), pp. 381-404.

(1) Reports the results of a study designed to assess the relationship between personality traits such as authoritarianism, need for independence, and flexibility and attitudes toward the budgetary system. The results indicate such variables predict the participativeness of the system but not an individual's attitude toward it.

(2) Categories: A. Psychology B. Field Study C. Budgeting

* * * * *

Categories: A--Source discipline. B--Method of analysis. C--Topic.

6.2. VARIANCE ANALYSIS AND INVESTIGATION (pp. 171-183)

The articles in this subcategory deal with the decision to investigate and the analysis of variances. Certain articles on standard costs and performance evaluation related to this topic are included in subcategory 6.5, Planning and Control-General (pp. 193-212).

Dean, J., "Correlation Analysis of Cost Variation," The Accounting Review (March 1937), pp. 55-60.

(1) Presents a method of variance analysis which uses multiple correlation analysis to identify that portion related statistically to cost factors which are beyond the control of the manager. This allows identification of the portion that can properly be held accountable to the manager. Introduces statistical sophistication to the literature of management accounting.

(2) Categories: A. Statistics B. Modeling C. Variance Analysis

* * * * *

Solomons, D., "A Diagrammatic Representation of Standard Cost Variances," Accounting Research (January 1951), pp. 46-51.

(1) Presents a graphical portrayal of standard cost variances with primary attention focused on overhead variances. Written for demonstration rather than measurement purposes, this article introduces the graphical variance analysis technique.

(2) Categories: A. Unspecified B. A Priori C. Variance Analysis

* * * * *

Amerman, G., "The Mathematics of Variance Analysis I," Accounting Research (July 1953a), pp. 258-269.

(1) Presents a mathematical and graphical discussion of standard cost variances with particular attention given to the order of separation of the variables and the resultant placement of the combined price-quantity variance. Discusses only direct cost variances.

(2) Categories: A. Unspecified B. Modeling C. Variance Analysis

* * * * *

Amerman, G., "The Mathematics of Variance Analysis II," Accounting Research (October 1953b), pp. 329-350.

(1) Extends the discussion in Amerman (1953a) to overhead variances. Includes discussion of controllable and volume variances and an indepth illustration.

(2) Categories: A. Unspecified B. Modeling C. Variance Analysis

---

Categories: A--Source discipline. B--Method of analysis. C--Topic.

Amerman, G., "The Mathematics of Variance Analysis III," Accounting Research (January 1954a), pp. 56-79.

(1) Extends the discussions in Amerman (1953a) and (1953b) to the case of n variances when calculating price, quantity, and mix variances. The analysis includes the case where constant price ratios exist and the more general case.

(2) Categories: A. Unspecified B. Modeling C. Variance Analysis

* * * * *

Patrick, A. W., "A Proposal for Determining the Significance of Variations from Standard," The Accounting Review (October 1957), pp. 587-592.

(1) Proposes the use of statistics and control charts to determine when to investigate variances. The technique uses a control line and control limits and is designed to replace rules of thumb in determining when variances should be investigated.

(2) Categories: A. Mathematics/Statistics B. Modeling C. Variance Investigation

* * * * *

Watson, R. H., "Two-variate Analysis," The Accounting Review (January 1960), pp. 96-99.

(1) Sets forth a method for calculating both the price and quantity variances so that both sum to the total variance as distinguished from the traditional method of computing one and calculating the other by subtracting from the total. Includes mention of combined variances and an illustrated example.

(2) Categories: A. Mathematics B. Modeling C. Variance Analysis

* * * * *

Bierman, H., L. Fouraker and R. Jaedicke, "A Use of Probability and Statistics in Performance Evaluation," The Accounting Review (July 1961), pp. 409-417.

(1) Describes a model for solving the decision problem of when to investigate a variance. The model uses the normal distribution, a budget amount, and an investigation range. The discussion develops the probability and statistical concepts used and an example is illustrated.

(2) Categories: A. Mathematics B. Modeling C. Variance Investigation

* * * * *

Categories: A--Source discipline. B--Method of analysis. C--Topic.

Kwang, C. and A. Slavin, "The Simple Mathematics of Variance Analysis," The Accounting Review (July 1962), pp. 415-433.

(1) Presents an algebraic approach to defining variances and illustrates the relationship between the price and quantity variances for both direct and overhead costs. An excellent discussion of two-way and three-way variances.

(2) Categories: A. Mathematics B. Modeling C. Variance Analysis

* * * * *

Zannetos, Z. S., "On the Mathematics of Variance Analysis," The Accounting Review (July 1963), pp. 528-533.

(1) Presents an algebraic formulation of two- and three-way analysis of overhead variances as an alternative to the method proposed by Kwang and Slavin (1962). Also includes discussion of the significance of variances.

(2) Categories: A. Mathematics B. Modeling C. Variance Analysis

* * * * *

Weber, C., "The Mathematics of Variance Analysis," The Accounting Review (July 1963), pp. 534-539.

(1) Reports on studies made in Switzerland regarding the various mathematical formulations for calculating variances.

(2) Categories: A. Mathematics B. A Priori C. Variance Analysis

* * * * *

Zannetos, Z. S., "Standard Costs as a First Step to Probabilistic Control: A Theoretical Justification, an Extension and Implications," The Accounting Review (April 1964), pp. 296-304.

(1) Discusses the distribution of actual costs and quantities about the standard and the use of Chebyshev's inequality and the normal distribution in analyzing variances from standard. Includes discussion of when variances should be investigated using these techniques.

(2) Categories: A. Mathematics/Statistics B. Modeling C. Variance Investigation

* * * * *

Categories: A--Source discipline. B--Method of analysis. C--Topic.

Hobbs, J. B., "Volume-Mix-Price/Cost Budget Variance Analysis: A Proper Approach," The Accounting Review (October 1964), pp. 905-913.

(1) Presents a quantitative variance analysis technique for evaluating variances from budget. Illustrates by means of a case problem and calculates the price/cost volume and mix variances.

(2) Categories: A. Unspecified B. Modeling C. Variance Analysis

* * * * *

Horngren, C. T., "A Contribution Margin Approach to the Analysis of Capacity Utilization," The Accounting Review (April 1967), pp. 254-264.

(1) Presents a conceptual framework for analyzing capacity utilization which uses an opportunity cost approach to valuation rather than a unitized historical-cost approach.

(2) Categories: A. Unspecified B. A Priori C. Variance Analysis

* * * * *

DeCoster, D. T., "Measurement of the Idle-Capacity Variance," The Accounting Review (April 1966), pp. 297-302.

(1) Discusses the theory and practice of overhead costing and in particular the nature of the idle-capacity variance.

(2) Categories: A. Unspecified B. A Priori C. Variance Analysis

* * * * *

Onsi, M., "Quantitative Models for Accounting Control," The Accounting Review (April 1967), pp. 321-330.

(1) Discusses the nature, criteria of whether to investigate, and basic requirements of three different control models: the traditional accounting model, the model based on classical statistics, and the model based on decision theory. A good review of control models.

(2) Categories: A. Statistics/Decision Theory B. A Priori C. Variance Investigation

* * * * *

Hasseldine, C. R., "Mix and Yield Variances," The Accounting Review (July 1967), pp. 497-515.

(1) Discusses and illustrates the mix and yield variances in algebraic and graphical terms when substitution of factors is permitted.

(2) Categories: A. Unspecified B. A Priori C. Variance Analysis

* * * * *

Categories: A--Source discipline. B--Method of analysis. C--Topic.

Frank, W. and R. Manes, "A Standard Cost Application of Matrix Algebra," The Accounting Review (July 1967), pp. 516-525.

(1) Presents an algebraic formulation of standard cost variances, a matrix formulation that permits efficient computation, and an economic interpretation of the results.

(2) Categories: A. Unspecified B. Modeling C. Variance Analysis

* * * * *

Dopuch, N., J. G. Birnberg and J. S. Demski, "An Extension of Standard Cost Variance Analysis," The Accounting Review (July 1967), pp. 526-536.

(1) Discusses the use of standard cost variance analysis to control the application and performance of the firm's decision models as well as its traditional use in controlling processes. Includes discussion of the possible reasons for variances and an illustrated example.

(2) Categories: A. Unspecified B. A Priori C. Variance Analysis

* * * * *

Demski, J. S., "An Accounting System Structured on a Linear Programming Model," The Accounting Review (October 1967a), pp. 701-712.

(1) Discusses the use of a linear programming model of a firm which allows comparisons among budget amounts, actual results, and a budget based on actual inputs. Follows Dopuch, Birnberg and Demski (1967).

(2) Categories: A. Mathematics/Operations Research B. Modeling C. Variance Analysis

* * * * *

Demski, J. S., "Analyzing the Effectiveness of the Traditional Standard Cost Variance Model," Management Accounting (October 1967b), pp. 9-19.

(1) Discusses the use of traditional standard cost variance analysis in a well-structured planning and control setting and proposes an ex post model designed to provide superior control information. Includes discussion of the management control process and the economic theory of the firm. Follows Dopuch, Birnberg and Demski (1967).

(2) Categories: A. Operations Research B. Modeling C. Variance Analysis

* * * * *

Categories: A--Source discipline. B--Method of analysis. C--Topic.

Luh, F. S., "Controlled Cost: An Operational Concept and Statistical Approach to Standard Costing," The Accounting Review (January 1968), pp. 123-132.

(1) Proposes that a probability distribution and not a single value be used as the standard cost of an item. Deviations from standard are determined by comparison of actual and standard probability distributions.

(2) Categories: A. Statistics B. A Priori C. Variance Analysis

* * * * *

Cushing, B. E., "Some Observations on Demski's Ex Post Accounting System," The Accounting Review (October 1968), pp. 668-671.

(1) Analyzes the assumptions underlying Demski's (1967a,b) variance analysis model and discusses its limitations.

(2) Categories: A. Unspecified B. A Priori C. Variance Analysis

* * * * *

Chumachenko, N. G., "Once Again: The Volume-Mix-Price/Cost Budget Variance Analysis," The Accounting Review (October 1968), pp. 753-762.

(1) Reviews several areas of cost accounting from both the American and Soviet points of view. Includes discussion of profit analysis, volume variance analysis, the mix variance, and the analysis of changes in sales volume.

(2) Categories: A. Unspecified B. A Priori C. Variance Analysis

* * * * *

Theil, H., "How to Worry About Increased Expenditures," The Accounting Review (January 1969), pp. 27-37.

(1) Discusses the use of the Shannon and Weaver measure of information to evaluate the significance of variations from budget.

(2) Categories: A. Unspecified B. A Priori C. Variance Analysis

* * * * *

Horngren, C. T., "Capacity Utilization and the Efficiency Variance," The Accounting Review (January 1969), pp. 86-89.

(1) Discusses the framework set forth in Horngren (1967) for the analysis of capacity utilization and the integration of an efficiency variance within the framework.

(2) Categories: A. Unspecified B. A Priori C. Variance Analysis

* * * * *

Categories: A—Source discipline. B—Method of analysis. C—Topic.

Kaplan, R. S., "Optimal Investigation Strategies with Imperfect Information," Journal of Accounting Research (Spring 1969), pp. 32-43.

(1) Discusses the implementation of optimal policies by the integration of the costs and probability distributions which arise in the case of imperfect information.
(2) Categories: A. Statistics B. Modeling C. Variance Analysis

* * * * *

Lev, B., "An Information Theory Analysis of Budget Variances," The Accounting Review (October 1969a), pp. 704-710.

(1) Discusses the use of the Shannon and Weaver measure of information from information theory to identify and analyze variances that are interdependent.

(2) Categories: A. Unspecified B. A Priori C. Variance Analysis

* * * * *

Dyckman, T. R., "The Investigation of Cost Variances," Journal of Accounting Research (Autumn 1969), pp. 215-244.

(1) Discusses including the costs and benefits of investigation in the analysis of variances. Uses a statistical decision theory approach and includes discussion of both discrete and continuous state sets.

(2) Categories: A. Statistics B. Modeling C. Variance Investigation

* * * * *

Lev. B., "Testing a Prediction Method for Multivariate Budgets," Journal of Accounting Research (Supplement 1969b), pp. 182-204.

(1) Reports the results of an empirical study designed to test the prediction model proposed by Thiel (1969) for analyzing variances from budget. The findings indicate the Thiel model outperforms actual forecasts made and forecasts from two naive models.

(2) Categories: A. Unspecified B. Empirical C. Variance Analysis

* * * * *

Ronen, J., "Capacity and Operating Variances: An Ex Post Approach," Journal of Accounting Research (Autumn 1970), pp. 232-252.

(1) Proposes a set of variances designed to improve the design and utilization of operating capacity.

(2) Categories: A. Unspecified B. A Priori C. Variance Analysis

* * * * *

Categories: A--Source discipline. B--Method of analysis. C--Topic.

Ozan, T. and T. Dyckman, "A Normative Model for Investigation Decisions Involving Multiorigin Cost Variances," Journal of Accounting Research (Spring 1971), pp. 88-115.

(1) Presents a model of a cost center, derives the probability distribution of the noncontrollable costs, and calculates the present value of the expected profit from investigating. Formulates the decision model as a linear program. Takes a cost-benefit approach to variance analysis.

(2) Categories: A. Unspecified B. Modeling C. Variance Investigation

* * * * *

Gonedes, N. J., "Optimal Timing of Control Messages for a Two-State Markov Process," Journal of Accounting Research (Autumn 1971), pp. 236-252.

(1) Presents an analysis of a goal model to determine the optimal timing of control messages. The goal model is a finite-state continuous time Markov process.

(2) Categories: A. Mathematics B. Modeling C. Variance Analysis

* * * * *

Wolk, H. I. and A. D. Hillman, "Materials Mix and Yield Variance: A Suggested Improvement," The Accounting Review (July 1972), pp. 549-555.

(1) Proposes a model of raw materials variances which overcomes the deficiencies of the traditional method and takes into account the possibility that the standard mix may be abandoned in the short-run because of changes in price.

(2) Categories: A. Unspecified B. Modeling C. Variance Analysis

* * * * *

Bashan, O., Y. Goldschmidt, G. Levkowitz and L. Shashua, "Laspeyres Indexes for Variance Analysis in Cost Accounting," The Accounting Review (October 1973), pp. 790-793.

(1) Illustrates the use of Laspeynes Indexes to formulate a variance analysis model. Although a teaching note this is an interesting application of economics to variance analysis.

(2) Categories: A. Economics B. Modeling C. Variance Analysis

* * * * *

Categories: A—Source discipline. B—Method of analysis. C—Topic.

Ronen, J., "Nonaggregation Versus Disaggregation of Variances," The Accounting Review (January 1974), pp. 50-60.

(1) Discusses the analysis of variances and proposes a conceptual framework for simultaneously evaluating the costs and benefits of various disaggregation strategies. Includes an illustrated example.

(2) Categories: A. Unspecified B. A Priori C. Variance Analysis

* * * * *

Abdel-khalik, A. R., "The Entropy Law, Accounting Data, and Relevance to Decision Making," The Accounting Review (April 1974), pp. 271-283.

(1) Discusses entropy and in particular the entropy measure used by Theil (1969) and Lev (1969) and reports the results of an empirical test of the difference in amount of information computed by the supplier and the amount by the user.

(2) Categories: A. Unspecified B. Empirical C. Variance-Analysis

* * * * *

Hughes, J., "Optimal Timing of Cost Information," Journal of Accounting Research (Autumn 1975), pp. 344-349.

(1) Presents a discussion and revision of Kaplan's (1969) model of process investigation based upon imperfect cost information.

(2) Categories: A. Unspecified B. Modeling C. Variance Analysis

* * * * *

Magee, R. P., "A Simulation Analysis of Alternative Cost Variance Investigation Models," The Accounting Review (July 1976), pp. 529-544.

(1) Presents a framework for chosing a decision model and a simulation analysis of the more popular cost variance investigation models in the literature.

(2) Categories: A. Operations Research B. Simulation Experiment C. Variance Investigation

* * * * *

Categories: A—Source discipline. B—Method of analysis. C—Topic.

Ansari, S. L., "Behavioral Factors in Variance Control: Report on a Laboratory Experiment," Journal of Accounting Research (Autumn 1976), pp. 189-211.

(1) Reports the results of a laboratory experiment designed to test the joint influence variance reports and leadership style have on employee satisfaction and productivity. The findings generally supported the framework of the study, however, the results for specific hypotheses were mixed.

(2) Categories: A. Psychology B. Laboratory Experiment C. Variance Analysis

* * * * *

Magee, R. P., "Cost Control with Imperfect Parameter Knowledge," The Accounting Review (January 1977a), pp. 190-199.

(1) Discusses parameter uncertainty in cost control and the robustness of a proposed dynamic programming cost variance investigation model to errors in parameter estimation. A model is then formulated which provides parameter information as a by-product of the investigation decision.

(2) Categories: A. Unspecified B. Modeling C. Variance Analysis

* * * * *

Magee, R. P., "The Usefulness of Commonality Information in Cost Control Decisions," The Accounting Review (October 1977b), pp. 869-880.

(1) Presents and illustrates a cost variance investigation model which takes into account the fact that multiple-cost process variances may be correlated and result in lower expected costs.

(2) Categories: A. Unspecified B. Modeling C. Variance Analysis

* * * * *

Categories: A--Source discipline. B--Method of analysis. C--Topic.

Lin, W. T., "Multiple Objective Budgeting Models: A Simulation," The Accounting Review (January 1978), pp. 61-76.

(1) Presents several multiple objective budgeting models which include two planning models (a satisficing goal programming model and an optimizing multiple objective linear programming model) and two performance evaluation models (a traditional standard cost variance analysis system and an expost variance analysis system.) A simulation analysis is performed on the models.

(2) Categories: A. Organizational Behavior B. Simulation Analysis C. Variance Analysis

* * * * *

Dittman, D. and P. Prakash, "Cost Variance Investigation: Markovian Control of Markov Processes," Journal of Accounting Research (Spring 1978), pp. 14-25.

(1) Proposes the use of a fixed critical cost to signal a need for cost variance investigation rather than dynamic programming or Bayesian models. Derives an explicit expression for the long-run average cost per period of controlled operations which can easily be used in practice.

(2) Categories: A. Mathematics B. Modeling C. Variance Investigation

* * * * *

Jacobs, F. H., "An Evaluation of the Effectiveness of Some Cost Variance Investigation Models," Journal of Accounting Research (Spring 1978), pp. 190-203.

(1) Reports the results of a study designed to evaluate the effectiveness of six specific variance investigation models, including control charts and Bayesian models. Specific settings under which the various models are most effective are discussed.

(2) Categories: A. Unspecified B. Field Study C. Variance Investigation

* * * * *

Categories: A--Source discipline. B--Method of analysis. C--Topic.

Magee, R. P. and J. W. Dickhaut, "Effects of Compensation Plans on Heuristics in Cost Variance Investigations," Journal of Accounting Research (Autumn 1978), pp. 294-314.

(1) Reports the results of an experiment designed to test the effect alternative compensaton plans have on the behavior of cost control decision makers in an uncertain environment. The findings indicate such environmental changes influence the choice of heuristic and the cost incurred by the organization.

(2) Categories: A. Psychology--Individual B. Laboratory Experiment C. Variance Investigation

* * * * *

Dittman, D. and P. Prakash, "Cost Variance Investigation: Markovian Control Versus Optimal Control," The Accounting Review (April 1979), pp. 358-373.

(1) Presents a comparison of the long-run expected costs per period of a Markovian control process (the process is investigated whenever cost exceeds a cutoff amount) and a Bayesian or optimal control process (the costs update the probability the process is out of control and investigation occurs when the cutoff probability is exceeded).

(2) Categories: A. Unspecified B. A Priori C. Variance Investigation

* * * * *

Brown, C., "Human Information Processing for Decision to Investigate Cost Variances," Journal of Accounting Research (Spring 1981), pp. 62-85.

(1) Reports the results of a simulation and a laboratory experiment designed to test the effects certain situational variables have on the decision to investigate variances.

(2) Categories: A. Psychology--Individual B. Laboratory Experiment C. Variance Analysis

* * * * *

Categories: A--Source discipline. B--Method of analysis. C--Topic.

Buckman, A. G. and B. L. Miller, "Optimal Investigation of a Multiple Cost Processes System," Journal of Accounting Research (Spring 1982), pp. 28-41.

(1) Presents a model of an n-cost processes system in which the processes are statistically independent but related by the assumption that corrective action takes place for all n-processes or none of them. It presents a myopic policy which is roughly comparable in accuracy to the one-cost process of Dittman and Prakash (1978).

(2) Categories: A. Unspecified B. Modeling C. Variance Investigation

* * * * *

Mensah, Y. M., "A Dynamic Approach to the Evaluation of Input-Variable Cost Center Performance," The Accounting Review (October 1982), pp. 681-700.

(1) Presents and discusses a variance analysis technique to be used in assessing the performance of cost center managers where materials and/or other production factors can be substituted for one another in specified ratios. Includes a linear programming formulation.

(2) Categories: A. Unspecified B. Modeling C. Variance Analysis

* * * * *

Categories: A--Source discipline. B--Method of analysis. C--Topic.

6.3 TRANSFER PRICING (pp. 184-189)

This subcategory contains articles relating to the various aspects of transfer pricing. Articles on decentralization and performance evaluation in general, without specific reference to transfer pricing, are included in subcategory 6.5, Planning and Control-General (pp. 193-212).

Hirshleifer, J., "On the Economics of Transfer Pricing," Journal of Business (July 1956), pp. 172-184.

(1) Discusses setting transfer prices to induce divisions to act so as to maximize firm profits. Includes discussion of transfer-price setting under competitive and imperfectly competitive market conditions and concludes market price is the correct transfer price only when the product is produced in a competitive market. In a noncompetitive setting, marginal cost is the correct transfer price. Classic economic viewpoint on transfer pricing.

(2) Categories: A. Economics B. A Priori C. Transfer Pricing

* * * * *

Stone, W. E., "Intracompany Pricing," The Accounting Review (October 1956), pp. 625-627.

(1) Discusses transfer pricing and the criteria that a transfer price must meet. Reviews four types of transfer prices: 1) arbitrary, 2) cost, 3) sales price, and 4) bargained price. Introduces transfer pricing to the accounting literature.

(2) Categories: A. Unspecified B. A Priori C. Transfer Pricing

* * * * *

Bierman, H., "Pricing Intracompany Transfers," The Accounting Review (July 1959), pp. 429-432.

(1) Discusses the decentralization and transfer pricing problem noting that the transfer price does not affect the profits of the total firm and that conflicts of interest arise in setting a transfer price. Defines several transfer prices and discusses their use for measuring performance and for decision-making.

(2) Categories: A. Economics B. A Priori C. Transfer Pricing

* * * * *

Categories: A--Source discipline. B--Method of analysis. C--Topic.

Stone, W. E., "Tax Considerations in Intra-Company Pricing," The Accounting Review (January 1960), pp. 51-59.

(1) Discusses the implications of the effects transfer prices have on subsidiary and parent taxable income and inventory values. References the tax code and tax court rulings.

(2) Categories: A. Legal B. A Priori C. Transfer Pricing

* * * * *

Shubik, M., "Incentives, Decentralized Control, the Assignment of Joint Costs and Internal Pricing," Management Science (April 1962) pp. 325-343.

(1) Discusses the control problems which arise from the use of joint cost allocations and transfer prices in a decentralized setting and presents a model for such allocations based on game theory work of Shapley. Includes a review of game theory and several examples. A classic article that was followed by considerable work in the accounting literature.

(2) Categories: A. Economics/Game Theory/OR B. Modeling C. Transfer Pricing

* * * * *

Stone, W. E., "Legal Implications of Intracompany Pricing," The Accounting Review (January 1964), pp. 38-42.

(1) Discusses the antitrust acts and court rulings affecting the use of transfer prices between segments of a corporation and the legal implications of such prices.

(2) Categories: A. Legal B. A Priori C. Transfer Pricing

* * * * *

Dopuch, N. and D. Drake, "Accounting Implications of a Mathematical Programming Approach to the Transfer Price Problem," Journal of Accounting Research (Spring 1964), pp. 10-24.

(1) Discusses the various transfer pricing methods and their relationships to management accounting. Includes discussion of the application of linear programming to transfer pricing.

(2) Categories: A. Mathematics/Operations Research B. A Priori C. Transfer Pricing

* * * * *

Categories: A—Source discipline. B—Method of analysis. C—Topic.

Goetz, B., "Transfer Prices: An Exercise in Relevancy and Goal Congruence," The Accounting Review (July 1967), pp. 435-440.

(1) Discusses transfer prices and goal congruence and concludes opportunity cost is the best transfer price to use to achieve goal congruence. Illustrates with an example.

(2) Categories: A. Unspecified B. A Priori C. Transfer Pricing

* * * * *

Wells, M. C., "Profit Centres, Transfer Prices and Mysticism," Abacus (December 1968), pp. 174-181.

(1) Discusses profit centers and transfer prices and whether they are useful management control techniques. Concludes that mystical transfer prices should be eliminated and instead transfer amounts should be used for divisional evaluation.

(2) Categories: A. Unspecified B. A Priori C. Transfer Pricing

* * * * *

Goetz, B., "The Effect of a Cost-Plus Contract on Transfer Prices," The Accounting Review (April 1969), pp. 398-400.

(1) Illustrates the effect of using transfer prices in a cost-plus contract situation. Although primarily a teaching note this expands Goetz (1967).

(2) Categories: A. Unspecified B. A Priori C. Transfer Pricing

* * * * *

Ronen, J. and G. McKinney, "Transfer Pricing for Divisional Automony," Journal of Accounting Research (Spring 1970), pp. 99-112.

(1) Discusses the use of a transfer price with a subsidy or tax which will give decentralized divisions essentially complete autonomy and induce decisions that will maximize total corporate profits. Compares this model with Hirshleifer's.

(2) Categories: A. Economics B. Modeling C. Transfer Pricing

* * * * *

Categories: A--Source discipline. B--Method of analysis. C--Topic.

Gordon, M. J., "A Method of Pricing for a Socialist Economy," The Accounting Review (July 1970), pp. 427-443.

(1) Discusses the problems of pricing in a socialist economy and proposes a set of rules for determining transfer prices which will result in efficient administration and control. The prices are set by each firm under rules of the central authority and under cost output and price models. This way price and output behave as if the system were a perfectly competitive market.

(2) Categories: A. Economics/OR B. Modeling C. Transfer Pricing

* * * * *

Onsi, M., "A Transfer Pricing System Based on Opportunity Cost," The Accounting Review (July 1970), pp. 535-543.

(1) Discusses the economic transfer pricing system and opportunity costs. Proposes that opportunity costs calculated from a linear programming model of the organization be used as the transfer price in the organization.

(2) Categories: A. Operations Research B. Modeling C. Transfer Pricing

* * * * *

Lemke, K. W., "In Defence of the 'Profit Centre' Concept," Abacus (December 1970), pp. 182-188.

(1) Discusses transfer pricing and whether the profit center concept is useful. Includes discussion of the use of incremental costs and market prices as transfer prices.

(2) Categories: A. Unspecified B. A Priori C. Transfer Pricing

* * * * *

Thomas, A. L., "Transfer Prices of the Multinational Firm: When will they be Arbitrary?" Abacus (June 1971), pp. 40-53.

(1) Discusses the setting of transfer prices by firms with divisions in different countries and the implications of these for the host country. Concludes transfer prices which do not approximate an arm's-length transaction and price can be set arbitrarily to the firm's advantage.

(2) Categories: A. Economics B. A Priori C. Transfer Pricing

* * * * *

Categories: A—Source discipline. B—Method of analysis. C—Topic.

Abdel-khalik, A. R. and E. J. Lusk, "Transfer Pricing--A Synthesis," The Accounting Review, (January 1974), pp. 8-23.

(1) Reviews the various approaches taken toward transfer pricing including the theory of the firm and mathematical programming approaches and offers several observations on the topic.

(2) Categories: A. Economics/Mathematics B. A Priori C. Transfer Pricing

* * * * *

Kornbluth, J. S. H., "Accounting in Multiple Objective Linear Programming," The Accounting Review (April 1974), pp. 284-295.

(1) Discusses the calculation of an efficient solution to a multiple objective linear program and the uses and interpretation of the multidimensional scheme of transfer prices.

(2) Categories: A. Mathematics/OR B. Modeling C. Transfer Pricing

* * * * *

Watson, D. J. H. and J. V. Baumler, "Transfer Pricing: A Behavioral Context," The Accounting Review (July 1975), pp. 466-474.

(1) Discusses mathematical programming and other transfer pricing models in a behavioral social-system context and presents a paradigm for evaluating the usefulness and limitations of proposed models.

(2) Categories: A. Economics B. A Priori C. Transfer Pricing

* * * * *

Bailey, A. D. and W. J. Boe, "Goal and Resource Transfers in the Multigoal Organization," The Accounting Review (July 1976), pp. 559-573.

(1) Reviews the economic, behavioral, and quantitative literature in transfer pricing and relates it to the generalized goal decomposition programming technique.

(2) Categories: A. Economics/Psychology/OR B. A Priori C. Transfer Pricing

* * * * *

Categories: A--Source discipline. B--Method of analysis. C--Topic.

Merville, L. J. and J. W. Petty, "Transfer Pricing for the Multinational Firm," The Accounting Review (October 1978), pp. 935-951.

(1) Discusses the implications the international business environment has on the setting of transfer prices. Presents a linear programming and goal programming framework which permits optimization of various factors including tax rates, profit, and risks around the world.

(2) Categories: A. Unspecified B. Modeling C. Transfer Pricing

* * * * *

Kanodia, C., "Risk Sharing and Transfer Price Systems Under Uncertainty," Journal of Accounting Research (Spring 1979), pp. 74-98.

(1) Presents an extension of the Hirshleifer (1956) analysis on transfer pricing to include an uncertain environment. Includes discussion of a system based on Arrow-Debreu contingent commodities and presentation of two models constructed to optimize central management's preferences and allow risk sharing.

(2) Categories: A. Economics B. Modeling C. Transfer Pricing

* * * * *

Tang, R. Y. W. and K. H. Chan, "Environmental Variables of International Transfer Pricing: A Japan-United States Comparison," Abacus (June 1979), pp. 3-12.

(1) Presents the results of a study of the environmental variables considered in setting international transfer prices by large U.S. and Japanese multinational corporations. The findings indicate that while profit was the strongest determinant other environmental variables such as market share, taxes, and foreign currency valuations were also important.

(2) Categories: A. Unspecified B. Survey (Questionnaire) C. Transfer Pricing

* * * * *

Swieringa, R. J. and J. H. Waterhouse, "Organizational Views of Transfer Pricing," Accounting, Organizations and Society (May 1982), pp. 149-165.

(1) Discusses four models of organization: the behavioral, garbage can, organizing, and markets and hierarchies models and their implications for decentralization and transfer pricing decisions.

(2) Categories: A. Psychology-Organization B. A Priori C. Transfer Pricing

---

Categories: A--Source discipline. B--Method of analysis. C--Topic.

6.4. PRINCIPAL-AGENT (pp. 190-192)

This subcategory contains articles using agency-type models on various aspects of control. Many of these articles could have been classified in other categories (e.g., Budgeting, Variance Analysis). As this is a new, rapidly growing area, we decided to set up a separate section for it.

Ross, S. A., "The Economic Theory of Agency: The Principal's Problem," American Economic Review (May 1973), pp. 134-139.

(1) Discusses the principal's problem in the agency setting and analyzes whether solution of this problem necessarily leads to a Pareto efficient situation for all. Concludes that there exists a class of payoffs that leads to both the solution of the principal's problem and to a Pareto efficient solution and that such a class is likely to arise in practice.

(2) Categories: A. Economics B. Modeling C. Principal-Agent

* * * * *

Itami, H., "Evaluation Measures and Goal Congruence Under Uncertainty," Journal of Accounting Research (Spring 1975), pp. 73-96.

(1) Presents a model for analyzing goal congruence under conditions of uncertainty and evaluates certain performance measures to determine if they lead to goal congruence (Also, see Itami's (1977) AAA monograph.)

(2) Categories: A. Economics/Decision Theory B. Modeling
C. Principal-Agent

* * * * *

Demski, J. S., "Uncertainty and Evaluation Based on Controllable Performance," Journal of Accounting Research (Autumn 1976), pp. 230-245.

(1) Analyzes the risk-sharing aspects of the controllable performance concept in a setting where uncertainty is explicitly recognized. The findings indicate the use of controlability filters is inconsistent with efficient risk sharing and incentive considerations may argue against a focus on the controllable aspects of performance.

(2) Categories: A. Economics B. Modeling C. Principal-Agent

* * * * *

Categories: A--Source discipline. B--Method of analysis. C--Topic.

Demski, J. S. and G. A. Feltham, "Economic Incentives in Budgetary Control Systems," The Accounting Review (April 1978), pp. 336-359.

(1) Analyzes the use of budgets in an economic setting and the conditions that may induce their use. The findings indicate market incompleteness is a necessary condition for the existence of budget-based contracts.

(2) Categories: A. Economics B. Modeling C. Principal-Agent

* * * * *

Groves, T. and M. Loeb, "Incentives in Divisionalized Firms," Management Science (March 1979), pp. 221-230.

(1) Discusses coordination and control in a multidivision firm and the problem of motivating division managers both to act in congruence with the firm's goals and to communicate truthful information to the corporate center for decision making purposes. Proposes a control structure which retains the benefits of decentralization and provides incentives for truthful reporting in a setting with intrafirm externalities.

(2) Categories: A. Economics B. Modeling C. Principal-Agent

* * * * *

Atkinson, A. A., "Information Incentives in a Standard-Setting Model of Control," Journal of Accounting Research (Spring 1979), pp. 1-22.

(1) Analyzes the incentive effect that a contract which combines profit sharing with standard setting has on the development of information. The findings indicate that standard setting combined with profit sharing dominates any existing fixed wage contract.

(2) Categories: A. Economics B. Modeling C. Principal-Agent

* * * * *

Baiman, S. and J. S. Demski, "Variance Analysis Procedures as Motivation Devices," Management Science (August 1980a), pp. 840-848.

(1) Analyzes the use of standard cost variance analysis as a motivational device within the principal-agent model. Concludes that the investigation of such variances can have desirable motivational effects.

(2) Categories: A. Economics B. Modeling C. Principal-Agent

* * * * *

Categories: A--Source discipline. B--Method of analysis. C--Topic.

Magee, R. P., "Equilibria in Budget Participation," Journal of Accounting Research (Autumn 1980), pp. 551-573.

(1) Analyzes the effect participation in the budgeting process has on various aspects of the owner-manager relationship. The implications both for the use of participative budgeting and for behavioral research in this area are presented.

(2) Categories: A. Economics B. Modeling C. Principal-Agent

* * * * *

Baiman, S. and J. S. Demski, "Economically Optimal Performance Evaluation and Control Systems," Journal of Accounting Research (Supplement 1980b), pp. 184-220.

(1) Analyzes the demand for and use of information in the performance evaluation and control system of a firm and distinguishes between a decision-influencing use of information and a decision-facilitating use.

(2) Categories: A. Economics B. Modeling C. Principal-Agent

* * * * *

Christensen, J., "The Determination of Performance Standards and Participation," Journal of Accounting Research (Autumn 1982), pp. 589-603.

(1) Presents an analysis of performance standards and participation in an agency setting. Investigates several aspects including the use of standards as signals from a predecision information system and as communication by an agent possessing superior information. Confines the analysis to pareto optimal contracts.

(2) Categories: A. Economics B. Modeling C. Principal-Agent

* * * * *

Categories: A--Source discipline. B--Method of analysis. C--Topic.

6.5. PLANNING AND CONTROL-GENERAL (pp. 193-212)

This subcategory contains those articles in the areas of planning and control not otherwise categorized. Included are articles on standard costs, cost control, decentralization, and performance evaluation.

Gibson, J. C., "A Standard Cost Problem," The Accounting Review (December 1927), pp. 362-387.

(1) Discusses standard costs and their use in directing the attention of management to variations. An early appearance of standard costs in the literature.

(2) Categories: A. Unspecified B. A Priori C. P&C-General (Standard Costs)

* * * * *

Scott, D. R., "Trends in the Technique and Tools of Management," The Accounting Review (June 1937), pp. 138-145.

(1) Discusses several aspects of the use of policy in business management including the place of the policy executive in the organization, the rise of "functional control," the use of business statistics to supplement and extend accounting data, and the rise of budgeting. The perspective is that of an organization/policy framework rather than accounting. The thread that runs through the entire discussion is the importance of a forward looking viewpoint.

(2) Categories: A. Unspecified B. A Priori C. P&C-General

* * * * *

Rucker, R. G., "Cost Analysis by Standards in the Accounts," The Accounting Review (December 1939), pp. 368-374.

(1) Argues for the extension of standard costs beyond their use for control purposes and into the actual accounts. Variances would then be charged off to current profit/loss rather than put into inventory. Advocates eliminating the cost of waste and efficiency from the cost of a product. The first appearance of this concept in the literature.

(2) Categories: A. Unspecified B. A Priori C. P&C-General (Standard Costs)

* * * * *

Categories: A--Source discipline. B--Method of analysis. C--Topic.

Edwards, H. R., M. S. Kem and H. W. Wilder, "The Use of Accounting in Business Policy Determination," The Accounting Review (October 1947), pp. 395-404.

(1) Discussion by each of the authors of the importance of accounting reports in guiding management in everyday business policies. The first lists the phases of policy determination which are influenced by accounting, the second focuses on budgeting and operations analysis and their effects, and the third discusses situations in which the accounting method used influences the business policies. An early discussion of the effect of the organization's accounting system has on the functioning of the organization.

(2) Categories: A. Unspecified B. A Priori C. P&C-General

* * * * *

Crossman, P., "The Function of the Cost Accountant in Cost Control," The Accounting Review (January 1953a), pp. 25-31.

(1) Examines the responsibilities of the cost accountant and management in a cost control program and delineates the cost accountant's tasks. Concludes with a summary of what constitutes good cost control.

(2) Categories: A. Unspecified B. A Priori C. P&C-General

* * * * *

Crum, L. R., "The Role of Cost Accounting in Cost Control," The Accounting Review (July 1953), pp. 363-372.

(1) Discusses management, cost accounting, and the need for cost control including a discussion of standards. Characterizes the cost accountant not as an inspector but as one partially responsible for the establishment of efficient production procedures.

(2) Categories: A. Unspecified B. A Priori C. P&C-General

* * * * *

Crossman, P., "The Genesis of Cost Control," The Accounting Review (October 1953b), pp. 522-527.

(1) Traces the beginnings of the idea that accounting should supply data useful to management in controlling costs to a well formed state by the close of the 19th century. A historical piece on the development of the accounting concept of cost control.

(2) Categories: A. Unspecified B. A Priori C. P&C-General

* * * * *

Categories: A--Source discipline. B--Method of analysis. C--Topic.

Benninger, L. J., "Cost Control as Applied to the Smaller Business Organization," The Accounting Review (January 1956), pp. 95-98.

(1) Discusses the usefulness of accounting in solving the cost control problems of small businesses. Includes coverage of control devices and procedures and concludes they may be of some use in small businesses.

(2) Categories: A. Unspecified B. A Priori C. P&C-General

* * * * *

Ridgway, V. F., "Dysfunctional Consequences of Performance Measurements," Administrative Science Quarterly (September 1956), pp. 240-247.

(1) Reviews the literature pertaining to the dysfunctional consequences of using quantitative measures of performance. Coverage includes studies on single, multiple, and composite measures of performance and the results indicate use of each can result in undesirable or unintended managerial behavior. One of the first articles to introduce behavioral considerations of accounting measures to the literature.

(2) Categories: A. Psychology (Behavioral) B. A Priori C. P&C-General

* * * * *

Richards, A. B., "Input-Output Accounting for Business," The Accounting Review (July 1960), pp. 429-436.

(1) Discusses the relationship between input-output analysis and accounting and illustrates an input-output accounting system by translating a conventional accounting system into a Leontief framework and using actual accounting data. Then indicates how input-output accounting can be used in financial analysis and planning. First indepth treatment of this topic and presentation of a method for predicting changes in balance sheet accounts given a level of operations.

(2) Categories: A. Mathematics B. Modeling C. P&C-General

* * * * *

Categories: A—Source discipline. B—Method of analysis. C—Topic.

Andersson, H. F., "Allowance for Setup Time Under Standard Costs," The Accounting Review (July 1960), pp. 497-500.

(1) Discusses the variances that arise in small versus large runs from not taking setup time into account, explains a formula for computing set up time, and illustrates the method by an example.

(2) Categories: A. Unspecified B. A Priori C. P&C-General (Standard (Costs)

* * * * *

Kemp, P. S., "Accounting Data for Planning, Motivation and Control," The Accounting Review (January 1962), pp. 44-50.

(1) Discusses the accumulation and presentation of costs and revenues, both historical and projected, for planning, motivation, and control purposes. Concludes that separate costs, revenues, and budgets are required for different purposes. Introduces the idea of setting different budget levels for each of the three purposes.

(2) Categories: A. Unspecified B. A Priori C. P&C-General

* * * * *

Jaedicke, R. K., "Accounting Data for Purposes of Control," The Accounting Review (April 1962), pp. 181-188.

(1) Discusses the concept of control and the uses of accounting data in control. Topics discussed include the human relations problems of control, the use of a standard cost system to measure opportunity costs, and feedback for mathematical and statistical models.

(2) Categories: A. Unspecified B. A Priori C. P&C-General

* * * * *

Shillinglaw, G., "Toward a Theory of Divisional Income Measurement," The Accounting Review (April 1962), pp. 208-216.

(1) Discusses the measurement of divisional income as a reflection of management performance. Includes a discussion of the postulates and standards proposed as a step toward a theory of divisional income measurement. A good discussion of financial accounting-type "principles" (objectivity, matching, etc.) in a division setting.

(2) Categories: A. Unspecified B. A Priori C. P&C-General

* * * * *

Categories: A—Source discipline. B--Method of analysis. C—Topic.

Benston, G. J., "The Role of the Firm's Accounting System for Motivation," The Accounting Review (April 1963), pp. 347-354.

(1) Surveys the literature relating to motivation and organizational theory and then discusses, in light of this literature, accounting systems and reports. The discussion includes coverage of centralization/decentralization, the motivation of small groups, the role of the manager, and the effects of budgets and responsibility reports on motivation. First thorough discussion of behavioral considerations in the literature in accounting.

(2) Categories: A. Psychology-Organization B. A Priori C. P&C-General

* * * * *

Charnes, A., W. W. Cooper, and Y. Ijiri, "Breakeven Budgeting and Programming to Goals," Journal of Accounting Research (Spring 1963), pp. 16-43.

(1) Discusses the use of linear programming in breakeven analysis and planning. Introduces the use of the spread sheet approach to breakeven budgeting.

(2) Categories: A. Mathematics B. Modeling C. P&C-General (Could also be CVP.)

* * * * *

Ijiri, Y., F. K. Levy and R. C. Lyon, "A Linear Programming Model for Budgeting and Financial Planning," Journal of Accounting Research (Autumn 1963), pp. 198-212.

(1) Discusses the application of linear programming techniques to accounting in providing data for financial planning and budgeting.

(2) Categories: A. Mathematics B. Modeling C. P&C-General (Could also be CVP.)

* * * * *

Graese, C. E., "Responsibility Reporting to Management," The Accounting Review (April 1964), pp. 387-391.

(1) Discusses responsibility accounting in general and describes the design and implementation of a responsibility accounting system in a flour mill.

(2) Categories: A. Unspecified B. A Priori C. P&C-General

* * * * *

Categories: A—Source discipline. B—Method of analysis. C—Topic.

Arrow, K. J., "Control in Large Organizations," Management Science (April 1964), pp. 397-406.

(1) Discusses the problems of control in three characteristic large organizations: large corporations, governments, and economic systems as a whole. Includes discussion of uncertainty and differential information as they apply to the control problem and the merits and demerits of the price mechanism as a control technique. A classic discussion of organizational control.

(2) Categories: A. Unspecified B. A Priori C. P&C-General

* * * * *

Luneski, C., "Some Aspects of the Meaning of Control," The Accounting Review (July 1964), pp. 591-597.

(1) Discusses the function of management and the concept of control and the relationship between control and the managerial function. Concludes with a discussion of the relationship between control and accounting.

(2) Categories: A. Unspecified B. A Priori C. P&C-General

* * * * *

Zannetos, Z. S., "Some Thoughts on Internal Control Systems of the Firm," The Accounting Review (October 1964), pp. 860-868.

(1) Discusses several models of the firm including the classical theory, Taylor's model of rational action, and a modern theory based on cooperative behavior and the implications each has for the control function of the organization. Discusses the effect of organizational structure on performance of the firm and introduces the concept of willful agents within the firm maximizing their own best interests thereby necessitating the use of control systems.

(2) Categories: A. Unspecified B. A Priori C. P&C-General

* * * * *

Categories: A--Source discipline. B--Method of analysis. C--Topic.

Bonini, C. P., R. K. Jaedicke and H. M. Wagner, Management Controls: New Directions in Basic Research (McGraw-Hill, 1964).

(1) Presents seventeen papers and discussion comments of a seminar on basic research in management control held at Stanford University in 1963. Topics include economic theory, simulation, budgeting, and behavioral science as related to control. An excellent collection of basic research papers on control from a group of very distinguished scholars.

(2) Categories: A. Economics/Psychology B. Multiple C. P&C-General

* * * * *

Ijiri, Y., Management Goals and Accounting for Control (Chicago: Rand McNally, 1965).

(1) Presents a discussion and analysis of the relationships between organizational planning and the accounting processes used for control. Includes coverage of specific planning models. Distinguishes between planning and control in analyzing management goals.

(2) Categories: A. Economics/Mathematics B. Modeling C. P&C-General

* * * * *

Solomons, D., Divisional Performance: Measurement and Control (New York: Financial Executives Research Foundations, 1965) also published by R. D. Irwin.

(1) Discusses and reports the results of a field study investigating the relationships between the central and divisional managers of a decentralized company. Includes discussion of divisional evaluation by profits, ROI, Residual Income, and nonprofit measures. Presents an empirical and personal view of the area of decentralized planning and control.

(2) Categories: A. Unspecified B. Field Study C. P&C-General

* * * * *

Ross, W. R., "PERT/Cost Resource Allocation Procedure," The Accounting Review (July 1966), pp. 464-473.

(1) Reviews the concepts and procedures of the PERT/Cost technique and illustrates its usefulness with an example for resource allocation. A good discussion of PERT/Cost.

(2) Categories: A. Mathematics B. Modeling C. P&C-General

* * * * *

Categories: A—Source discipline. B—Method of analysis. C—Topic.

Caplan, E. H., "Behavioral Assumptions of Management Accounting," The Accounting Review (July 1966), pp. 496-509.

(1) Discusses the behavioral assumptions of the traditional management accounting model (work is unpleasant, economic motivation, etc.) and contrasts these with the assumptions of a modern organization-theory model. Classic discussion of the connection between management accounting and the field of human behavior in organizations and a good source of definitions.

(2) Categories: A. Psychology-Organization B. A Priori C. P&C-General

* * * * *

Charnes, A. and W. W. Cooper, "Some Network Characterizations for Mathematical Programming and Accounting Approaches to Planning and Control," The Accounting Review (January 1967), pp. 24-52.

(1) Discusses and illustrates the relationship between accounting and mathematical programming and the possible extensions of accounting to planning and control that might be revealed by such analysis. Network models are used to develop the analysis.

(2) Categories: A. Mathematics/Operations Research B. Modeling C. P&C-General

* * * * *

Cook, D. M., "The Effect of Frequency of Feedback on Attitudes and Performance," Journal of Accounting Research (Supplement 1967), pp. 213-224.

(1) Presents the results of a study designed to test the effect frequency of feedback has on managerial attitude and performance. The findings indicate both interest and satisfaction are related to frequency of performance feedback. An early behavioral study in the area of performance feedback.

(2) Categories: A. Psychology B. Laboratory Study C. P&C-General

* * * * *

Farag, S. M., "A Planning Model for the Divisionalized Enterprise," The Accounting Review (April 1968), pp. 312-320.

(1) Discusses the use of input-output analysis in a planning model of a firm. Includes discussion of the limitations of the method.

(2) Categories: A. Unspecified B. Modeling C. P&C-General

* * * * *

Categories: A—Source discipline. B--Method of analysis. C--Topic.

Caplan, E. H., "Behavioral Assumptions of Management Accounting: Report of a Field Study," The Accounting Review (April 1968), pp. 342-362.

(1) Reports the results of a study designed to determine the behavioral assumptions held by accountants and managers. The findings indicate most held assumptions consistent with the traditional accounting model (see Caplan 1966).

(2) Categories: A. Unspecified B. Field Study C. P&C-General

* * * * *

Livingstone, J. L., "Input-Output Analysis for Cost Accounting, Planning and Control," The Accounting Review (January 1969), pp. 48-64.

(1) Discusses the use of input-output analysis in planning and in evaluating incremental and opportunity costs. Presents a general input-output model and shows that the matrix cost allocation model is a special case of the general model. Illustrated with an example.

(2) Categories: A. Unspecified B. Modeling C. P&C-General (Could also be classified under cost allocation.)

* * * * *

Kinney, W. R., "An Environmental Model for Performance Measurement In Multi-Outlet Businesses," Journal of Accounting Research (Spring 1969), pp. 44-52.

(1) Proposes a performance measurement model which uses statistical estimates of the effects noncontrollable environmental factors have on the manager's peformance, thus providing an objective measure of performance.

(2) Categories: A. Statistics B. Modeling C. P&C-General (Performance Measurement)

* * * * *

Demski, J. S., "Predictive Ability of Alternative Performance Measurement Models," Journal of Accounting Research (Spring 1969a), pp. 96-115.

(1) Presents the results of a simulation study of alternative models of management information designed to test the ability of such models to predict losses. Based on models presented in Demski (1967a).

(2) Categories: A. Unspecified B. A Priori/Simulation C. P&C-General (Performance Measurement) (Could also be under variance analysis.)

Categories: A--Source discipline. B--Method of analysis. C--Topic.

Demski, J. S., "Decision-Performance Control," The Accounting Review (October 1969b), pp. 669-679.

(1) Discusses a broad conceptual view of the management decision process and the interaction between planning and control. Includes discussion of feedback and feed forward. Introduces a new perspective on the process that is different from the traditional planning and control view.

(2) Categories: A. Unspecified B. A Priori C. P&C-General

* * * * *

Demski, J. S., "The Decision Implementation Interface: Effects of Alternative Performance Measurement Models," The Accounting Review (January 1970a), pp. 76-87.

(1) Presents the results of a simulation experiment on three different performance measurement models: direct costing, absorption costing, and an ex post model. The decision setting is single variable. Compare to Demski (1969a) and (1971).

(2) Categories: A. Unspecified B. Simulation C. P&C-General (Also, a modern view of the direct/absorption cost controversy.)

* * * * *

Feltham, G. A., "Some Quantitative Approaches to Planning for Multiproduct Productive Systems," The Accounting Review (January 1970), pp. 11-26.

(1) Discusses the use of linear algebra, linear programming, and goal programming in planning production in a multiproduct process. Includes an example of each technique. Good review of the quantitative methods introduced in the prior ten years.

(2) Categories: A. Unspecified B. A Priori C. P&C-General

* * * * *

Gonedes, N. J., "Accounting for Managerial Control: An Application of Chance-Constrained Programming," Journal of Accounting Research (Spring 1970), pp. 1-20.

(1) Proposes the use of chance-constrained programming in formulating recommendations for optimal managerial control decisions.

(2) Categories: A. Mathematics/Operations Research B. Modeling C. P&C-General

* * * * *

Categories: A—Source discipline. B—Method of analysis. C—Topic.

Livingstone, J. L. and G. L. Salamon, "Relationship Between the Accounting and the Internal Rate of Return Measures: A Synthesis and an Analysis," Journal of Accounting Research (Autumn 1970), pp. 199-216.

(1) Reviews the prior literature on the relationships between the accounting and internal rates of return and draws out some propositions on dealing with reinvestment of cash flows.

(2) Categories: A. Unspecified B. A Priori C. P&C-General

* * * * *

Burns,, T. J., ed., The Behavioral Aspects of Accounting Data for Performance Evaluation (Columbus: College of Administrative Science, The Ohio State University, 1970).

(1) Presents the proceedings of the 1968 accounting symposium held at Ohio State University. Includes the papers and critiques presented and the discussions held at the symposium all relating to the organizational and motivational aspects of accounting for performance evaluation. Coverage includes Human Resource Accounting, PERT, and ROI.

(2) Categories: A. Psychology B. Multiple C. P&C-General

* * * * *

Probst, F. R., "Probabilistic Cost Controls: A Behavioral Dimension," The Accounting Review (January 1971), pp. 113-118.

(1) Reports the results of a field study implementing labor cost control charts in a manufacturing firm. The findings indicated that the foremen would not use charts based on sampling probabilities but would rely on charts based on their subjective probability estimates. An interesting behavioral field study on the use of a decision aid (and the use of subjective probability estimates).

(2) Categories: A. Unspecified B. Field Study C. P&C-General

* * * * *

Demski, J. S., "Implementation Effects of Alternative Performance Measurement Models in a Multivariable Context," The Accounting Review (April 1971), pp. 268-278.

(1) Presents the results of a simulation experiment on three different performance measurement models in a multivariable decision setting. Compare to Demski (1970).

(2) Categories: A. Unspecified B. Simulation C. P&C-General (Performance Measurement)

* * * * *

Categories: A—Source discipline. B—Method of analysis. C—Topic.

Godfrey, J. T., "Short-Run Planning in a Decentralized Firm," The Accounting Review (April 1971), pp. 282-297.

(1) Presents a short-run planning model based on linear programming and contrasts this model with the decomposition model.

(2) Categories: A. Unspecified B. Modeling C. P&C-General

* * * * *

Hinomoto, H., "Optimum Strategies for Management Information Processing and Control," Journal of Accounting Research (Autumn 1971), pp. 253-267.

(1) Analyzes the control process when task performance tends to deteriorate over time in a multiactivity setting.

(2) Categories: A. Unspecified B. Modeling C. P&C-General

* * * * *

Brenner, V. C., C. W. Carmack and M. G. Weinstein, "An Empirical Test of the Motivation-Hygiene Theory," Journal of Accounting Research (Autumn 1971), pp. 359-366.

(1) Reports the results of a questionnaire study designed to test Herzberg's Motivation-Hygiene Theory as an alternative to Maslow's Theory. The findings indicate a lack of support for Herzberg's theory. While not run in a management accounting setting this study discusses many topics of interest to those involved in motivating professionals.

(2) Categories: A. Psychology B. Field Study C. P&C-General

* * * * *

Butterworth, J. E. and B. A. Sigloch, "A Generalized Multi-Stage Input-Output Model and Some Derived Equivalent Systems," The Accounting Review (October 1971), pp. 700-716.

(1) Presents a general multi-stage input-output model from which alternative forms are derived for specific cases. Models which have previously appeared in the literature are analyzed and related to this general model.

(2) Categories: A. Unspecified B. Modeling C. P&C-General

* * * * *

Categories: A--Source discipline. B--Method of analysis. C--Topic.

Caplan, E. H., Management Accounting and Behavioral Science (Reading, Mass.: Addison Wesley Publishing Company, 1971).

(1) Discusses the classical and modern organization theories of management and the implications of each for the theory and practice of accounting. Includes specific coverage of budgeting and performance measurement and evaluation. An early synthesis of accounting and the behavioral sciences. Topical coverage is similar to Caplan (1966 and 1968).

(2) Categories: A. Organization Theory/Economics B. A Priori C. P&C-General

* * * * *

Sorensen, J. E. and D. D. Franks, "The Relative Contribution of Ability, Self-Esteem and Evaluative Feedback to Performance: Implications for Accounting Systems," The Accounting Review (October 1972), pp. 735-746.

(1) Reports the results of a study on the influence that ability, self-esteem, and style of feedback have on performance of goal setting. Discusses the results and their implications for management accounting including form of reports, feedback, and evaluation of budget estimates.

(2) Categories: A. Unspecified B. Laboratory/Field Experiment C. P&C-General

* * * * *

Stallman, J. C., "A Framework for Evaluating Cost Control Procedures for a Process," The Accounting Review (October 1972), pp. 774-790.

(1) Discusses cost control and presents a framework for evaluating the control procedures of a manufacturing firm. The model includes both efficiency costs and the costs of the various control procedures and allows calculation of the optimum amount of control effort.

(2) Categories: A. Unspecified B. Modeling C. P&C-General

* * * * *

Demski, J. S., "Optimal Performance Measurement," Journal of Accounting Research (Autumn 1972b), pp. 243-258.

(1) Discusses the concept of optimal performance measurement in a multi-person world and discusses several management accounting constructs including allocation and controllable/non-controllable costs.

(2) Categories: A. Economics B. Modeling C. P&C-General

* * * * *

Categories: A—Source discipline. B—Method of analysis. C—Topic.

Khandwalla, P. N., "The Effect of Different Types of Competition on the Use of Management Controls," Journal of Accounting Research (Autumn 1972), pp. 275-285.

(1) Reports the extent to which competitive conditions affect the management controls utilized by an organization. An interesting organization/environment-accounting system study.

(2) Categories: A. Unspecified B. Empirical C. P&C-General

* * * * *

Ishikawa, A. and C. H. Smith, "A Feedforward Control System for Organizational Planning and Control," Abacus (December 1972), pp. 163-180.

(1) Discusses the role of anticipatory control in planning and control systems as differentiated from feedback and adaptive control and illustrates its use in an actual setting by reference to a mathematical programming model.

(2) Categories: A. Engineering B. Modeling C. P&C-General

* * * * *

Hopwood, A. G., "An Empirical Study of the Role of Accounting Data in Performance Evaluation," Journal of Accounting Research (Supplement 1972), pp. 156-193.

(1) Reports the results of a questionnaire study designed to determine how accounting data are used in evaluating the performance of managers and the relationship of its use to job tension and to cost tension measures.

(2) Categories: A. Psychology B. Field Study C. P&C-General (Performance Evaluation)

* * * * *

Corcoran, A. W. and W. E. Leininger, "Stochastic Process Costing Models," The Accounting Review (January 1973), pp. 105-114.

(1) Proposes two models of process costing based on stochastic flows of the product through the production process. Illustrates both models and discusses the analysis of variances. Continues the mathematical modeling of accounting systems and specifically the input-output literature (Livingstone (1969) and Feltham (1970)).

(2) Categories: A. Unspecified B. Modeling C. P&C-General

* * * * *

Categories: A--Source discipline. B--Method of analysis. C--Topic.

Hopwood, A. G., "Leadership Climate and the Use of Accounting Data in Performance Evaluation," The Accounting Review (July 1974), pp. 485-495.

(1) Reports the results of a study designed to investigate the relationship between certain managerial factors and the use which is made of accounting data in performance evaluation. The findings indicated several relationships with implications for mangerial accounting.

(2) Categories: A. Psychology B. Field Study C. P&C-General (Performance Evaluation)

* * * * *

Gonedes, N. J. and Y. Ijiri, "Improving Subjective Probability Assessments for Planning and Control in Team-Like Organizations," Journal of Accounting Research (Autumn 1974), pp. 251-269.

(1) Discusses the use of scoring rules and a model based on Bayes' Theorem to improve planning and control probability assessments in a team-like organization.

(2) Categories: A. Mathematics B. Modeling C. P&C-General

* * * * *

Parker, L. D., "Goal Congruence: A Misguided Accounting Concept," Abacus (June 1976), pp. 3-13.

(1) Discusses organization goals and the concept of goal congruence and argues that congruence within the context of budgeting is neither attainable nor usable.

(2) Categories: A. Unspecified B. A Priori C. P&C-General

* * * * *

Cammann, C., "Effects of the Use of Control Systems," Accounting, Organizations and Society (November 1976), pp. 301-314.

(1) Presents the results of a study on the moderating effects subordinate participation in decision making and subordinate job difficulty have on the behavioral responses to the use of control systems. The findings indicate both factors moderate the ways subordinates responded to the use of control systems.

(2) Categories: A. Psychology B. Field Study C. P&C-General

* * * * *

Categories: A—Source discipline. B—Method of analysis. C—Topic.

Rahman, M. and A. M. McCosh, "The Influence of Organizational and Personal Factors on the Use of Accounting Information: An Empirical Study," Accounting, Organizations and Society (November 1976), pp. 339-355.

(1) Reports the results of a study on the relationship between styles of using accounting information for control and performance measurement and job related traits and organizational factors. Concludes that several relevant social and psychological aspects need to be considered in the design of a system.

(2) Categories: A. Organizational Theory B. Field Study C. P&C-General

* * * * *

Hopwood, A. G., Accounting and Human Behavior (Englewood Cliffs, N.J.: Prentice-Hall, 1976).

(1) Discusses the developments in the behavioral and social aspects of accounting. Includes coverage of control, budgeting, performance evaluation, decision making, the use of external reports, and designing accounting systems. Presents a good synthesis of the work in the area of accounting and human behavior.

(2) Categories: A. Psychology B. A Priori/Review C. P&C-General

* * * * *

Sorensen, J. E. and H. D. Grove, "Cost-Outcome and Cost-Effectiveness Analysis: Emerging Nonprofit Performance Evaluation Techniques," The Accounting Review (July 1977), pp. 658-675.

(1) Discusses several contemporary approaches to performance evaluation in nonprofit service organizations and proposes cost-outcome and cost-effectiveness methods for improving their usefulness. Illustrates with a combined example.

(2) Categories: A. Unspecified B. Modeling C. P&C-General (Performance Evaluation)

* * * * *

San Miguel, J., "The Behavioral Sciences and Concepts and Standards for Management Planning and Control," Accounting, Organizations and Society (November 1977), pp. 177-186.

(1) Reviews the literature on individuals, small groups, and organizations and the implications of this research for management accounting. Concludes that studies on individuals and small groups are inseparable from studies of complex organizations.

(2) Categories: A. Behavioral B. A Priori C. P&C-General

* * * * *

Categories: A--Source discipline. B--Method of analysis. C--Topic.

Birnberg, J. G., I. H. Frieze and M. D. Shields, "The Role of Attribution Theory in Control Systems," Accounting, Organizations and Society (December 1977), pp. 189-200.

(1) Presents a model of the management control process from the perspective of attribution theory, which describes how people seek and use information to structure and control their social environment. Includes discussion of feedback and performance reports.

(2) Categories: A. Psychology B. A Priori C. P&C-General

* * * * *

Loeb, M. and W. A. Magat, "Soviet Success Indicators and the Evaluation of Divisional Management," Journal of Accounting Research (Spring 1978), pp. 103-121.

(1) Presents the results of research on Soviet success indicators and relates it to the study of such indicators in the accounting literature. Suggests a new indicator for use in motivating management.

(2) Categories: A. Economics B. Modeling C. P&C-General (Performance Measurement)

* * * * *

Otley, D. T., "Budget Use and Managerial Performance," Journal of Accounting Research (Spring 1978), pp. 122-149.

(1) Reports the results of a study designed to test the effect style of budget use has on manager performance. The findings indicated different effects than those found in Hopwood (1972).

(2) Categories: A. Unspecified B. Field Study C. P&C-General

* * * * *

Neumann, B. R., "An Empirical Investigation of the Relationship Between an AID Hospital Classification Model and Accounting Measures of Performance," Journal of Accounting Research (Spring 1979), pp. 123-139.

(1) Presents the results of a study which relates certain decision variables that can be used to control hospital costs to a classification of hospitals derived from an AID (Automatic Interaction Detector) analysis. An analysis of the cost structures of 5 hospitals is shown.

(2) Categories: A. Unspecified B. Empirical Analysis of Data Bases C. P&C-General

* * * * *

Categories: A--Source discipline. B--Method of analysis. C--Topic.

Jiambalvo, J., "Performance Evaluation and Directed Job Effort: Model Development and Analysis in a CPA Firm Setting," Journal of Accounting Research (Autumn 1979), pp. 436-455.

(1) Presents and tests a model of the effect that the performance evaluation process has on the motivation of CPAs to engage in certain classes of job behaviors. The results indicate that perceptions of effort-reward relationships and intrinsic aspects of the job predict job effort better than job performance. While oriented toward a CPA Firm setting, this study continues the literature on the behavioral aspects of accounting.

(2) Categories: A. Psychology B. Field Study C. P&C-General (Performance Evaluation)

* * * * *

Maher, M. W., K. V. Ramanathan and R. B. Peterson, "Preference Congruence, Information Accuracy, and Employee Performance: A Field Study," Journal of Accounting Research (Autumn 1979), pp. 476-503.

(1) Reports the results of a study designed to test the relationship between the existence of goal conflicts and employee peformance in a costly and incomplete information system setting. The findings indicate that performance is related to the sources of conflict studied.

(2) Categories: A. Economics/Psychology B. Field Study C. P&C-General (Performance Evaluation)

* * * * *

Jacobs, F. and K. S. Lorek, "A Note on the Time-Series Properties of Control Data in an Accounting Environment," Journal of Accounting Research (Autumn 1979), pp. 618-621.

(1) Presents empirical evidence on the time-series properties of actual direct materials usage and electric power consumption of a large firm. The results indicate that the Box-Jenkins ARIMA models fit the data.
(2) Categories: A. Unspecified B. Empirical Study C. P&C-General

* * * * *

Vancil, R. F., Decentralization: Managerial Ambiguity by Design (Homewood, Illinois: Dow Jones-Irwin, 1979).

(1) Presents a theory of decentralization that includes autonomy, measurements and rewards, and responsibility and control. Includes a detailed presentation of the results of a survey designed to measure the various theoretical concepts in an exploratory manner. Contributes a synthesized theory of decentralized management.

(2) Categories: A. Unspecified B. Survey C. P&C-General

Categories: A--Source discipline. B--Method of analysis. C--Topic.

Amey, L. R., "Towards a New Perspective on Accounting Control," Accounting, Organizations and Society (March 1980), pp. 247-258.

(1) Discusses the objectives and performance measures appropriate to complex open system organizations and concludes the objective should be to maximize adaptability subject to a minimum level of stability. Includes discussion of aggregate (accounting period) and costing period (variance analysis) performance measures which this implies.

(2) Categories: A. Systems/Organization Theories B. A Priori C. P&C-General

* * * * *

Otley, D. T. and A. J. Berry, "Control, Organization and Accounting," Accounting, Organizations and Society (July 1980), pp. 231-244.

(1) Discusses the applicability of a cybernetic model of control to control in organizations and in particular to the role of accounting information systems.

(2) Categories: A. Unspecified B. A Priori C. P&C-General

* * * * *

Shields, M. D., "Some Effects of Information Load on Search Patterns Used to Analyze Performance Reports," Accounting, Organizations and Society (December 1980), pp. 429-442.

(1) Reports the results of a study designed to test how the amount of information in a performance report influences the report analysis procedure. The findings in general did not support the hypotheses.

(2) Categories: A. Psychology B. Process Tracing/Experiment C. P&C-General

* * * * *

Hirst, M. K., "Accounting Information and the Evaluation of Subordinates Performance: A Situational Approach," The Accounting Review (October 1981), pp. 771-784.

(1) Discusses the perception of accounting performance measures as incomplete in an uncertain task setting and considers whether the existence of dysfunctional effects of performance measures is also a function of task uncertainty.

(2) Categories: A. Psychology B. A Priori C. P&C-General (Performance Evaluation)

* * * * *

Categories: A—Source discipline. B—Method of analysis. C—Topic.

Brownell, P., "The Role of Accounting Data in Performance Evaluation, Budgetary Participation, and Organizational Effectiveness," Journal of Accounting Research (Spring 1982), pp. 12-27.

(1) Reports the results of a study designed to reconcile the different results reported in Hopwood (1972) and Otley (1978). The results indicate that budgetary participation moderates the effect evaluation style has on performance and that budget-focused leadership in most effective under conditions of high participation.

(2) Categories: A. Psychology B. Field Study C. P&C-General

* * * * *

Jiambalvo, J., "Measures of Accuracy and Congruence in the Performance Evaluation of CPA Personnel: Replication and Extentions," Journal of Accounting Research (Spring 1982), pp. 152-161.

(1) Presents the results of a study designed to test the importance of performance measure accuracy and congruence in CPA firms. The study replicates Maher, et al. (1979) and finds support for the hypothesis that information accuracy and goal congruence are positively correlated with job satisfaction and performance.

(2) Categories: A. Psychology--Organization B. Field Study C. P&C-General

* * * * *

REVIEW PAPERS

7. REVIEW PAPERS AND ANNOTATED BIBLIOGRAPHIES (pp. 213-217)

This is a subset of other recently produced bibliographies and review papers which could reduce costs of reviewing the literature. Each provides a good overview of a subset of the literature. (The papers in this category are listed alphabetically instead of chronologically.)

AAA, Committee on Concepts and Standards-Management Planning and Control, Managerial Accounting Literature Abstracts (AAA, 1976).

This annotated bibliography contains more than 300 management accounting articles from 1955 through 1975, including about 130 articles in professional journals. This is a very good source of information about articles published in that period.

Baiman, S., "Agency Research in Managerial Accounting: A Survey," Journal of Accounting Literature (Spring 1982), pp. 154-213.

A very comprehensive review of agency research. Includes a short annotated bibliography.

Brownell, P., "Participation in the Budgeting Process - When it Works and When it Doesn't," Journal of Accounting Literature (Spring 1982), pp. 124-153.

Comprehensive review of participation in budgeting literature. Includes a short annotated bibliography.

Demski, J. and D. Kreps, "Models in Managerial Accounting," Journal of Accounting Research (Supplement 1982), pp. 117-148.

Extensive review of the modeling literature from 1970-1982, including management science applications, information economics, and the incentive contracting literature.

Dopuch, N. and L. Revsine, eds., Accounting Research 1960-1970: A Critical Evaluation (Center for International Education and Research in Accounting: University of Illinois, 1973).

Presents the proceedings of a conference on research in accounting held at the University of Illinois in 1971. The section on management accounting research contains addresses by R. N. Anthony, J. S. Demski, and T. R. Dyckman.

Epstein, M. J. and Epstein, J. B., "An Annotated Bibliography of Scientific Management and Standard Costing to 1920," Abacus (December 1974), pp. 165-174.

An annotated bibliography covering eighty-one articles.

Horngren, C. T., "Management Accounting: Where Are We?" in Management Accounting and Control (Robert Beyer Lecture Series: University of Wisconsin-Madison, 1975).

Discusses the evolution of management accounting from its early "search for truth" orientation through its focus on decision-making to its present treatment of information as an economic good.

Jensen, R. E., , "Some Thoughts on Quantitative Models and Applications in Managerial Accounting," The Accounting Journal (Winter 1977/78), pp. 244-276.

Annotated comprehensive bibliography of quantitative methods in accounting. Includes about 200 items.

Kaplan, R. S., "The Significance and Investigation of Cost Variances: Survey and Extensions," Journal of Accounting Research (Autumn 1975), pp. 311-337.
Reviews the models proposed in the literature for assessing the significance of cost variances within a taxonomy based on the assumptions and purposes of the models. Includes discussion of models from the statistics, management science, and accounting literatures. A good review and taxonomy of the various variance investigation models.

Kaplan, R. S., "Application of Quantitative Models in Mangerial Accounting: A State of the Art Survey," in Management Accounting - State of the Art (Robert Beyer Lecture Series: University of Wisconsin - Madison, 1977). Reprinted in The Accounting Journal (Winter 1977-78).

A classic review, focusing on applications of management science models to managerial accounting.

Kaplan, R. S., "The Impact of Management Accounting Research on Policy and Practice," The Impact of Accounting Research on Policy and Practice, 1981 Proceedings of the Arthur Young Professors' Roundtable, J. Buckley, ed. (Reston, VA: The Council of Arthur Young Professors, 1981).

Brief survey of management accounting research. Review of evidence that quantitative methods in managerial accounting are (not) being applied by practitioners.

Kaplan, R. S., "Measuring Manufacturing Performance: A New Challenge for Managerial Accounting Research," The Accounting Review (October 1983), pp. 686-705.

Reviews implications of managerial accounting literature. Recommends shifting research from externally imposed financial measures to internal non-financial performance measures.

Maher, M. W., "Management Accounting Literature: Past, Present and Future," Unpublished paper presented at the 1982 AAA meetings (University of Michigan, 1982).

Reviews the literature and predicts directions for future research. Emphasizes the importance of positive, economics-based theory.

Prickett, A. L., Classified Cost Accounting Bibliography, Indiana Business Studies, Study No. 29 (Bloomington: The School of Business, Indiana University, 1946).

A classified bibliography containing references from 1890 to 1946. Previously published in 1945 as Indiana Business Study No. 28.

Scapens, R., "Management Accounting - A Survey Paper," Unpublished paper (1982).

A comprehensive review of management accounting covering much of the 1960's, through 1982. Compares practitioner and research literature.

Spicer, B. and V. Ballew, "Management Accounting Systems and the Economics of Internal Organization," Accounting, Organizations, and Society (March 1983), pp. 73-96.

Relates themes in management accounting and control to Williamson's organizational framework and other work in the economics of internal organization.

Sundem, G. L., "Future Directions in Management Accounting Research," Paper presented at the Seventh Accounting Research Convocation at the University of Alabama (November 1981).

Develops taxonomy, evaluates current research, and discusses prospects for managerial accounting research in the taxonomy's three major classes: (1) information system choice, (2) information system design, (3) and information processing.

Tantral, P., "Accounting Literature in Non-Accounting Periodicals: An Assessment and Annotated Bibliography," Doctoral thesis, (New York: New York University School of Business Administration, 1983).

Includes a comprehensive list of accounting references in other journals. Although primarily emphasizing financial accounting it includes many references of interest to students of management accounting literature.

Tiessen, P. and J. H. Waterhouse, "Towards a Descriptive Theory of Management Accounting," Accounting, Organizations, and Society (July 1983), pp. 251-267.

Integrates agency theory, the literature on markets and hierarchies, and contingency theory, and discusses implications for management accounting.

Wells, M. C., A Bibliography of Cost Accounting: Its Origins and Development to 1914 (Urbana: Center for International Education and Research in Accounting, University of Illinois Press, 1978).

A comprehensive bibliography with over 2,000 references.

ALPHABETICAL BIBLIOGRAPHY

ALPHABETICAL BIBLIOGRAPHY

	Page
AAA, "Report of the Committee on Cost Concepts and Standards," The Accounting Review (April 1952), pp. 174-188.	31
AAA, "Tentative Statement of Cost Concepts Underlying Reports for Management Purposes," The Accounting Review (April 1956), pp. 182-193.	32
AAA, "Report of the Committee on Management Accounting," The Accounting Review (April 1959), pp. 207-214.	35
AAA, "Report of the Committee on Management Accounting," The Accounting Review (July 1960), pp. 400-404.	35
AAA, "Report of the Management Accounting Committee," The Accounting Review (July 1962), pp. 523-537.	36
AAA, "Report of the Committee on Managerial Decision Models," The Accounting Review (Supplement 1969), pp. 43-76.	39
AAA, "Report of the Committee on Managerial Accounting," The Accounting Review (Supplement 1970), pp. 1-8.	39
AAA, "Report of the Committee on Managerial Accounting, 1969-1971," The Accounting Review (Supplement 1972), pp. 317-335.	39
AAA, "Report of the Committee on Internal Measurement and Reporting," The Accounting Review (Supplement 1973), pp. 209-241.	40
AAA, "Report of the Committee on Concepts and Standards-Internal Planning and Control," The Accounting Review (Supplement 1974), pp. 79-96.	40
AAA, Committee on Concepts and Standards-Management Planning and Control, Managerial Accounting Literature Abstracts (AAA, 1976).	214
AAA, "Report of the Committee on Concepts and Standards-Managerial Planning and Control," The Accounting Review (Supplement 1977), pp. 55-63.	41
Abdel-khalik, A. R., "The Entropy Law, Accounting Data, and Relevance to Decision Making," The Accounting Review (April 1974), pp. 271-283.	179
Abdel-khalik, A. R. and E. J. Lusk, "Transfer Pricing--A Synthesis," The Accounting Review, (January 1974), pp. 8-23.	188

Page

Adar, Z., A. Barnea and B. Lev, "A Comprehensive Cost-Volume-Profit Analysis Under Uncertainty," The Accounting Review (January 1977), pp. 137-149. 126

Albery, M., "Analysis Versus Interpretation of Cost," The Accounting Review (July 1953), pp. 425-430. 97

Alchian, A. A., and H. Demsetz, "Production, Information Costs, and Economic Organization," American Economic Review (December 1972), pp. 777-795. 69

Amerman, G., "The Mathematics of Variance Analysis I," Accounting Research (July 1953a), pp. 258-269. 171

Amerman, G., "The Mathematics of Variance Analysis II," Accounting Research (October 1953b), pp. 329-350. 171

Amerman, G., "The Mathematics of Variance Analysis III," Accounting Research (January 1954a), pp. 56-79. 172

Amerman, G., "Facts About Direct Costing for Profit Determination," Accounting Research (April 1954b), pp. 154-166. 82

Amey, L. R., "Towards a New Perspective on Accounting Control," Accounting, Organizations and Society (March 1980), pp. 247-258. 211

Anderson, D. R., "The Function of Industrial Controllership," The Accounting Review (January 1944), pp. 55-65. 73

Andersson, H. F., "Allowance for Setup Time Under Standard Costs," The Accounting Review (July 1960), pp. 497-500. 196

Ansari, S. L., "Behavioral Factors in Variance Control: Report on a Laboratory Experiment," Journal of Accounting Research (Autumn 1976), pp. 189-211. 180

Ansari, S. L., "An Integrated Approach to Control System Design," Accounting, Organizations and Society (June 1977), pp. 101-112. 66

Ansari, S. L., "Towards an Open Systems Approach to Budgeting," Accounting, Organizations and Society (February 1980), pp. 149-162. 168

Anthony, R. N., "Cost Concepts for Control," The Accounting Review (April 1957), pp. 229-234. 34

Anton, H. R., "The Funds Statement as an Internal Report to Management," The Accounting Review (January 1955), pp. 71-79. 56

	Page
Argyris, C., The Impact of Budgets on People (The Controllership Foundation, 1952).	161
Argyris, C., "Organizational Learning and Management Information Systems," Accounting, Organizations and Society (June 1977), pp. 113-124.	66
Arrow, K. J., "Control in Large Organizations," Management Science (April 1964), pp. 397-406.	198
Arrow, K. J., The Limits of Organization, (New York: W. W. Norton and Co. Inc., 1974).	69
Ashton, A. H., "An Emprical Study of Budget-Related Predictions of Corporate Executives," Journal of Accounting Research (Autumn 1982), pp. 440-449.	169
Ashton, R. H., "Deviation-Amplifying Feedback and Unintended Consequences of Management Accounting Systems," Accounting, Organizations and Society (November 1976), pp. 289-300.	167
Ashton, R. H., "A Descriptive Study of Information Evaluation," Journal of Accounting Research (Spring 1981), pp. 42-61.	144
Atkinson, A. A., "Information Incentives in a Standard-Setting Model of Control," Journal of Accounting Research (Spring 1979), pp. 1-22.	191
Atwood, P. W., "The Manufacturer Looks at His Cost of Distribution," The Accounting Review (March 1934), pp. 23-28.	91
Avery, H. G., "Accounting for Joint Costs," The Accounting Review (April 1951), pp. 232-238.	101
Avery, H. G. and M. Pollack, "Cost and Output Relationships," The Accounting Review (October 1946), pp. 419-424.	114
Bailey, A. D., "A Dynamic Programming Approach to the Analysis of Different Costing Methods in Accounting for Inventory," The Accounting Review (July 1973), pp. 560-574.	88
Bailey, A. D. and W. J. Boe, "Goal and Resource Transfers in the Multigoal Organization," The Accounting Review (July 1976), pp. 559-573.	188
Baiman, S., "The Evaluation and Choice of Internal Information Systems Within a Multi-person World," Journal of Accounting Research (Spring 1975), pp. 1-15.	47
Baiman, S., "Agency Research in Managerial Accounting: A Survey," Journal of Accounting Literature (Spring 1982), pp. 154-213.	214

	Page
Baiman, S. and J. S. Demski, "Variance Analysis Procedures as Motivation Devices," Management Science (August 1980a), pp. 840-848.	191
Baiman, S. and J. S. Demski, "Economically Optimal Performance Evaluation and Control Systems," Journal of Accounting Research (Supplement 1980b), pp. 184-220.	192
Baker, K. R. and R. E. Taylor, "A Linear Programming Framework for Cost Allocation and External Acquisition When Reciprocal Services Exist," The Accounting Review (October 1979), pp. 784-790.	108
Balachandran, B. and R. Ramakrishnan, "Joint Cost Allocation: A Unified Approach," The Accounting Review (January 1981), pp. 85-96.	110
Balch, J., "Some Aspects of Standard Costs," The Accounting Review (March 1934), pp. 29-32.	94
Baloff, N. and J. W. Kennelly, "Accounting Implications of Product and Process Start-Ups," Journal of Accounting Research (Autumn 1967), pp. 131-143.	116
Banbury, J. and J. E. Nahapiet, "Towards a Framework for the Study of the Antecedents and Consequences of Information Systems in Organizations," Accounting, Organizations and Society (February 1980), pp. 163-178.	67
Banerjee, K. C., "Cost, Price, Profit and Volume Reactions," Accounting Research (October 1954), pp. 343-362.	120
Barefield, R. M., "The Effect of Aggregation on Decision Making Success: A Laboratory Study," Journal of Accounting Research (Autumn 1972), pp. 229-242.	139
Barhydt, D., R. H. Clement, D. W. Lufkin and A. J. Yorke, "Planning Concepts in the 'Tentative Statement of Cost Concepts'," The Accounting Review (October 1957), pp. 593-597.	34
Barton, R. F., "An Experimental Study of the Impact of Competitive Pressures on Overhead Allocation Bids," Journal of Accounting Research (Spring 1969), pp. 116-122.	138
Bashan, O., Y. Goldschmidt, G. Levkowitz and L. Shashua, "Laspeyres Indexes for Variance Analysis in Cost Accounting," The Accounting Review (October 1973), pp. 790-793.	178
Becker, S. W. and D. Green, "Budgeting and Employee Behavior," Journal of Business (October 1962), pp. 392-402.	161

Page

Becker, S. W., J. Ronen and G. H. Sorter, "Opportunity Costs--An Experimental Approach," Journal of Accounting Research (Autumn 1974), pp. 317-329. 140

Beckett, J. A., "A Study of the Principles of Allocating Costs," The Accounting Review (July 1951), pp. 327-333. 101

Bedford, N. M., "The Nature of Business Costs, General Concepts," The Accounting Review (January 1957), pp. 8-14. 33

Beer, S., "Operational Research and Financial Management," Accounting Research (January 1957), pp. 1-13. 148

Benbasat, I. and A. S. Dexter, "Individual Differences in the Use of Decision Support Aids," Journal of Accounting Research (Spring 1982), p. 1-11. 144

Bennett, G. E., "Some Observations on the Application of Manufacturing Expense to Production," The Accounting Review (March 1926), pp. 1-7. 93

Benninger, L. J., "The Traditional vs. the Cost Accounting Concept of Cost," The Accounting Review (October 1949), pp. 387-391. 96

Benninger, L. J., "A Proposed Reconciliation of Standard and Current Material Costs," The Accounting Review (April 1950a), pp. 156-160. 96

Benninger, L. J., "Standard Costs for Income Determination, Control, and Special Studies," The Accounting Review (October 1950b), pp. 378-383. 96

Benninger, L. J., "Development of Cost Accounting Concepts and Principles," The Accounting Review (January 1954), pp. 27-37. 32

Benninger, L. J., "Cost Control as Applied to the Smaller Business Organization," The Accounting Review (January 1956), pp. 95-98. 195

Benninger, L. J., "Accounting Theory and Cost Accounting," The Accounting Review (July 1965), pp. 547-557. 38

Benston, G. J., "The Role of the Firm's Accounting System for Motivation," The Accounting Review (April 1963), pp. 347-354. 197

Benston, G. J., "Multiple Regression Analysis of Cost Behavior," The Accounting Review (October 1966), pp. 657-672. 116

Beranek, W., "A Note on the Equivalence of Certain Capital Budgeting Criteria," The Accounting Review (October 1964), pp. 914-916. 131

Page

Berkow, W. F., "Need for Engineering Influence Upon Accounting Procedures," The Accounting Review (April 1964), pp. 377-386. 98

Bernhard, R. H., "Some Problems in Applying Mathematical Programming to Opportunity Costing," Journal of Accounting Research (Spring 1968), pp. 143-148. 151

Bierman, H., "Pricing Intracompany Transfers," The Accounting Review (July 1959), pp. 429-432. 184

Bierman, H., "Probability, Statistical Decision Theory, and Accounting," The Accounting Review (July 1962), pp. 400-405. 76

Bierman, H., "Inventory Valuation: The Use of Market Prices," The Accounting Review (October 1967), pp. 731-737. 103

Bierman, H., L. Fouraker and R. Jaedicke, "A Use of Probability and Statistics in Performance Evaluation," The Accounting Review (July 1961), pp. 409-417. 172

Billera, L. J., D. C. Heath and R. E. Verrecchia, "A Unique Procedure for Allocating Common Costs from a Production Process," Journal of Accounting Research (Spring 1981), pp. 185-196. 110

Birnberg, J. G. and R. Nath, "Implications of Behavioral Science for Management Accounting," The Accounting Review (July 1967), pp. 468-479. 138

Birnberg, J. G., I. H. Frieze and M. D. Shields, "The Role of Attribution Theory in Control Systems," Accounting, Organizations and Society (December 1977), pp. 189-200. 209

Blocker, J. G., "Budgeting in Relation to Standard Costs," The Accounting Review (June 1936), pp. 117-124. 160

Blocher, E. and C. Stickney, "Duration and Risk Assessments in Capital Budgeting," The Accounting Review (January 1979), pp. 180-188. 136

Bodenhorn, D., "An Economist Looks at Industrial Accounting and Depreciation," The Accounting Review (October 1961), pp. 583-588. 129

Bodnar, G. and E. J. Lusk, "Motivational Considerations in Cost Allocation Systems: A Conditioning Theory Approach," The Accounting Review (October 1977), pp. 857-868. 108

Bonini, C. P., R. K. Jaedicke and H. M. Wagner, Management Controls: New Directions in Basic Research (McGraw-Hill, 1964). 199

	Page
Bornemann, A., "Empirical Cost Study and Economic Theory," The Accounting Review (July 1945), pp. 327-331.	114
Boyd, V. and D. Taylor, "The Magic Words-Managerial Accounting," The Accounting Review (January 1961), pp. 105-112.	35
Bray, F. S., C. Smith and D. R. B. Smith, "Worsted Spinning Costs: A Specific Application of the General Principles of Standard Costing," Accounting Research (July 1949), pp. 163-204.	54
Brenner, V. C., C. W. Carmack and M. G. Weinstein, "An Empirical Test of the Motivation-Hygiene Theory," Journal of Accounting Research (Autumn 1971), pp. 359-366.	204
Brief, R. P. and J. Owen, "A Least Squares Allocation Model," Journal of Accounting Research (Autumn 1968).	104
Brief, R. P. and J. Owen, "Present Value Models and the Multi-Asset Problem," The Accounting Review (October 1973), pp. 690-695.	134
Brown, C., "Human Information Processing for Decision to Investigate Cost Variances," Journal of Accounting Research (Spring 1981), pp. 62-85.	182
Brown, V. H., "Rate of Return: Some Comments on Its Applicability in Capital Budgeting," The Accounting Review (January 1961), pp. 50-62.	129
Brownell, P., "Participation in Budgeting, Locus of Control, and Organizational Effectiveness," The Accounting Review (October 1981), pp. 844-860.	169
Brownell, P., "Participation in the Budgeting Process - When it Works and When it Doesn't," Journal of Accounting Literature (Spring 1982), pp. 124-153.	214
Brownell, P., "A Field Study Examination of Budgetary Participation and Locus of Control," The Accounting Review (October 1982), pp. 766-777.	169
Brownell, P., "The Role of Accounting Data in Performance Evaluation, Budgetary Participation, and Organizational Effectiveness," Journal of Accounting Research (Spring 1982), pp. 12-27.	212
Brummet, R. L., "Direct Costing - Should It Be a Controversial Issue?" The Accounting Review (July 1955), pp. 439-443.	82
Brummet, R. L., E. G. Flamholtz and W. C. Pyle, "Human Resource Measurement - A Challenge for Accountants," The Accounting Review (April 1968), pp. 217-224.	58

Page

Bruns, W. J., "Inventory Valuation and Management Decisions," The Accounting Review (April 1965), pp. 345-357. 137

Bruns, W. J., "The Accounting Period and Its Effect Upon Management Decisions," Journal of Accounting Research (Supplement 1966), pp. 1-20. 137

Bruns, W. J., "Accounting Information and Decision Making: Some Behavioral Hypotheses," The Accounting Review (July 1968), pp. 469-480. 138

Bruns, W. J., and J. Waterhouse, "Budgetary Control and Organization Structure," Journal of Accounting Research (Autumn 1975), pp. 177-203. 166

Brush, L. F., "Graphic Analysis of Expense," The Accounting Review (October 1943), pp. 331-338. 119

Buckman, A. G. and B. L. Miller, "Optimal Investigation of a Multiple Cost Processes System," Journal of Accounting Research (Spring 1982), pp. 28-41. 183

Burke, W. L., "Cost Allocation and Distribution - Merchandise Accounting," The Accounting Review (October 1963), pp. 802-812. 102

Burns,, T. J., ed., The Behavioral Aspects of Accounting Data for Performance Evaluation (Columbus: College of Administrative Science, The Ohio State University, 1970). 203

Butterworth, J. E., "The Accounting System as An Information Function," Journal of Accounting Research (Spring 1972), pp. 1-27. 46

Butterworth, J. E. and B. A. Sigloch, "A Generalized Multi-Stage Input-Output Model and Some Derived Equivalent Systems," The Accounting Review (October 1971), pp. 700-716. 204

Buzby, S., "Extending the Applicability of Probabilistic Management Planning and Control Models," The Accounting Review (January 1974), pp. 42-49. 117

Byrne, R., A. Charnes, W. W. Cooper and K. Kortanek, "Some New Approaches to Risk," The Accounting Review (January 1968), pp. 18-37. 132

Callen, J., "Financial Cost Allocation: A Game Theoretic Approach," The Accounting Review (April 1978), pp. 303-308. 108

Cammann, C., "Effects of the Use of Control Systems," Accounting, Organizations and Society (November 1976), pp. 301-314. 207

	Page
Canning, J. B., "Cost of Production and Market Price," The Accounting Review (September 1931), pp. 161-164.	93
Caplan, E. H., "Behavioral Assumptions of Management Accounting," The Accounting Review (July 1966), pp. 496-509.	200
Caplan, E. H., "Behavioral Assumptions of Management Accounting: Report of a Field Study," The Accounting Review (April 1968), pp. 342-362.	201
Caplan, E. H., Management Accounting and Behavioral Science (Reading, Mass.: Addison Wesley Publishing Company, 1971).	205
Carlisle, H. M., "Cost Accounting for Advanced Technology Programs, The Accounting Review (January 1966), pp. 115-120.	56
Castenholz, W. B., "The Proper Treatment of Distribution Costs." The Accounting Review (March 1927), pp. 19-27.	89
Castenholz, W. B., "Selling and Administrative Expense as a Basis for Sales Control and Cost Reduction," The Accounting Review (June 1931), pp. 125-130.	90
Castenholz, W. B., "What Constitutes Material Cost of Production," The Accounting Review (October 1958), pp. 650-653.	98
Charnes, A., C. Colantoni, W. W. Cooper and K. O. Kortanek, "Economic, Social, and Enterprise Accounting and Mathematical Models," The Accounting Review (January 1972), pp. 85-108.	153
Charnes, A. and W. W. Cooper, "Some Network Characterizations for Mathematical Programming and Accounting Approaches to Planning and Control," The Accounting Review (January 1967), pp. 24-52.	200
Charnes, A., W. W. Cooper, and Y. Ijiri, "Breakeven Budgeting and Programming to Goals," Journal of Accounting Research (Spring 1963), pp. 16-43.	197
Chenault, L. R., "Business Behavior and the Theory of the Firm," The Accounting Review (October 1954), pp. 645-651.	68
Cherrington, D. J. and J. O. Cherrington, "Appropriate Reinforcement Contingencies in the Budgeting Process," Journal of Accounting Research (Supplement 1973), pp. 225-253.	164
Chiu, J. S. and D. T. DeCoster, "Multiple Product Costing by Multiple Correlation Analysis," The Accounting Review (October 1966), pp. 673-681.	103
Christensen, C., "Construction of Present Value Tables for Use in Evaluation of Capital Investment Opportunities," The Accounting Review (October 1955), pp. 666-672.	128

Page

Christensen, J., "The Determination of Performance Standards and Participation," Journal of Accounting Research (Autumn 1982), pp. 589-603. 192

Chumachenko, N. G., "Once Again: The Volume-Mix-Price/Cost Budget Variance Analysis," The Accounting Review (October 1968), pp. 753-762. 176

Churchill, N., "Linear Algebra and Cost Allocations: Some Examples," The Accounting Review (October 1964), pp. 894-904. 102

Clark, J. M., Studies in the Economics of Overhead Costs (University of Chicago Press, 1923). 145

Coase, R. H., "The Nature of the Firm," Economica, (November 1937), pp. 386-405. 68

Cohen, M. A. and R. Halperin, "Optimal Inventory Order Policy for a Firm Using the LIFO Inventory Costing Method," Journal of Accounting Research (Autumn 1980), pp. 375-389. 155

Cohen, S. I. and M. Loeb, "Public Goods, Common Inputs, and the Efficiency of Full Cost Allocations," The Accounting Review (April 1982), pp. 336-347. 111

Colantoni, C. S., R. P. Manes and A. Whinston, "Programming, Profit Rates and Pricing Decisions," The Accounting Review (July 1969), pp. 467-481. 123

Colantoni, C. S., R. P. Manes and A. Whinston, "A Unified Approach to the Theory of Accounting and Information Systems," The Accounting Review (January 1971), pp. 90-102. 65

Collins, F., "The Interaction of Budget Characteristics and Personality Variables with Budgetary Response Attitudes," The Accounting Review (April 1978), pp. 324-335. 167

Collins, F., "Managerial Accounting Systems and Organizational Control: A Role Perspective," Accounting, Organizations and Society (May 1982), pp. 107-122. 67

Comiskey, E. E., "Cost Control by Regression Analysis," The Accounting Review (April 1966), pp. 235-238. 115

Cook, D. M., "The Effect of Frequency of Feedback on Attitudes and Performance," Journal of Accounting Research (Supplement 1967), pp. 213-224. 200

Corcoran, A. W. and W. E. Leininger, "Stochastic Process Costing Models," The Accounting Review (January 1973), pp. 105-114. 206

	Page
Coughlan, J., "Industrial Accounting," The Accounting Review (July 1959), pp. 415-428.	129
Cox, C. E., "What is Cost?" The Accounting Review (December 1930), pp. 288-297.	93
Crandall, R. H., "Information Economics and Its Implications for the Further Development of Accounting Theory," The Accounting Review (July 1969), pp. 457-466.	44
Crawford, J. R., "Statistical Accounting Procedures," The Accounting Review (July 1944), pp. 266-270.	30
Crossman, P. T., "The Function of the Cost Accountant in Cost Control," The Accounting Review (January 1953a), pp. 25-31.	194
Crossman, P. T., "The Genesis of Cost Control," The Accounting Review (October 1953b), pp. 522-527.	194
Crossman, P. T., "The Nature of Management Accounting," The Accounting Review (April 1958), pp. 222-227.	76
Crum, L. R., "The Role of Cost Accounting in Cost Control," The Accounting Review (July 1953), pp. 363-372.	194
Cushing, B. E., "Some Observations on Demski's Ex Post Accounting System," The Accounting Review (October 1968), pp. 668-671.	176
Cyert, R. M. and J. March, Behavioral Theory of the Firm (Englewood Cliffs, N.J.: Prentice Hall, Inc., 1963).	68
Dalton, F. E. and J. B. Miner, "The Role of Accounting Training in Top Management Decision Making," The Accounting Review (January 1970), pp. 134-139.	138
Danford, F., "Some Modern Developments in Accounting for Manufacturing Enterprises," The Accounting Review (June 1933), pp. 119-121.	52
Davidson, H. J. and R. M. Trueblood, "Accounting for Decision-Making," The Accounting Review (October 1961), pp. 577-582.	149
Davidson, S., "Old Wine into New Bottles," The Accounting Review (April 1963a), pp. 278-284.	36
Davidson, S., "The Day of Reckoning: Managerial Analysis and Accounting Theory," Journal of Accounting Research (Autumn 1963b), pp. 117-126.	37
Davis, P. M., "Marginal Analysis of Credit Sales," The Accounting Review (January 1966), pp. 121-126.	150

	Page
Dean, J., "Correlation Analysis of Cost Variation," The Accounting Review (March 1937), pp. 55-60.	171
DeCoster, D. T., "Measurement of the Idle-Capacity Variance," The Accounting Review (April 1966), pp. 297-302.	174
DeCoster, D. T. and J. P. Fertakis, "Budget-Induced Pressure and Its Relationship to Supervisory Behavior," Journal of Accounting Research (Autumn 1968), pp. 237-246.	162
Demski, J. S., "An Accounting System Structured on a Linear Programming Model," The Accounting Review (October 1967a), pp. 701-712.	175
Demski, J. S., "Analyzing the Effectiveness of the Traditional Standard Cost Variance Model," Management Accounting (October 1967b), pp. 9-19.	175
Demski, J. S., "Predictive Ability of Alternative Performance Measurement Models," Journal of Accounting Research (Spring 1969a), pp. 96-115.	201
Demski, J. S., "Decision-Performance Control," The Accounting Review (October 1969b), pp. 669-679.	202
Demski, J. S., "The Decision Implementation Interface: Effects of Alternative Performance Measurement Models," The Accounting Review (January 1970a), pp. 76-87.	202
Demski, J. S., "Some Decomposition Results for Information Evaluation," Journal of Accounting Research (Autumn 1970b), pp. 178-198.	45
Demski, J. S., "Implementation Effects of Alternative Performance Measurement Models in a Multivariable Context," The Accounting Review (April 1971), pp. 268-278.	203
Demski, J. S., "Information Improvement Bounds," Journal of Accounting Research (Spring 1972a), pp. 58-76.	46
Demski, J. S., "Optimal Performance Measurement," Journal of Accounting Research (Autumn 1972b), pp. 243-258.	205
Demski, J. S., "Uncertainty and Evaluation Based on Controllable Performance," Journal of Accounting Research (Autumn 1976), pp. 230-245.	190
Demski, J. S., Information Analysis, Second Edition, (Reading, Mass.: Addison-Wesley Publishing Company, 1980).	50

Page

Demski, J. S. and G. A. Feltham, Cost Determination: A Conceptual Approach, (Ames, Iowa: Iowa State University Press, 1976). 48

Demski, J. S. and G. A. Feltham, "Economic Incentives in Budgetary Control Systems," The Accounting Review (April 1978), pp. 336-359. 191

Demski, J. S. and D. Kreps, "Models in Managerial Accounting," Journal of Accounting Research (Supplement 1982), pp. 117-148. 214

Dermer, J. D., "Cognitive Characteristics and the Perceived Importance of Information," The Accounting Review (July 1973), pp. 511-519. 139

Dermer, J. and J. P. Siegel, "The Role of Behavioral Measures in Accounting for Human Resources," The Accounting Review (January 1974), pp. 88-97. 59

de Swardt, G. D., "A Theory of Cost and Cost Accounting I," Accounting Research (April 1952a), pp. 150-167. 32

de Swardt, G. D., "A Theory of Cost and Cost Accounting II," Accounting Research (July 1952b), pp. 237-265. 32

Devine, C. T., "Cost Accounting and Pricing Policies," The Accounting Review (October 1950), pp. 384-389. 147

Dhaliwal, D. S., G. L. Salamon and E. D. Smith, "The Effect of Owner versus Management Control on the Choice of Accounting Methods," Journal of Accounting and Economics (July 1982), pp. 41-56. 71

Dickinson, J. P., "Cost-Volume-Profit Analysis Under Uncertainty," Journal of Accounting Research (Spring 1974), pp. 182-187. 125

Dillon, R. D. and J. F. Nash, "The True Relevance of Relevant Costs," The Accounting Review (January 1978), pp. 11-17. 154

Dittman, D. and P. Prakash, "Cost Variance Investigation: Markovian Control of Markov Processes," Journal of Accounting Research (Spring 1978), pp. 14-25. 181

Dittman, D. and P. Prakash, "Cost Variance Investigation: Markovian Control Versus Optimal Control," The Accounting Review (April 1979), pp. 358-373. 182

Dixon, R. L., "Fixed and Variable Costs," The Accounting Review (June 1940), pp. 218-222. 95

Page

Dixon, R. L., "The Need for a Statement of the Principles Underlying Cost Accounting," The Accounting Review (July 1943), pp. 256-258. 30

Dohr, J. L., "Budgetary Control and Standard Costs in Industrial Accounting," The Accounting Review (March 1932), pp. 31-33. 159

Donner, F. G., "General Motors Budgetary Control," The Accounting Review (March 1932), pp. 22-30. 159

Dopuch, N., "Mathematical Programming and Accounting Approaches to Incremental Cost Analysis," The Accounting Review (October 1963). 121

Dopuch, N., J. G. Birnberg and J. S. Demski, "An Extension of Standard Cost Variance Analysis," The Accounting Review (July 1967), pp. 526-536. 175

Dopuch, N. and D. Drake, "Accounting Implications of a Mathematical Programming Approach to the Transfer Price Problem," Journal of Accounting Research (Spring 1964), pp. 10-24. 185

Dopuch, N. and L. Revsine, eds., Accounting Research 1960-1970: A Critical Evaluation (Center for International Education and Research in Accounting: University of Illinois, 1973). 214

Dopuch, N. and J. Ronen, "The Effects of Alternative Inventory Valuation Methods," Journal of Accounting Research (Autumn 1973), pp. 191-211. 139

Doyle, L. A., "Uses of Cost Data for Production and Investment Policies," The Accounting Review (July 1950), pp. 274-282. 146

Driver, M. J. and T. J. Mock, "Human Information Processing, Decision Style Theory, and Accounting Information Systems," The Accounting Review (July 1975), pp. 490-508. 140

Drucker, A. P. R., "Budgeting and the Sales Quota," The Accounting Review (September 1929), pp. 175-180. 157

Drucker, A. P. R., "Factory Production Under Budgetary Control," The Accounting Review (December 1930), pp. 301-304. 158

Drucker, A. P. R., "Budgeting and Control of Machinery," The Accounting Review (September 1931), pp. 192-196. 158

Duvall, R. M. and J. Bullock, "Adjusting Rate of Return and Present-Value for Price Level Changes," The Accounting Review (July 1965), pp. 569-573. 132

	Page
Dyckman, T. R., "The Effects of Alternative Accounting Techniques on Certain Management Decisions," Journal of Accounting Research (Spring 1964), pp. 91-107.	137
Dyckman, T. R., "The Investigation of Cost Variances," Journal of Accounting Research (Autumn 1969), pp. 215-244.	177
Eckel, L. G., "Arbitrary and Incorrigible Allocations," The Accounting Review (October 1976), pp. 764-777.	107
Edwards, H. R., M. S. Kem and H. W. Wilder, "The Use of Accounting in Business Policy Determination," The Accounting Review (October 1947), pp. 395-404.	194
Edwards, J. D., "Reports to Top Management," The Accounting Review (January 1957), pp. 56-59.	75
Edwards, J. D., "This New Costing Concept - Direct Costing?" The Accounting Review (October 1958), pp. 561-567.	83
Elliott, V. L., "Functions and Activities of the Controller's Department," The Accounting Review (June 1940), pp. 185-190.	72
Epstein, M. J. and Epstein, J. B., "An Annotated Bibliography of Scientific Management and Standard Costing to 1920," Abacus (December 1974), pp. 165-174.	214
Ewusi-Mensah, K., "The External Organizational Environment and Its Impact on Management Information Systems," Accounting, Organizations and Society (December 1981), pp. 301-316.	43
Farag, S. M., "A Planning Model for the Divisionalized Enterprise," The Accounting Review (April 1968), pp. 312-320.	200
Fekrat, M. A., "The Conceptual Foundations of Absorption Costing," The Accounting Review (April 1972), pp. 351-355.	88
Feltham, G. A., "The Value of Information," The Accounting Review. (October 1968), pp. 684-696.	44
Feltham, G. A., "Some Quantitative Approaches to Planning for Multiproduct Productive Systems," The Accounting Review (January 1970), pp. 11-26.	202
Feltham, G. A., Information Evaluation, Studies in Accounting Research #5, (American Accounting Association, 1972).	47
Feltham, G. A., "Cost Aggregation: An Information Economic Analysis," Journal of Accounting Research (Spring 1977), pp. 42-70.	48

	Page
Feltham, G. A. and J. S. Demski, "The Use of Models in Information Evaluation," The Accounting Review (October 1970), pp. 623-640.	45
Ferrara, W. L., "Idle Capacity as a Loss - Fact or Fiction," The Accounting Review (July 1960), pp. 490-496.	84
Ferrara, W. L., "Overhead Costs and Income Measurement," The Accounting Review (January 1961), pp. 63-70.	84
Ferrara, W. L., "Relevant Costing - Two Points of View," The Accounting Review (October 1963), pp. 719-722.	86
Ferrara, W. L., "Probabilistic Approaches to Return on Investment and Residual Income," The Accounting Review (July 1977), pp. 597-604.	135
Ferrara, W. L. and J. C. Hayya, "Toward Probabilistic Profit Budgets," Management Accounting (October 1970), pp. 23-28.	163
Ferrara, W. L., J. C. Hayya and D. A. Nachman, "Normalcy of Profit in the Jaedicke-Robichek Model," The Accounting Review (April 1972), pp. 299-307.	124
Fess, P. E., "The Theory of Manufacturing Costs," The Accounting Review (July 1961), pp. 446-453.	85
Fess, P. E., "The Relevant Costing Concept for Income Measurement-Can it Be Defended," The Accounting Review (October 1963), pp. 723-732.	86
Fess, P. E. and W. L. Ferrara, "The Period Cost Concept for Income Measurement - Can It be Defended?" The Accounting Review (October 1961), pp. 598-602.	85
Feyerharm, R. W., "Budgetary Accounting Procedures and Accounting Forms for Small Colleges and Universities," The Accounting Review (January 1955), pp. 80-85.	56
Field, J. E., "Inventory Valuation and the Short-Run Cost Function," The Accounting Review (January 1960), pp. 104-110.	115
Field, J. E., "Toward a Multi-Level, Multi-Goal Information System," The Accounting Review (July 1969), pp. 593-599.	64
Fill, W. L., "The Break-Even Chart," The Accounting Review (April 1952), pp. 202-209.	119
Finn, F. J., "Integer Programming, Linear Programming and Capital Budgeting," Abacus (December 1973), pp. 180-192.	134

	Page
Firmin, P. A. and J. J. Linn, "Information Systems and Managerial Accounting," The Accounting Review (January 1968), pp. 75-82.	64
Flamholtz, E. G., "A Model for Human Resource Valuation: A Stochastic Process with Service Rewards," The Accounting Review (April 1971), pp. 253-267.	58
Flamholtz, E. G., "Assessing the Validity of a Theory of Human Resource Value: A Field Study," Journal of Accounting Research (Supplement 1972a), pp. 241-282.	58
Flamholtz, E. G., "Towards a Theory of Human Resource Value in Formal Organizations," The Accounting Review (October 1972b), pp. 666-676.	59
Flamholtz, E. G., "The Impact of Human Resource Valuation on Management Decisions: A Laboratory Experiment," Accounting, Organizations and Society (August 1976), pp. 153-165.	60
Folger, H. R., "Ranking Techniques and Capital Budgeting," The Accounting Review (January 1972), pp. 134-143.	133
Foran, M. F. and D. T. DeCoster, "An Experimental Study of the Effects of Participation, Authoritarianism, and Feedback on Cognitive Dissonance in a Standard Setting Situtation," The Accounting Review (October 1974), pp. 751-763.	165
Frank, W. and R. P. Manes, "A Standard Cost Application of Matrix Algebra," The Accounting Review (July 1967), pp. 516-525.	175
Fremgen, J. M., "Variable Costing for External Reporting - A Reconsideration," The Accounting Review (January 1962), pp. 76-81.	85
Fremgen, J. M., "The Direct Costing Controversy - An Identification of the Issues," The Accounting Review (January 1964), pp. 43-51.	86
Friedman, L. A. and B. R. Neuman, "The Effects of Opportunity Costs on Project Investment Decisions: A Replication and Extension," Journal of Accounting Research (Autumn 1980), pp. 407-419.	143
Gangolly, J. S., "On Joint Cost Allocation: Independent Cost Proportional Scheme (ICPS) and Its Properties," Journal of Accounting Research (Autumn 1981), pp. 299-312.	110
Garner, S. P., "Historical Development of Cost Accounting," The Accounting Review (October 1947), pp. 385-389.	31

	Page
Gibbs, G., "New Cost Accounting Concepts," The Accounting Review (January 1958), pp. 96-101.	97
Gibson, J. C., "A Standard Cost Problem," The Accounting Review (December 1927), pp. 362-387.	193
Gibson, J. L., "Accounting in the Decision-Making Process: Some Empirical Evidence," The Accounting Review (July 1963), pp. 492-500.	150
Ginzberg, M. J., "An Organizational Contingencies View of Accounting and Information Systems Implementation," Accounting, Organizations and Society (December 1980), pp. 369-383.	67
Givens, H. R., "An Application of Curvilinear Break-Even Analysis," The Accounting Review (January 1966), pp. 141-143.	122
Glover, F., "Management Decision and Integer Programming," The Accounting Review (April 1969), pp. 300-303.	152
Godfrey, J. T., "Short-Run Planning in a Decentralized Firm," The Accounting Review (April 1971), pp. 282-297.	204
Godfrey, J. T. and T. R. Prince, "The Accounting Model from an Information Systems Perspective," The Accounting Review (January 1971), pp. 75-89.	65
Goetz, B., "Transfer Prices: An Exercise in Relevancy and Goal Congruence," The Accounting Review (July 1967), pp. 435-440.	186
Goetz, B., "The Effect of a Cost-Plus Contract on Transfer Prices," The Accounting Review (April 1969), pp. 398-400.	186
Goggans, T. P., "Breakeven Analysis with Curvilinear Functions," The Accounting Review (October 1965), pp. 867-871.	122
Golembiewski, R. T., "Accountancy as a Function of Organization Theory," The Accounting Review (April 1964), pp. 333-341.	37
Goliger, J., "Analysis of Semi-Variable Expenses," The Accounting Review (July 1949), pp. 308-310.	95
Gonedes, N. J., "Accounting for Managerial Control: An Application of Chance-Constrained Programming," Journal of Accounting Research (Spring 1970), pp. 1-20.	202
Gonedes, N. J., "Optimal Timing of Control Messages for a Two-State Markov Process," Journal of Accounting Research (Autumn 1971), pp. 236-252.	178

Page

Gonedes, N. J. and Y. Ijiri, "Improving Subjective Probability Assessments for Planning and Control in Team-Like Organizations," Journal of Accounting Research (Autumn 1974), pp. 251-269. 207

Gordon, L. A. and H. Cook, "Absorption Costing and Fixed Factors of Production," The Accounting Review (January 1973), pp. 128-129. 88

Gordon, L. A., D. F. Larcker and F. D. Tuggle, "Strategic Decision Processes and the Design of Accounting Information Systems: Conceptual Linkages," Accounting, Organizations and Society (May 1979), pp. 203-214. 154

Gordon, L. A. and D. Miller, "A Contingency Framework for the Design of Accounting Information Systems," Accounting, Organizations and Society, (June 1976), pp. 59-69. 41

Gordon, M. J., "Cost Allocations and the Design of Accounting Systems for Control," The Accounting Review (April 1951), pp. 209-220. 80

Gordon, M. J., "A Method of Pricing for a Socialist Economy," The Accounting Review (July 1970), pp. 427-443. 187

Gorelick, G., "Soviet Accounting, Planning and Control," Abacus (June 1974), pp. 13-25. 62

Graese, C. E., "Responsibility Reporting to Management," The Accounting Review (April 1964), pp. 387-391. 197

Greer, H. C., "The Technique of Distribution Cost Accounting," The Accounting Review (June 1931), pp. 136-139. 91

Greer, H. C., "Managerial Accounting - Twenty Years From Now," The Accounting Review (April 1954), pp. 175-185. 75

Greer, W. R., "Capital Budgeting Analysis with the Timing of Events Uncertain," The Accounting Review (January 1970), pp. 103-114. 133

Gregory, J. C., "Capital Expenditure Evaluation by Direct Discounting," The Accounting Review (April 1962), pp. 308-314. 130

Gregory, R. H. and T. V. V. Atwater, "Cost and Value of Management Information as Functions of Age," Accounting Research (January 1957), pp. 42-69. 33

Gross, H., "Make or Buy Decisions in Growing Firms," The Accounting Review (October 1966), pp. 745-753. 151

Page

Groves, R., R. Manes and R. Sorensen, "The Application of the Hirsch-Dantzig 'Fixed Charge' Algorithm to Profit Planning: A Formal Statement of Product Profitability Analysis," The Accounting Review (July 1970), pp. 481-489. 152

Groves, T. and M. Loeb, "Incentives in Divisionalized Firms," Management Science (March 1979), pp. 221-230. 191

Hakanson, N., "An Induced Theory of Accounting Under Risk," The Accounting Review (July 1969), pp. 495-514. 38

Hamlen, S. S., W. A. Hamlen, and J. T. Tschirhart, "The Use of Core Theory in Evaluating Joint Cost Allocation Schemes," Accounting Review (July 1977), pp. 616-627. 107

Hamlen, S. S., W. A. Hamlen and J. T. Tschirhart, "The Use of the Generalized Shapley Allocation in Joint Cost Allocation," The Accounting Review (April 1980), pp. 269-287. 109

Hansen, P., "An Operational Cost Information Model," Abacus (December 1970), pp. 154-168. 153

Hanson, A. W., "The Relation of Cost Accounting to the Budgetary Control Problem," The Accounting Review (March 1932), pp. 34-37. 159

Hanson, E. I., "The Budgetary Control Function," The Accounting Review (April 1966), pp. 239-243. 162

Harrell, A. M., "The Decision-Making Behavior of Air Force Officers and the Management Control Process," The Accounting Review (October 1977), pp. 833-841. 141

Harrell, A. M. and H. D. Klick, "Comparing the Impact of Monetary and Nonmonetary Human Asset Measures on Executive Decision Making," Accounting, Organizations and Society (December 1980), pp. 393-400. 60

Harris, G. L., "An Application of Standard Costs in the Field of Distribution," The Accounting Review (June 1931), pp. 118-124. 90

Hartley, R. V., "Operations Research and Its Implications for the Accounting Profession," The Accounting Review (April 1968), pp. 321-332. 77

Hartley, R. V., "Some Extensions of Sensitivity Analysis," The Accounting Review (April 1970), pp. 223-234. 152

Hartley, R. V., "Decision Making When Joint Products Are Involved," The Accounting Review (October 1971), pp. 746-755. 105

Page

Harvey, D. W., "Financial Planning Information for Production Start-ups," The Accounting Review (October 1976), pp. 838-845. 135

Haseman, W. C., "An Interpretive Framework for Cost," The Accounting Review (October 1968), pp. 738-752. 38

Haseman, W. D. and A. B. Whinston, "Design of a Multidimensional Accounting System," The Accounting Review (January 1976), pp. 65-79. 66

Hasseldine, C. R., "Mix and Yield Variances," The Accounting Review (July 1967), pp. 497-515. 174

Hayes, D. C., "The Contingency Theory of Managerial Accounting," The Accounting Review (January 1977), pp. 22-39. 41

Heebink, D. V., "The Optimum Capital Budget," The Accounting Review (January 1964), pp. 90-93. 131

Heimann, S. R. and E. J. Lusk, "Decision Flexibility: An Alternative Evaluation Criterion," The Accounting Review (January 1976), pp. 51-64. 153

Hepworth, S. R., "Direct Costing--The Case 'Against'," The Accounting Review (January 1954), pp. 94-99. 81

Hilliard, J. E. and R. A. Leitch, "Cost-Volume-Profit Analysis Under Uncertainty: A Log Normal Approach," The Accounting Review (January 1975), pp. 69-80. 125

Hilton, R. W., "The Determinants of Cost Information Value: An Illustrative Analysis," Journal of Accounting Research (Autumn 1979), pp. 411-435. 50

Hilton, R. W. and R. J. Swieringa, "Perception of Initial Uncertainty as a Determinant of Information Value," Journal of Accounting Research (Spring 1981), pp. 109-119. 51

Hilton, R. W., R. J. Swieringa, and R. E. Hoskin, "Perception of Accuracy as a Determinant of Information Value," Journal of Accounting Research (Spring 1981), pp. 86-108. 51

Hinomoto, H., "Optimum Strategies for Management Information Processing and Control," Journal of Accounting Research (Autumn 1971), pp. 253-267. 204

Hirsch, M., "Disaggregated Probabilistic Accounting Information: The Effect of Sequential Events on Expected Value Maximization Decisions," Journal of Accounting Research (Autumn 1978), pp. 254-269. 142

Page

Hirschman, R. W., "Direct Costing and the Law," The Accounting Review (January 1965), pp. 176-183. 87

Hirshleifer, J., "On the Economics of Transfer Pricing," Journal of Business (July 1956), pp. 172-184. 184

Hirst, M. K., "Accounting Information and the Evaluation of Subordinates Performance: A Situational Approach," The Accounting Review (October 1981), pp. 771-784. 211

Hobbs, J. B., "Volume-Mix-Price/Cost Budget Variance Analysis: A Proper Approach," The Accounting Review (October 1964), pp. 905-913. 174

Holstrum, G. L., "The Effect of Budget Adaptiveness and Tightness on Managerial Decision Behavior," Journal of Accounting Research (Autumn 1971), pp. 268-277. 163

Hopwood, A. G., "An Empirical Study of the Role of Accounting Data in Performance Evaluation," Journal of Accounting Research (Supplement 1972), pp. 156-193. 206

Hopwood, A. G., "Leadership Climate and the Use of Accounting Data in Performance Evaluation," The Accounting Review (July 1974), pp. 485-495. 207

Hopwood, A. G., Accounting and Human Behavior (Englewood Cliffs, N.J.: Prentice-Hall, 1976). 208

Hopwood, A. G., "Towards an Organizational Perspective for the Study of Accounting and Information Systems," Accounting, Organizations and Society (August 1978), pp. 3-13. 42

Horngren, C. T., "A Contribution Margin Approach to the Analysis of Capacity Utilization," The Accounting Review (April 1967), pp. 254-264. 174

Horngren, C. T., "Capacity Utilization and the Efficiency Variance," The Accounting Review (January 1969), pp. 86-89. 176

Horngren, C. T., "Management Accounting: Where Are We?" in Management Accounting and Control (Rober Beyer Lecture Series: University of Wisconsin-Madison, 1975). 215

Horngren, C. T. and G. H. Sorter, "'Direct' Costing for External Reporting," The Accounting Review (January 1961), pp. 84-93. 84

Huefner, R. J., "Analyzing and Reporting Sensitivity Data," The Accounting Review (October 1971), pp. 717-732. 133

Page

Hughes, J., "Optimal Timing of Cost Information," Journal of Accounting Research (Autumn 1975), pp. 344-349. 179

Hughes, J. and J. Scheiner, "Efficiency Properties of Mutually Satisfactory Allocations," The Accounting Review (January 1980), pp. 85-95. 109

Hungate, T. L., "Unit Costs in Institutions of Higher Education," The Accounting Review (March 1934), pp. 38-43. 52

Ijiri, Y., Management Goals and Accounting for Control (Chicago: Rand McNally, 1965). 199

Ijiri, Y. and H. Itami, "Quadratic Cost-volume Relationship and Timing of Demand Information," The Accounting Review (October 1973), pp. 724-737. 124

Ijiri, Y., R. K. Jaedicke and J. L. Livingstone, "The Effect of Inventory Costing Methods on Full and Direct Costing," Journal of Accounting Research (Spring 1965), pp. 63-74. 87

Ijiri, Y., J. Kinard and F. Putney, "An Integrated Evaluation System for Budget Forecasting and Operating Performance with a Classfied Budgeting Bibliography," Journal of Accounting Research (Spring 1968), pp. 1-28. 162

Ijiri, Y., F. K. Levy and R. C. Lyon, "A Linear Programming Model for Budgeting and Financial Planning," Journal of Accounting Research (Autumn 1963), pp. 198-212. 197

Ijiri, Y. and G. L. Thompson, "Applications of Mathematical Control Theory to Accounting and Budgeting (The Continuous Wheat Trading Model)," The Accounting Review (April 1970), pp. 246-258. 162

Ilersic, A. R., "The Theory and Practice of Stock Control," Accounting Research (April 1955), pp. 123-132. 148

Ishikawa, A. and C. H. Smith, "A Feedforward Control System for Organizational Planning and Control," Abacus (December 1972), pp. 163-180. 206

Itami, H., "Evaluation Measures and Goal Congruence Under Uncertainty," Journal of Accounting Research (Spring 1975), pp. 73-96. 190

Itami, H., Adaptive Behavior: Management Control and Information Analysis, Studies in Accounting Research #15 (American Accounting Association, 1977). 48

Jacobs, F. H., "An Evaluation of the Effectiveness of Some Cost Variance Investigation Models," Journal of Accounting Research (Spring 1978), pp. 190-203. 181

	Page
Jacobs, F. H. and K. S. Lorek, "A Note on the Time-Series Properties of Control Data in an Accounting Environment," Journal of Accounting Research (Autumn 1979), pp. 618-621.	210
Jaedicke, R. K., "Some Notes on Product-Combination Decisions," The Accounting Review (October 1958), pp. 596-601.	148
Jaedicke, R. K., "Improving Break-Even Analysis by Linear Programming Techniques," NAA Bulletin (March 1961), pp. 5-12.	120
Jaedicke, R. K., "Accounting Data for Purposes of Control," The Accounting Review (April 1962), pp. 181-188.	196
Jaedicke, R. K. and A. A. Robichek, "Cost-Volume-Profit Analysis Under Conditions of Uncertainty," The Accounting Review (October 1964), pp. 917-926.	121
Jaggi, B. and H. Lau, "Toward a Model for Human Resource Valuation," The Accounting Review (April 1974), pp. 321-329.	59
Jensen, D. L., "The Role of Cost in Pricing Joint Products: A Case of Production in Fixed Proportions," The Accounting Review (July 1974), pp. 465-476.	106
Jensen, D. L., "A Class of Mutually Satisfactory Allocations," The Accounting Review (October 1977), pp. 842-856.	107
Jensen, M. C., and W. M. Meckling, "Theory of the Firm: Managerial Behavior, Agency Costs, and Ownership Structure," Journal of Financial Economics (October 1976), pp. 305-360.	70
Jensen, R. E., "A Multiple Regression Model for Cost Control-Assumptions and Limitations," The Accounting Review (April 1967), pp. 265-273.	116
Jensen, R. E., "Sensitivity Analysis and Integer Linear Programming," The Accounting Review (July 1968), pp. 425-446.	123
Jensen, R. E., "Some Thoughts on Quantitative Models and Applications in Managerial Accounting," The Accounting Journal (Winter 1977/78), pp. 244-276.	215
Jensen, R. E., and C. T. Thomsen, "Statistical Analysis in Cost Measurement and Control," The Accounting Review (January 1968), pp. 83-93.	116
Jiambalvo, J., "Performance Evaluation and Directed Job Effort: Model Development and Analysis in a CPA Firm Setting," Journal of Accounting Research (Autumn 1979), pp. 436-455.	210

	Page
Jiambalvo, J., "Measures of Accuracy and Congruence in the Performance Evaluation of CPA Personnel: Replication and Extensions," Journal of Accounting Research (Spring 1982), pp. 152-161.	212
Johnson, G. L. and S. S. Simik, "Multiproduct C-V-P Analysis Under Uncertainty," Journal of Accounting Research (Autumn 1971), pp. 278-286.	124
Johnson, G. L. and S. S. Simik, "The Use of Probability Inequalities in Multiproduct C-V-P Analysis Under Uncertainty," Journal of Accounting Research (Spring 1974), pp. 67-79.	124
Jonsson, S., "Budgetary Behavior in Local Government--A Case Study Over 3 Years," Accounting, Organizations and Society (December 1982), pp. 287-304.	169
Judd, F., "Development of Cost Accounting Concepts of Scheduled Airlines," The Accounting Review (January 1949), pp. 61-67.	54
Kanodia, C., "Risk Sharing and Transfer Price Systems Under Uncertainty," Journal of Accounting Research (Spring 1979), pp. 74-98.	189
Kaplan, R. S., "Optimal Investigation Strategies with Imperfect Information," Journal of Accounting Research (Spring 1969), pp. 32-43.	177
Kaplan, R. S., "Variable and Self-Service Costs in Reciprocal Allocation Models," The Accounting Review (October 1973), pp. 738-748.	105
Kaplan, R. S., "The Significance and Investigation of Cost Variances: Survey and Extensions," Journal of Accounting Research (Autumn 1975), pp. 311-337.	215
Kaplan, R. S., "Application of Quantitative Models in Managerial Accounting: A State of the Art Survey," in Management Accounting - State of the Art (Robert Beyer Lecture Series: University of Wisconsin - Madison, 1977). Reprinted in The Accounting Journal (Winter 1977-78).	215
Kaplan, R. S., "The Impact of Management Accounting Research on Policy and Practice," The Impact of Accounting Research on Policy and Practice, 1981 Proceedings of the Arthur Young Professors' Roundtable, J. Buckley, ed. (Reston, VA: The Council of Arthur Young Professors, 1981).	215
Kaplan, R. S., "Measuring Manufacturing Performance: A New Challenge for Managerial Accounting Research," The Accounting Review (October 1983), pp. 686-705.	215
Kaplan, R. S., and G. Thompson, "Overhead Allocation via Mathematical Programming Models," The Accounting Review (April 1971), pp. 352-364.	105

Page

Kaplan, R. S., and U. P. Welam, "Overhead Allocation with Imperfect Markets and Nonlinear Technology," The Accounting Review (July 1974), pp. 477-484. 106

Keane, S. M., "The Internal Rate of Return and the Reinvestment Fallacy," Abacus (June 1979), pp. 48-55. 136

Kelley, A. C., "Cost Analysis of a Cost-Plus Contract," The Accounting Review (October 1942), pp. 370-376. 73

Kemp, P. S., "Accounting Data for Planning, Motivation and Control," The Accounting Review (January 1962), pp. 44-50. 196

Kenis, I., "Effects of Budgetary Goal Characteristics on Managerial Attitudes and Performance," The Accounting Review (October 1979), pp. 707-721. 168

Khandwalla, P. N., "The Effect of Different Types of Competition on the Use of Management Controls," Journal of Accounting Research (Autumn 1972), pp. 275-285. 206

Kinney, W. R., "An Environmental Model for Performance Measurement In Multi-Outlet Businesses," Journal of Accounting Research (Spring 1969), pp. 44-52. 201

Kircher, P., "Theory and Research in Management Accounting," The Accounting Review (January 1961), pp. 43-49. 36

Klammer, T., "The Association of Capital Budgeting Techniques with Firm Performance," The Accounting Review (April 1973), pp. 353-364. 134

Koch, A. P., "A Fallacy in Accounting for Spoiled Goods," The Accounting Review (July 1960), pp. 501-502. 98

Kohler, E. L. and W. W. Cooper, "Costs, Prices and Profits: Accounting in the War Program," The Accounting Review (July 1945), pp. 267-308. 74

Kopta, W. A., "Managerial Utility of Accounting in a Period of Adjustment," The Accounting Review (July 1954), pp. 369-372. 147

Kornbluth, J. S. H., "Accounting in Multiple Objective Linear Programming," The Accounting Review (April 1974), pp. 284-295. 188

Kottas, J. F., A. H. Lau and H. Lau, "A General Approach to Stochastic Management Planning Models: An Overview," The Accounting Review (April 1978), pp. 389-401. 126

Kottas, J. F. and H. Lau, "Direct Simulation in Stochastic CVP Analysis," The Accounting Review (July 1978), pp. 698-707. 126

	Page
Kwang, C. and A. Slavin, "The Simple Mathematics of Variance Analysis," The Accounting Review (July 1962), pp. 415-433.	173
Ladin, E., "The Role of the Accountant in Operations Analysis," The Accounting Review (April 1962), pp. 289-294.	76
Langholm, O., "Cost Structure and Costing Method: An Empirical Study," Journal of Accounting Research (Autumn 1965), pp. 218-227.	87
Larcker, D. F., "The Perceived Importance of Selected Information Characteristics for Strategic Capital Budgeting Decisions," The Accounting Review (July 1981), pp. 519-538.	136
Largay, J. A., "Microeconomic Foundations of Variable Costing," The Accounting Review (January 1973), pp. 115-119.	88
LaValle, I. H. and A. Rappaport, "On the the Economics of Acquiring Information of Imperfect Reliability," The Accounting Review (April 1968), pp. 225-230.	44
Lawrence, W. B., "Cost Accounting versus the Pricing System," The Accounting Review (April 1945), pp. 177-182.	146
Lea, R. B., "A Note on the Definition of Cost Coefficients in a Linear Programming Model," The Accounting Review (April 1972), pp. 346-350.	153
Lehnberg, V. B., "Cost Accounting for Motor Freight Lines," The Accounting Review (April 1950), pp. 184-191.	54
Lehnberg, V. B., "Cost Accounting for Motor Freight Terminals," The Accounting Review (April 1952), pp. 215-220.	55
Lemke, B. C., "Is Manufacturing Cost an Objective Concept?" The Accounting Review (January 1951), pp. 77-79.	96
Lemke, K. W., "In Defence of the 'Profit Centre' Concept," Abacus (December 1970), pp. 182-188.	187
Lentilhon, R. W., "Direct Costing - Either ... Or?" The Accounting Review (October 1964), pp. 880-883.	87
Lev, B., "An Information Theory Analysis of Budget Variances," The Accounting Review (October 1969a), pp. 704-710.	177
Lev. B., "Testing a Prediction Method for Multivariate Budgets," Journal of Accounting Research (Supplement 1969b), pp. 182-204.	177
Lewis, R. B., "The Role of Accounting in Decision Making," The Accounting Review (January 1960), pp. 37-44.	148

Page

Liao, M., "Model Sampling: A Stochastic Cost-Volume-Profit Analysis," The Accounting Review (October 1975), pp. 780-790. 125

Lieberman, A. Z. and A. B. Whinston, "A Structuring of an Events - Accounting Information System," The Accounting Review (April 1975), pp. 246-258. 65

Lin, W. T., "Multiple Objective Budgeting Models: A Simulation," The Accounting Review (January 1978), pp. 61-76. 181

Livingstone, J. L., "Matrix Algebra and Cost Allocation," The Accounting Review (July 1968), pp. 503-508. 104

Livingstone, J. L., "Input-Output Analysis for Cost Accounting, Planning and Control," The Accounting Review (January 1969), pp. 48-64. 201

Livingstone, J. L., "Organization Goals and the Budget Process," Abacus (June 1975), pp. 37-48. 165

Livingstone, J. L. and G. L. Salamon, "Relationship Between the Accounting and the Internal Rate of Return Measures: A Synthesis and an Analysis," Journal of Accounting Research (Autumn 1970), pp. 199-216. 203

Lobo, G. J. and M. W. Maher, Information Economics and Accounting Research (Ann Arbor, Michigan: Division of Research, Graduate School of Business Administration, The University of Michigan, 1980). 50

Loeb, M. and W. A. Magat, "Soviet Success Indicators and the Evaluation of Divisional Management," Journal of Accounting Research (Spring 1978), pp. 103-121. 209

Lorig, A. N., "Cost Accounting and the Classification of Municipal Expenditures," The Accounting Review (September 1936), pp. 291-295. 53

Lorig, A. N., "Joint Cost Analysis as an Aid to Management," The Accounting Review (October 1955), pp. 634-637. 102

Lowles, D. C., "Some Results of Cost Analysis in Industrial Distribution," The Accounting Review (June 1931), pp. 131-135. 90

Lucas, H. C., "The Use of an Accounting Information System, Action and Organizational Performance," The Accounting Review (October 1975), pp. 735-746. 66

Luh, F. S., "Controlled Cost: An Operational Concept and Statistical Approach to Standard Costing," The Accounting Review (January 1968), pp. 123-132. 176

	Page
Luneski, C., "Some Aspects of the Meaning of Control," The Accounting Review (July 1964), pp. 591-597.	198
Luneski, C., "Continuous Versus Discrete Compounding for Capital Budgeting Decisions," The Accounting Review (October 1967), pp. 767-771.	132
Lusk, E. J., "Discriminant Analysis as Applied to the Resource Allocation Decision," The Accounting Review (July 1972), pp. 567-575.	134
Lusk, E. J., "A Test of Differential Performance Peaking for a Disembedding Task," Journal of Accounting Research (Spring 1979), pp. 286-294.	143
Luttrell, W. F., "Some Problems of Inter-Plant Cost Comparisons," Accounting Research (April 1954), pp. 107-120.	97
Ma, R., "Project Appraisal in a Divisionalized Company," Abacus (December 1969), pp. 132-142.	133
Ma, R., P. Pandey and M. Scott, "Capital Budgeting and Discounted Cash Equivalents," Abacus (December 1978), pp. 180-187.	135
Magee, R. P., "Cost-Volume-Profit Analysis, Uncertainty and Capital Market Equilibrium," Journal of Accounting Research (Autumn 1975), pp. 257-266.	126
Magee, R. P., "A Simulation Analysis of Alternative Cost Variance Investigation Models," The Accounting Review (July 1976), pp. 529-544.	179
Magee, R. P., "Cost Control with Imperfect Parameter Knowledge," The Accounting Review (January 1977a), pp. 190-199.	180
Magee, R. P., "The Usefulness of Commonality Information in Cost Control Decisions," The Accounting Review (October 1977b), pp. 869-880.	180
Magee, R. P., "Equilibria in Budget Participation," Journal of Accounting Research (Autumn 1980), pp. 551-573.	192
Magee, R. P. and J. W. Dickhaut, "Effects of Compensation Plans on Heuristics in Cost Variance Investigations," Journal of Accounting Research (Autumn 1978), pp. 294-314.	182
Maher, M. W., "Regulation and Controls: Firms' Response to the Foreign Corrupt Practices Act," The Accounting Review (October 1981).	71

	Page
Maher, M. W., "Management Accounting Literature: Past, Present and Future," Unpublished paper presented at the 1982 AAA meetings (University of Michigan, 1982).	216
Maher, M. W., K. V. Ramanathan and R. B. Peterson, "Preference Congruence, Information Accuracy, and Employee Performance: A Field Study," Journal of Accounting Research (Autumn 1979), pp. 476-503.	210
Manes, R. P., "A New Dimension to Break Even Analysis," Journal of Accounting Research (Spring 1966), pp. 87-100.	122
Manes, R. P., S. H. Park and R. Jensen, "Relevant Costs of Intermediate Goods and Services," The Accounting Review (July 1982), pp. 594-606.	111
Manes, R. P. and V. L. Smith, "Economic Joint Cost Theory and Accounting Practice," The Accounting Review (January 1965), pp. 31-35.	103
Mann, E. J., "Management and Industrial Accounting in Western Europe," The Accounting Review (April 1956), pp. 244-252.	61
Marple, R. P., "Combining the Forecast and Flexible Budgets," The Accounting Review (April 1946), pp. 140-148.	160
Marple, R. P., "Direct Costing and the Uses of Cost Data," The Accounting Review (July 1955), pp. 430-438.	82
Marshall, R. M., "Determining an Optimal Accounting Information System for an Unidentified User," Journal of Accounting Research (Autumn 1972), pp. 286-307.	46
Mason, P., "The Use of Costs in Setting Selling Prices," The Accounting Review (June 1926), pp. 72-76.	145
Mattessich, R., "The Constellation of Accountancy and Economics," The Accounting Review (October 1956), pp. 551-564.	33
Mattessich, R., "Budgeting Models and System Simulation," The Accounting Review (July 1961), pp. 384-397.	161
Matz, A., "Cost Accountng in Germany," The Accounting Review (September 1940), pp. 371-379.	61
Matz, A., "Problems in Designing an Accounting System," The Accounting Review (April 1945), pp. 216-222.	63
Matz, A., "Electronics in Accounting," The Accounting Review (October 1946), pp. 371-379.	63

	Page
Mauldon, R. G., H. P. Schapper and D. W. G. Treloar, "A Managerial Accounting System for Australian Agriculture," Abacus (August 1968), pp. 39-50.	62
Mayer, R. R., "The Role of the Accountant in Equipment Replacement Analyses," The Accounting Review (October 1958), pp. 637-644.	128
McClenon, P. R., "Cost Finding Through Multiple Correlation Analysis," The Accounting Review (July 1963), pp. 540-548.	115
McDonough, J. J., "The Accountant, Data Collection and Social Exchange," The Accounting Review (October 1971), pp. 676-685.	39
McFarland, W. B., "The Basic Theory of Standard Costs," The Accounting Review (June 1939), pp. 151-158.	94
McFarland, W. B., "The Economics of Business Costs," The Accounting Review (June 1940), pp. 196-205.	95
McFarland, W. B., "Cost Analysis for Equipment Replacement," The Accounting Review (January 1947), pp. 58-64.	128
McFarland, W. B., "Research in Management Accounting by the National Association of Accountants," The Accounting Review (January 1961), pp. 21-25.	76
McLean, H. I., "Unit Costs of Instruction at the University of Pennsylvania," The Accounting Review (March 1934), pp. 33-37.	53
McRae, T. W., "Opportunity and Incremental Cost: An Attempt to Define in Systems Terms," The Accounting Review (April 1970), pp. 315-321.	152
Mellman, M., "Marketing Cost Analysis - Development and Current Practice," The Accounting Review (January 1963), pp. 118-123.	149
Mensah, Y. M., "A Dynamic Approach to the Evaluation of Input-Variable Cost Center Performance," The Accounting Review (October 1982), pp. 681-700.	183
Merchant, K. A., "The Design of the Corporate Budgeting System: Influences on Managerial Behavior and Performance," The Accounting Review (October 1981), pp. 813-829.	168
Merville, L. J. and J. W. Petty, "Transfer Pricing for the Multinational Firm," The Accounting Review (October 1978), pp. 935-951.	189
Milani, K., "The Relationship of Participation in Budget-Setting to Industrial Supervisor Performance and Attitudes: A Field Study," The Accounting Review (April 1975), pp. 274-284.	165

Page

Millians, P. M., "Profit Planning and Budgetary Control," The Accounting Review (January 1947), pp. 65-68. 160

Minch, R., and E. Petri, "Matrix Models of Reciprocal Service Cost Allocation," The Accounting Review (July 1972), pp. 576-80. 105

Mock, T. J., "Comparative Values of Information Structures," Journal of Accounting Research (Supplement 1969), pp. 124-159. 45

Mock, T. J., "Concepts of Information Value and Accounting," The Accounting Review (October 1971), pp. 765-778. 45

Mock, T. J., "The Value of Budget Information," The Accounting Review (July 1973), pp. 520-534. 164

Mock, T. J., Measurement and Accounting Information Criteria, Studies in Accounting Research #13 (American Accounting Association, 1976). 40

Mock, T. J., T. L. Estrin and M. A. Vasarhelyi, "Learning Patterns, Decision Approach, and Value of Information," Journal of Accounting Research (Spring 1972), pp. 129-153. 46

Mock, T. J. and M. A. Vasarhelyi, "A Synthesis of the Information Economics and Lens Models," Journal of Accounting Research (Autumn 1978), pp. 414-423. 49

Moore, C., "The Concepts of the P/V Graph Applied to Capital Investment Planning," The Accounting Review (October 1962), pp. 721-729. 130

Moriarity, S., "Another Approach to Allocating Joint Costs," Accounting Review (October 1975), pp. 791-795. 107

Moriarity, S., "Communicating Financial Information Through Multidimensional Graphics," Journal of Accounting Research (Spring 1979), pp. 205-224. 142

Moriarity, S., ed., Joint Cost Allocation, Proceedings of the University of Oklahoma Conference on Cost Allocations (Center for Economic and Management Research, Norman OK, 1981). 111

Morrison, T. A., and E. Kaczka, "A New Application of Calculus and Risk Analysis to Cost-Volume-Profit Changes," The Accounting Review (April 1969), pp. 330-343. 123

Morse, W. J., "Reporting Production Costs That Follow the Learning Curve Phenomenon," The Accounting Review (October 1972), pp. 761-773. 117

Page

Moss, M. F. and W. C. Haseman, "Some Comments on the Applicability of Direct Costing to Decision Making," The Accounting Review (April 1957), pp. 184-193. 83

Nash, J. F., "A Note on Cost-Volume-Profit Analysis and Price Elasticity," The Accounting Review (April 1975), pp. 384-386. 125

Neilsen, O., "Direct Costing--The Case 'For'," The Accounting Review (January 1954), pp. 89-93. 81

Nelson, O. S., "Cost Principles in Termination Settlements," The Accounting Review (October 1944), pp. 422-430. 74

Neuman, B. R. and L. A. Friedman, "Opportunity Costs: Further Evidence Through an Experimental Replication," Journal of Accounting Research (Autumn 1978), pp. 400-410. 142

Neumann, B. R., "An Empirical Investigation of the Relationship Between an AID Hospital Classification Model and Accounting Measures of Performance," Journal of Accounting Research (Spring 1979), pp. 123-139. 209

Newman, D. P., "Prospect Theory: Implications for Information Evaluation," Accounting, Organizations and Society (July 1980), pp. 217-230. 50

Nichols, A. C. and D. E. Grawig, "Accounting Reports with Time as a Variable," The Accounting Review (October 1968), pp. 631-639. 77

Noble, H. S., "Some Cost Accounting Concepts of Wider Application," The Accounting Review (December 1926), pp. 48-54. 28

Noble, H. S., "The Relation of Business Organization to Accounting," The Accounting Review (September 1927), pp. 232-236. 29

Noble, H. S., "Cost Accounting in Great Britain," The Accounting Review (June 1929), pp. 88-93. 61

Onsi, M., "Quantitative Models for Accounting Control," The Accounting Review (April 1967), pp. 321-330. 174

Onsi, M., "A Transfer Pricing System Based on Opportunity Cost," The Accounting Review (July 1970), pp. 535-543. 187

Onsi, M., "Factor Analysis of Behavioral Variables Affecting Budgeting Slack," The Accounting Review (July 1973), pp. 535-550. 164

Osborn, R. C., "The Relative Efficiency of Large, Medium-Sized and Small Business," The Accounting Review (July 1950), pp. 262-273. 55

Page

Ostlund, H. J., "Cost Research in the Field of Distribution," The Accounting Review (March 1932), pp. 48-53. 91

Otley, D. T., "Budget Use and Managerial Performance," Journal of Accounting Research (Spring 1978), pp. 122-149. 209

Otley, D. T., "The Contingency Theory of Management Accounting: Achievement and Prognosis," Accounting, Organizations and Society (December 1980), pp. 413-428. 43

Otley, D. T. and A. J. Berry, "Control, Organization and Accounting," Accounting, Organizations and Society (July 1980), pp. 231-244. 211

Otley, D. T. and F. J. B. Dias, "Accounting Aggregation and Decision-Making Performance: An Experimental Investigation," Journal of Accounting Research (Spring 1982), pp. 171-188. 144

Ouchi, W., "A Conceptual Framework for the Design of Organizational Control Mechanisms," Management Science (September, 1979), pp. 833-848. 71

Ozan, T. and T. Dyckman, "A Normative Model for Investigation Decisions Involving Multiorigin Cost Variances," Journal of Accounting Research (Spring 1971), pp. 88-115. 178

Paddock, H. E., "Production Waste - Its Nature and Its Accounting," The Accounting Review (January 1958), pp. 50-55. 97

Paine, N. R., "Uncertainty and Capital Budgeting," The Accounting Review (April 1964), pp. 330-332. 131

Pape, M. E., "Costs and Inventory Values in the Glue Industry," The Accounting Review (January 1959), pp. 52-58. 56

Parker, L. D., "Goal Congruence: A Misguided Accounting Concept," Abacus (June 1976), pp. 3-13. 207

Paton, W. A., "Distribution Costs and Inventory Values," The Accounting Review (September 1927), pp. 246-253. 89

Patrick, A. W., "A Proposal for Determining the Significance of Variations from Standard," The Accounting Review (October 1957), pp. 587-592. 172

Patrick, A. W., "Some Observations on the Breakeven Chart," The Accounting Review (October 1958), pp. 573-580. 120

Peacock, R. B., "The Assessment of a Project in the Heavy Chemical Industry," Accounting Research (October 1954), pp. 275-288. 55

Page

Peasnell, K. V., "On Capital Budgeting and Income Measurement," Abacus (June 1981), pp. 52-67. 136

Peloubet, M. E., "Observations on Cost," The Accounting Review (January 1943), pp. 9-16. 29

Perry, K. W., "Accounting and Economics Reciprocally Indebted," The Accounting Review (July 1958), pp. 450-454. 35

Pfenning, R. E., "Business Information Systems," The Accounting Review (April 1962), pp. 234-243. 64

Prakash, P. and A. Rappaport, "Information Interdependencies: System Structure Induced by Accounting Information," The Accounting Review (October 1975), pp. 723-734. 65

Prickett, A. L., "Labor Turnover Rate and Cost," The Accounting Review (December 1931), pp. 261-276. 94

Prickett, A. L., "General Principles of Cost Accounting," The Accounting Review (April 1944), pp. 169-180. 30

Prickett, A. L., Classified Cost Accounting Bibliography, Indiana Business Studies, Study No. 29 (Bloomington: The School of Business, Indiana University, 1946). 216

Probst, F. R., "Probabilistic Cost Controls: A Behavioral Dimension," The Accounting Review (January 1971), pp. 113-118. 203

Purdy, C. R., "Industry Patterns of Capacity or Volume Choice: Their Existence and Rationale," Journal of Accounting Research (Autumn 1965), pp. 228-241. 99

Rahman, M. and A. M. McCosh, "The Influence of Organizational and Personal Factors on the Use of Accounting Information: An Empirical Study," Accounting, Organizations and Society (November 1976) pp. 339-355. 208

Rappaport, A., "Sensitivity Analysis for Decision Making," The Accounting Review (July 1967), pp. 441-456. 151

Rappaport, A., "Integer Programming and Managerial Analysis," The Accounting Review (April 1969), pp. 297-299. 151

Raun, D. L., "The Problem of Fixed Charges," The Accounting Review (July 1951), pp. 338-346. 81

Raun, D. L., "Accounting for Decisions," The Accounting Review (July 1961), pp. 460-471. 149

Page

Raun, D. L., "The Application of Monte Carlo Analysis to an Inventory Problem." The Accounting Review (October 1963), pp. 751-758. 150

Raun, D. L., "The Limitations of Profit Graphs, Breakeven Analysis, and Budgets," The Accounting Review (October 1964), pp. 927-945. 122

Read, W. H., C. L. Stanford, H. W. Kendrick and R. L. Dixon, "Report of Committee on Statement of Cost Accounting Concepts," The Accounting Review (January 1948), pp. 28-43. 31

Revsine, L., "Change in Budget Pressure and Its Impact on Supervisor Behavior," Journal of Accounting Research (Autumn 1970), pp. 290-292. 163

Rice, W. B., "Statistical Uses of Accounting Data," The Accounting Review (July 1944), pp. 260-266. 30

Richards, A. B., "Input-Output Accounting for Business," The Accounting Review (July 1960), pp. 429-436. 195

Ridgway, V. F., "Dysfunctional Consequences of Performance Measurements," Administrative Science Quarterly (September 1956), pp. 240-247. 195

Rockness, H. O., "Expectancy Theory in a Budgeting Setting: An Experimental Examination," The Accounting Review (October 1977), pp. 893-903. 167

Ronen, J., "Capacity and Operating Variances: An Ex Post Approach," Journal of Accounting Research (Autumn 1970), pp. 232-252. 177

Ronen, J., "Some Effects of Sequential Aggregation in Accounting on Decision Making," Journal of Accounting Research (Autumn 1971), pp. 307-332. 139

Ronen, J., "Nonaggregation Versus Disaggregation of Variances," The Accounting Review (January 1974), pp. 50-60. 179

Ronen, J. and G. Falk, "Accounting Aggregation and the Entropy Measure: An Experimental Approach," The Accounting Review (October 1973), pp. 696-717. 47

Ronen, J. and J. L. Livingstone, "An Expectancy Theory Approach to the Motivational Impacts of Budgets," The Accounting Review (October 1975), pp. 671-685. 165

Ronen, J. and G. McKinney, "Transfer Pricing for Divisional Automony," Journal of Accounting Research (Spring 1970), pp. 99-112. 186

	Page
Rorem, C. R., "Similarities of Accounting and Statistical Methods," The Accounting Review (March 1927), pp. 10-18.	29
Rorem, C. R., "Differential Costs," The Accounting Review (December 1928), pp. 333-341.	145
Rorem, C. R., "Cost Analysis for Hospitals," The Accounting Review (June 1930), pp. 159-161.	52
Rorem, C. R., "The Costs of Medical Care," The Accounting Review (March 1932), pp. 38-41.	94
Rosenzweig, K., "An Exploratory Field Study of the Relationships Between the Controller's Department and Overall Organizational Characteristics," Accounting, Organizations and Society (December 1981), pp. 339-354.	78
Ross, S. A., "The Economic Theory of Agency: The Principal's Problem," American Economic Review (May 1973), pp. 134-139.	190
Ross, W. R., "PERT/Cost Resource Allocation Procedure," The Accounting Review (July 1966), pp. 464-473.	199
Roth, A., and R. E. Verrecchia, "The Shapley Value as Applied to Cost Allocation: A Reinterpretation," Journal of Accounting Research (Spring 1979), pp. 295-303.	109
Rucker, R. G., "Cost Analysis by Standards in the Accounts," The Accounting Review (December 1939), pp. 368-374.	193
Saliers, E. A., "Differential Costs," The Accounting Review (October 1943), pp. 338-340.	146
Samuels, J. M., "Opportunity Costing: An Application of Mathematical Programming," Journal of Accounting Research (Autumn 1965), pp. 182-191.	150
Sanders, T. H., "The Uses of Differential Costs," The Accounting Review (March 1929), pp. 9-12.	146
San Miguel, J., "The Behavioral Sciences and Concepts and Standards for Management Planning and Control," Accounting, Organizations and Society (November 1977), pp. 177-186.	208
Sathe, V., "The Relevance of Modern Organization Theory for Managerial Accounting," Accounting, Organizations and Society (August 1978), pp. 89-92.	42
Savich, R. S., "The Use of Accounting Information in Decision Making," The Accounting Review (July 1977), pp. 642-652.	141

Page

Scapens, R., "Management Accounting - A Survey Paper," Unpublished paper (University of Manchester, 1982). 216

Schaefer, H. P., "The Distribution Cost Problem," The Accounting Review (October 1958), pp. 625-631. 92

Schiff, M. and A. Y. Lewin, "The Impact of People on Budgets," The Accounting Review (April 1970), pp. 259-268. 163

Schlatter, C. F., "Fixed Expense," The Accounting Review (April 1945), pp. 156-163. 80

Scott, D. R., "Trends in the Technique and Tools of Management," The Accounting Review (June 1937), pp. 138-145. 193

Searfoss, D. G., "Some Behavioral Aspects of Budgeting for Control: An Empirical Study," Accounting, Organizations and Society (November 1976), pp. 375-385. 167

Seiler, R. E., "Improvements in External Reporting by Use of Direct Costing," The Accounting Review (January 1959), pp. 59-66. 83

Seiler, R. E. and R. W. Bartlett, "Personality Variables as Predictors of Budget System Characteristics," Accounting, Organizations and Society (December 1982), pp. 381-404. 170

Shields, M. D., "Some Effects of Information Load on Search Patterns Used to Analyze Performance Reports," Accounting, Organizations and Society (December 1980), pp. 429-442. 211

Shih, W., "A General Decision Model for Cost-Volume-Profit Analysis Under Uncertainty," The Accounting Review (October 1979), pp. 687-706. 127

Shillinglaw, G., "Toward a Theory of Divisional Income Measurement," The Accounting Review (April 1962), pp. 208-216. 196

Shillinglaw, G., "The Concept of Attributable Cost," Journal of Accounting Research (Spring 1963), pp. 73-85. 149

Shubik, M., "Incentives, Decentralized Control, the Assignment of Joint Costs and Internal Pricing," Management Science (April 1962) pp. 325-343. 185

Silverman, O. J., "Pretermination Planning," The Accounting Review (July 1945), pp. 316-320. 74

Simon, S. I., "Cost Accounting and the Law," The Accounting Review (October 1964), pp. 884-889. 77

	Page
Singer, F. A., "Management Accounting," The Accounting Review (January 1961), pp. 112-118.	36
Skinner, R. C., "Process Costing," Abacus (December 1978), pp. 160-170.	99
Smith, F. P., "Lot Release Cost Accounting in the Aviation Industry," The Accounting Review (January 1947), pp. 68-74.	53
Smyth, E. B., "Management Accounting in Australia," The Accounting Review (July 1960), pp. 464-470.	62
Solomons, D., "A Diagrammatic Representation of Standard Cost Variances," Accounting Research (January 1951), pp. 46-51.	171
Solomons, D., Divisional Performance: Measurement and Control (New York: Financial Executives Research Foundations, 1965) also published by R. D. Irwin.	199
Solomons, D., "Breakeven Analysis Under Absorption Costing," The Accounting Review (July 1968), pp. 447-452.	123
Solomons, D. ed., Studies in Cost Analysis, Second Edition (Homewood, IL: Irwin, 1968).	38
Sorensen, J. E. and D. D. Franks, "The Relative Contribution of Ability, Self-Esteem and Evaluative Feedback to Performance: Implications for Accounting Systems," The Accounting Review (October 1972), pp. 735-746.	205
Sorensen, J. E. and H. D. Grove, "Cost-Outcome and Cost-Effectiveness Analysis: Emerging Nonprofit Performance Evaluation Techniques," The Accounting Review (July 1977), pp. 658-675.	208
Sorter, G. H. and C. T. Horngren, "Asset Recognition and Economic Attributes - The Relevant Costing Approach," The Accounting Review (July 1962), pp. 391-399.	85
Spence, A. M., "The Economics of Internal Organization: An Introduction," The Bell Journal of Economics (Spring 1975), pp. 163-172.	70
Spicer, B. and V. Ballew, "Management Accounting Systems and the Economics of Internal Organization," Accounting, Organizations, and Society (March 1983), pp. 73-96.	216
Spruce, W. E., "The Integration of Standard and Current Cost for Profit Measurement," Accounting Research (October 1951), pp. 362-398.	147

Page

Stallman, J. C., "A Framework for Evaluating Cost Control Procedures for a Process," The Accounting Review (October 1972), pp. 774-790. 205

Staubus, G. J., "Direct, Relevant or Absorption Costing?" The Accounting Review (January 1963), pp. 64-74. 86

Stedry, A., Budget Control and Cost Behavior (Prentice-Hall, 1960). 161

Stettler, H. F., "Breakeven Analysis: Its Uses and Misuses," The Accounting Review (July 1962), pp. 460-463. 121

Stone, W. E., "Intracompany Pricing," The Accounting Review (October 1956), pp. 625-627. 184

Stone, W. E., "Tax Considerations in Intra-Company Pricing," The Accounting Review (January 1960), pp. 51-59. 185

Stone, W. E., "Legal Implications of Intracompany Pricing," The Accounting Review (January 1964), pp. 38-42. 185

Sundem, G. L., "Evaluating Simplified Capital Budgeting Models Using a Time-State Preference Metric," The Accounting Review (April 1974), pp. 306-320. 135

Sundem, G. L., "A Game Theory Model of the Information Evaluator and the Decision Maker," Journal of Accounting Research (Spring 1979), pp. 243-261. 49

Sundem, G. L., "Future Directions in Management Accounting Research," Paper presented at the Seventh Accounting Research Convocation at the University of Alabama (November 1981). 216

Sussman, M. R., "Present-Value Shortcuts," The Accounting Review (April 1965), pp. 407-413. 132

Swieringa, R. J. and R. H. Moncur, "The Relationship Between Managers' Budget-Oriented Behavior and Selected Attitude, Position, Size, and Performance Measures," Journal of Accounting Research (Supplement 1972), pp. 194-209. 164

Swieringa, R. J. and R. H. Moncur, Some Effects of Participative Budgeting on Managerial Behavior (NAA, 1975). 166

Swieringa, R. J., M. Gibbins, L. Larsson, and J. L. Sweeney, "Experiments in the Heuristics of Human Information Processing," Journal of Accounting Research (Supplement 1976), pp. 159-187. 140

Swieringa, R. J., and J. H. Waterhouse, "Organizational Views of Transfer Pricing," Accounting, Organizations and Society (May 1982), pp. 149-165. 189

Page

Taggart, H. F., "The Relation of a Cost Accountant to the NRA Codes," The Accounting Review (June 1934), pp. 149-157. 72

Taggart, H. F., "Accounting and Code Regulation," The Accounting Review (March 1935), pp. 69-76. 72

Taggart, H. F., "Accounting in the National-Defense Program," The Accounting Review (March 1941), pp. 33-40. 73

Tang, R. Y. W. and K. H. Chan, "Environmental Variables of International Transfer Pricing: A Japan-United States Comparison," Abacus (June 1979), pp. 3-12. 189

Tantral, P., "Accounting Literature in Non-Accounting Periodicals: An Assessment and Annotated Bibliography," Doctoral thesis, (New York: New York University School of Business Administration, 1983). 216

Taussig, R., "Information Requirements of Replacement Models," Journal of Accounting Research (Spring 1964), pp. 67-69. 131

Theil, H., "How to Worry About Increased Expenditures," The Accounting Review (January 1969), pp. 27-37. 176

Theiss, E. L., "Budgetary Procedure as a Means of Administrative Control," The Accounting Review (March 1932), pp. 11-21. 158

Theiss, E. L., "Accounting and Budgeting," The Accounting Review (June 1935), pp. 156-161. 159

Theiss, E. L., "The Beginnings of Business Budgeting," The Accounting Review (March 1937), pp. 43-55. 160

Thomas, A. L., The Allocation Problem, Studies in Accounting Research #3 (American Accounting Association, 1969). 104

Thomas, A. L., "Transfer Prices of the Multinational Firm: When will they be Arbitrary?" Abacus (June 1971), pp. 40-53. 187

Thomas, A. L., The Allocation Problem: Part Two, Studies in Accounting Research #9 (American Accounting Association, 1974). 106

Thomas, A. L., A Behavioral Analysis of Joint-Cost Allocation and Transfer Pricing (Champaign, Illinois: Stipes Publishing Company, 1980). 110

Thomas, A. L., "Goals for Joint-Cost Allocation: An Incompatibility in the Literature," Abacus (December 1982), pp. 166-174. 112

Thompson, W. W. and E. L. Kemper, "Probability Measures for Estimated Data," The Accounting Review (July 1965), pp. 574-578. 115

	Page
Tiessen, P. and J. H. Waterhouse, "Towards a Descriptive Theory of Management Accounting," Accounting, Organizations, and Society (July 1983), pp. 251-267.	216
Tiffany, K. C., "Reports for Management," The Accounting Review (April 1950), pp. 142-148.	74
Tomassini, L. A., "Behavioral Research on Human Resource Accounting: A Contingency Framework," Accounting, Organizations and Society (August 1976), pp. 239-252.	59
Tomassini, L. A., "Assessing the Impact of Human Resource Accounting: An Experimental Study of Managerial Decision Preferences," The Accounting Review (October 1977), pp. 904-914.	60
Trueblood, R. M., and W. W. Cooper, "Research and Practice in Statistical Applications to Accounting, Auditing, and Management Control," The Accounting Review (April 1955), pp. 221-229.	75
Uecker, W. C., "A Behavioral Study of Information System Choice," Journal of Accounting Research (Spring 1978), pp. 169-189.	49
Uecker, W. C., "The Effects of Knowledge of the User's Decision Model in Simplified Information Evaluation," Journal of Accounting Research (Spring 1980), pp. 191-213.	143
Vancil, R. F., Decentralization: Managerial Ambiguity by Design (Homewood, Illinois: Dow Jones-Irwin, 1979).	210
Vasarhelyi, M., "Man-Machine Planning Systems: A Cognitive Style Examination of Interactive Decision Making," Journal of Accounting Research (Spring 1977), pp. 138-153.	141
Vatter, W. J., "Limitations of Overhead Allocation," The Accounting Review (April 1945), pp. 163-176.	101
Vatter, W. J., "The Use of Operations Research in American Companies," The Accounting Review (October 1967), pp. 721-730.	57
Verrecchia, R. E., "An Analysis of Two Cost Allocation Cases," The Accounting Review (July 1982), pp. 579-593.	111
Vickers, D., "On the Economics of Breakeven," The Accounting Review (July 1960), pp. 405-412.	120
Walden, R. E., "Cost Analysis for Electric Utilities," The Accounting Review (July 1942), pp. 257-264.	53
Wallace, E. L., "Some Comments on the Statement of Planning Costs," The Accounting Review (July 1957), pp. 448-466.	34

	Page
Warriner, P., "How Statistical Analysis Can Serve Accountants," The Accounting Review (July 1951), pp. 362-370.	75
Wasserman, M. J., "Costs and Volume in the Milk Pasteurizing Industry," The Accounting Review (October 1946), pp. 425-429.	114
Waterhouse, J. H. and P. Tiessen, "A Contingency Framework for Management Accounting System Research," Accounting, Organizations and Society (August 1978), pp. 65-76.	42
Watson, D. J. H. and J. V. Baumler, "Transfer Pricing: A Behavioral Context," The Accounting Review (July 1975), pp. 466-474.	188
Watson, R. H., "Two-variate Analysis," The Accounting Review (January 1960), pp. 96-99.	172
Weber, C., "The Mathematics of Variance Analysis," The Accounting Review (July 1963), pp. 534-539.	173
Weil, R. L., "Allocating Joint Costs," American Economic Review (December 1968), p. 1342-1345.	104
Weingartner, H., "The Excess Present Value Index-A Theoretical Basis and Critique," Journal of Accounting Research (Autumn 1963).	130
Weinwurm, E. H., "The Importance of Idle Capacity Costs," The Accounting Review (July 1961), pp. 418-421.	84
Wells, M. C., "Profit Centres, Transfer Prices and Mysticism," Abacus (December 1968), pp. 174-181.	186
Wells, M. C., A Bibliography of Cost Accounting: Its Origins and Development to 1914 (Urbana: Center for International Education and Research in Accounting, University of Illinois Press, 1978).	217
White, W. L., "Problems in Determining Total Costs of Distribution," The Accounting Review (March 1934), pp. 15-22.	91
Whitin, T. M., "Some Business Applications of Marginal Analysis with Particular Reference to Inventory Control," Accounting Research (July 1952), pp. 205-219.	147
Whittaker, E., "Realism and Cost Accounting," The Accounting Review (January 1946), pp. 13-19.	95
Wiener, J., "Separation of Fixed and Variable Costs," The Accounting Review (October 1960), pp. 686-690.	98

Page

Wiener, J., "The Cost Structure of the Industrial Enterprise: Pattern of Analysis," The Accounting Review (July 1962), pp. 438-451. 121

Williams, J. J., "Zero-base Budgeting: Prospects for Developing a Semi-Confusing Budgeting Information System," Accounting, Organizations and Society (August 1981), pp. 153-164. 168

Williams, T. H., and C. H. Griffin, "Matrix Theory and Cost Allocation," The Accounting Review (July 1964), pp. 671-678. 102

Williamson, O. E., "Markets and Hierarchies: Some Elementary Considerations," American Economic Review (May 1973), pp. 316-325. 69

Williamson, O. E., Markets and Hierarchies: Analysis and Antitrust Implications (New York: Free Press, 1975). 70

Willingham, J. J., "The Accounting Entity: A Conceptual Model," The Accounting Review (July 1964), pp. 543-552. 37

Wolk, H. I. and A. D. Hillman, "Materials Mix and Yield Variance: A Suggested Improvement," The Accounting Review (July 1972), pp. 549-555. 178

Woodbury, N. F., "A Treatment of Distribution Cost," The Accounting Review (June 1927), pp. 124-128. 89

Woods, R. S., "Some Dimensions of Integrated Systems," The Accounting Review (July 1964), pp. 598-614. 64

Wright, F. K., "Measuring Project Profitability: Rate of Return or Present Value," The Accounting Review (July 1962), pp. 433-437. 130

Wright, H. W., "Allocation of General and Administrative Expenses," The Accounting Review (October 1966), pp. 626-633. 103

Wright, W. H., "Observations of an American Cost Accountant Abroad," The Accounting Review (January 1957), pp. 107-111. 62

Yetton, P. W., "The Interaction Between a Standard Time Incentive Payment Scheme and a Simple Accounting Information System," Accounting, Organizations and Society (June 1976), pp. 81-87. 154

Zanetos, Z. S., "Mathematics as a Tool of Accounting Instruction and Research, The Accounting Review (April 1963), pp. 326-335. 77

Zannetos, Z. S., "On the Mathematics of Variance Analysis," The Accounting Review (July 1963), pp. 528-533. 173

Page

Zannetos, Z. S., "Standard Costs as a First Step to Probabilistic Control: A Theoretical Justification, an Extension and Implications," The Accounting Review (April 1964), pp. 296-304. 173

Zannetos, Z. S., "Some Thoughts on Internal Control Systems of the Firm," The Accounting Review (October 1964), pp. 860-868. 198

Zimmerman, J. L., "Budget Uncertainty and the Allocation Decision in a Nonprofit Organization," Journal of Accounting Research (Autumn 1976), pp. 301-319. 166

Zimmerman, J. L., "The Costs and Benefits of Cost Allocations," The Accounting Review (July 1979), pp. 504-521. 108

Zlatkovich, C. T., "Some Principles of Accounting System Design," The Accounting Review (July 1958), pp. 419-422. 63

Zraick, L. E., "Packing House Accounting," The Accounting Review (July 1947), pp. 299-303. 54